A Golden Civilization

&

The Map of Mindfulness

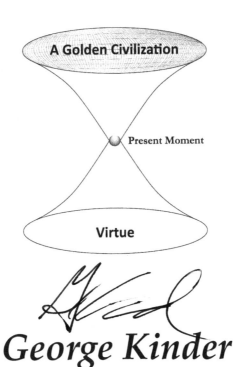

George Kinder

ISBN: 978-1-7327927-0-8

Copyright © George D. Kinder 2018

First Edition

Printed in the United States of America

www.serenitypoint.org

Serenity Point Press

Acknowledgments:

Cover and book design by Katelyn Comeau

Illustrations by Katelyn Comeau, Nadine Mazzola, and George Kinder

With tremendous gratitude to my scrupulous readers:
Kathy Lubar, Drexel Ace, Tom Kinder, Lora Woodward, Joan Luzier,
Vicki Sanders, Louis Vollebregt, Julian Powe, Alan Simons, Jonathan Clark,
Randy Gardner, Lisa Marble, Katelyn Comeau, and Chris Booth.

The most special thanks goes to Maryellen Grady, whose thoughtfulness, patience, and daily attention to text and image over many years brought this book to life.

Testimonials

George Kinder has, once again, opened our eyes to some inescapable, fundamental truths that we should all be mindful of. He reconnects us with what really matters and asks probing questions of introspection that encourage the reader to realign our vision, velocity and even values. Perhaps most importantly, George has the courage and commitment in his book to not only envision for us what is possible; he also sets out a roadmap to get us there. His ideas seem perfectly plausible, because they are—the idea of a Golden Civilization is something that we can collectively work towards. I kept finding myself thinking about John Lennon's masterpiece "Imagine" because the book is a wonderful enabler for free thinking and creativity; releasing the reader from any sense of learned helplessness, intellectual impotency and constrained expectations of the future; the book is that good. Anybody can profit enormously from letting this book into their lives but I'd suggest it's a must for those of us that want the financial services sector to harness the transformational power of transparency, integrity and purposefulness.

~Andy Agathangelou, Founding Chair, Transparency Task Force

A brilliant and energizing synthesis brimming with insightful and hopeful directions that could—if we only would—create a golden civilization wherein, among other things, institutions are our servants, deep presence counts as wealth, and media delivers peace.

Thus forms a golden circle of outer and inner freedom. May it be so.

~Prof. Anne C. Klein, Lama Rigzin Drolma, Dept of Religion, Rice University; Founding spiritual director, Dawn Mountain; author of Meeting the Great Bliss Queen and Heart Essence of the Vast Expanse, a Story of Transmission.

Great men in history did not start with their obstacles, they started with their dreams!! Together we desperately need to develop a vision for the world that gives us enough energy to overcome any obstacle. Who better than George Kinder, the Father of Life Planning, to understand what it takes to get to that energy? To start thinking and feeling about what would really be a great future for the world and all the creatures in it. This might be the most ambitious Life Plan ever but let's believe in the power of the dream. As Kinder shows, it is time to Life Plan civilization and make the Life Plan stick.

~Louis Vollebregt, Global Trainer in Life Planning Leadership, CEO Means in Progress

In this brilliant book, George espouses a new world order, known as a Golden Civilization. It is a perfect society, marked by an absence of war, hunger and poverty, and filled with kindness, harmony, self-knowledge, creativity and desire to reach humanity's potential. It is a paradise on earth.

The Golden Civilization is built on 7 principles: entrepreneurial spirit, democracy, media freedom, trusted advice, trusted products, free markets, and free leadership. Freedom, trust, and great leadership then lie at the heart of this visionary society.

Everyone has a role to play in this inclusive society, by being mindful or aware of the present. Mindfulness practice is important because it brings peace and releases energy that arises from engagement with the present. This book is powerful and truly motivational and will stimulate many interesting discussions and debates.

~Dr Lien Luu, Principal Lecturer (Associate Professor) & Associate Head of School (E&C) Coventry Business School UK

A Golden Civilization has real capacity to galvanise thinking and action at a personal, community, organizational, and national/international level. It carries a universal, timeless message, drawing as it does on music, literature, philosophy, and all the wisdom George Kinder has developed in his life. We need voices like George's that can offer us all a sense of vision and possibility and agency.

What a pleasure to bathe in George's passion, wisdom, spirit, and lucid prose! He guides us into taking responsibility for tackling the many challenges of our day with a beautiful mix of far-sighted imagination and deep-rooted empathy. And he leaves us with a profound message about our role and obligations as supporters of our fellow human beings. This is a book for the whole world.

~*Julian Powe, Trusted Advisor Associates*

A Golden Civilization is a vision and a blueprint for establishing a human society that is both sustainable and allows everyone to flourish to their fullest extent.

~*Leigh Brasington, Meditation Teacher, Author of*
Right Concentration: A Practical Guide to the Jhanas

Kinder provides an unabashedly positive message of hope so desperately needed in these uncertain times. His wisdom provides us with a real chance to remake ourselves and our society by creating a better future for all humanity. Kinder's vision is inspiring and a necessary first step in transforming the world we would seek to pass on to our children and grandchildren.

~Dan Boyce, a founding partner at the Center for Financial Planning in Southfield, Michigan and former Board Chair of Prescott College in Prescott, AZ

A massive project of vision and detail, starting with the values we need to evolve and sustain a dynamic world. Kinder's mind ranges through mindfulness and wisdom teaching to the many ways wisdom must be enacted in political, economic, and cultural life. The range he covers is immense, but even greater is the scope of this heart-felt map for humanity, with freedom to create as its north star.

~Kathy Brownback, Instructor Emeritus in Religion and Philosophy, Phillips Exeter Academy

A Golden Civilization is a profound and timely book that raises the bar for a global vision of leadership—one based on wisdom. This is a must-read guide for leaders primed to create a better world out of these complex times.

~Dr. Joel & Michelle Levey, Founders, Wisdom at Work; Faculty, University of Minnesota Medical School; Authors, Living in Balance: A Mindful Guide for Thriving in a Complex World; Mindfulness, Meditation, and Mind Fitness; and Wisdom at Work. *http://WisdomAtWork.com*

George's vision of a Golden Civilization is transformative. It will change your view of freedom, government, war, work, leaders, and yourself.

~Randy Gardner, Educator and Author,
Founder, Goals Gap Planning, LLC

Model Integrity, Deliver Freedom... Sounds perfect to me! Thought leader, George Kinder, explores themes and innovations that will help us move from our current state to an enlightened state... a Golden Civilization. With no time to wait, mindful change must be our highest priority, for ourselves and our society.

~Sheryl Garrett, Founder, Garrett Planning Network

Awesome book! Financial advice pioneer, George Kinder, elegantly calls our attention to a new way of being and permits us to adjust our societal model to one that mirrors what we truly want to be.

~Stacey Tisdale, On-Air Financial Journalist,
President, CEO, Mind Money Media Inc

The world needs healing and people are screaming out for new direction. George Kinder has the answer. With his immense wisdom and contagious passion he sets out a blueprint for a more meaningful way to live that is not governed by greed and self interest. If you have been yearning for a way to make a difference, trust in the rich teachings of this book.

~Tina Weeks, founder of Serenity Financial Planning

Not since Walt Whitman have I heard as visionary a voice of inclusion and longing, seeking to free the spirit of humankind, and setting us on a path of wise, honorable, authentic, participative life. George Kinder has envisioned a new world, a leap of civilization based on the foundation of fulfilling the true potential of the conscious human in a world hungry for change. He sets in motion the examined life of democratic freedom along with our global need for a new economic system rooted in true democratic principles of virtue and equality. Kinder points us toward a global renaissance. This is big! This is true integrity in action. I want to help create and live in the world that Kinder teaches us is possible.

~Eido Frances Carney Roshi, Olympia Zen Center, author
of Kakurenbo or the Whereabouts of Zen Priest Ryokan

To Mother Earth and her Golden Civilizations

Table of Contents

Part I

A GOLDEN CIVILIZATION

Part II

CODA

APPENDICES

Charts & Images

PREFACE

For a manifesto to succeed, it must speak to our hearts like a poem while infecting the mind with images and ideas that are dazzlingly new. It needs to open our eyes to the true causes of the bewildering, disturbing, exciting changes occurring around us, exposing the possibilities our current reality is pregnant with. It should make us feel hopelessly inadequate for not having recognized these truths ourselves, and it must lift the curtain on the unsettling realization that we have been acting as petty accomplices, reproducing a deadened past. Lastly, it needs to have the power of a Beethoven symphony, urging us to become agents of a future that ends unnecessary mass suffering and inspire humanity to realize its potential for authentic freedom.[1]

~Yanis Varoufakis

When I started *A Golden Civilization*, I wanted to address two crises: the banking crisis and the crisis in democracy. I have come to realize that we face many more crises, and with many more to come, all as a consequence of how we have framed our world and the structures we have built to maintain that frame.

> *In particular, there will be no end to our regrets as long as our response to the complexities of the knowledge we acquire is to create unaccountable hierarchies of profit and power.*

A Golden Civilization intentionally calls to mind the Golden Age of prehistory as well as the great civilizations that followed in India, China, Egypt, Greece, Rome, and elsewhere. But it primarily calls us to the future, to imagine a civilization that includes the best of all that has come before us, to fix the flaws that led to their collapse, and to address the cracks in the foundation of our own civilization.

Chaotically lurching from one crisis to the next is no way to create a Golden Civilization. Rather, we must build the strongest of foundations, we must move toward greater humanity in all spheres, toward our great hearts.

> *The frame of civilization goes far beyond economics and politics. A Golden Civilization requires, if it is to be sustainable, a radical restructuring of how we think about the world, and how we experience it—even to how we understand time and space, and the balance between the world outside us and the world within.*

As we succeed, we will come to the end of humanity's warring states period that extends back in time as far as we can remember. War has no place in a global culture.

To help us envision a new frame and a more accurate one, in these early pages I will introduce concepts that come from studies of mindfulness, both ancient and modern, along with a brief description of the mechanics of black holes. Then, incorporating those mechanics, I will talk about how we accumulate virtue and introduce a map of our universe that includes both our outer and inner worlds. The map gives more significance to the dynamic nature of the present moment where all our actions occur, than to any other aspects of time and space. It is from this new map and frame that we will construct a Golden Civilization.

You may find yourselves, as you read these early pages, eager to rush forward to the political and economic ideas and proposals for action that occupy most of the book and that can propel us into a Golden Civilization. I have written the book with that thought in mind, and so each chapter includes reminders of the major themes in the book. That said, I encourage you instead to pause with this early section of the book, whether to savor it or struggle with it. Both are possible, as coming to understand a new frame of how the world works is as challenging as it is exhilarating. It requires careful reading. The more you absorb and internalize it, the more obvious the structures of a Golden Civilization become.

> *As we contrast these two frames, old and new, it will become obvious why our politicians cannot lead us into a Golden Civilization, and why it is that we must show them how. In a Golden Civilization, wisdom is our foundation. It is there freedom finds peace and then flourishes.*

A Golden Civilization requires a great vision that stimulates the passion and the vigor of a people as it calls forth their authenticity and their compassion. It is time to create that vision and to hold to it. It is not a time for compromise. It is time to build the movement that will ensure a Golden Civilization for a thousand generations. We must end corruption and abuses of power. Without integrity in all our systems, planet Earth is not a sustainable home for *Homo sapiens* and *Homo sapiens* are not the proper guardians for the species of Mother Earth.

Part I

A GOLDEN CIVILIZATION AND THE MAP OF MINDFULNESS

*If you want a Golden Civilization, you must start with
what is golden inside of you.*

*If you want a civilization that will thrive for a thousand years,
you must start with what is timeless inside of you.*

*If you want a civilization that is universal, reaching into all realms,
you must start with profound respect for all sentient being.*

Introduction
to
A Golden Civilization

When I imagine a Golden Civilization, I imagine a world of harmony, learning, creativity, and endeavor, where daily the old and young, rich and poor, and all the cultures of humanity and all its creatures intermingle, thrive, engage with, and learn from one another, fulfilling their own potential as we fulfill humanity's potential. People are kind to one another. There is no war, no hunger. Decisions are made democratically. There is poverty only where chosen as a life of simplicity.

If we are to create a Golden Civilization, we must envision it clearly and then we must choose to enact it. If we wish to send a satellite to Saturn's rings, our aim must be impeccable. If we miss by even a few inches for every mile we travel, we will never arrive. How much clearer we must be in our vision of that foundation on which a Golden Civilization will be built, the root structures from which it will grow. How deeply and with what wisdom must we understand the very best of our nature, for what other foundation can there be? And we must have courage and constancy, for if we shy away from the ideals that would deliver us into a Golden Civilization, the complexity of our modern machinery will carry us irretrievably far away from where we wish to go. As impossible as it might seem, it is time for us to craft the vision and go for it. Our alternative is untenable. As William Blake once said,

> *If the Sun & Moon should doubt*
> *They'd immediately Go out.*

The Challenge of Human Virtue: We Must Learn to Be Wise

For generations, great thinkers have pondered the brilliance of the human species, how great its accomplishments, reaching in knowledge to the farthest expanse of the universe and beyond, deep into the subtlest of subatomic particles and to dimensions we can hardly imagine. How rapid has been our progress: in science, in commerce, in culture—in fact, in all things except the human spirit, except basic human kindness, except virtue and wisdom. In all things we have progressed dramatically, except in these.

With the pace of human history quickening, with humanity in the thrall of our many advances, both for good and for ill, and with the ill threatening now not only our immediate neighbors, but the whole planet, it is time for us to take on the challenge of actualizing human virtue, kindness, and wisdom and to seek to advance as rapidly on those fronts as we are on all others. It is time for us to understand how to embed wisdom inside each of us, and to place kindness and virtue into the structures and systems of civilization for generations to come.

If we want our children to live in a Golden Civilization, the first step is for each of us to imagine it.

It is time for us to look out a thousand generations and to imagine ourselves in a Golden Civilization. From that vantage we can look back to here and now and ask ourselves, what are the changes we need to make to get there, the course corrections that will guarantee that this Golden Civilization comes into being and resiliently self-generates, starting even now with our generation and our children's, and moving forward for a thousand generations to come?

A Golden Civilization: The Threats

Most threats to a Golden Civilization do not arise because the earth is a dangerous place, or because it does not give us enough resources to sustain ourselves, and even thrive. Most of the threats arise because of us, because of our brilliance of invention, our brilliant scientific minds unearthing the fundamental laws of nature and implementing new commerce as we utilize and exploit those laws, unaware of—or disregarding—the darker consequences to ourselves or to Mother Earth that might occur.

Among the threats that we legitimately fear are the consequences of pollution, global warming, and species extinction occurring on our watch. We fear false news and demagogues, and corruption and deceit in high office. We fear the effects of bio-engineering, of cloning, of using synthetic DNA to create whole new species without fully understanding the consequences to ourselves, our fellow creatures, and Mother Earth. We fear war and terrorists and cultures of violence and surveillance and guns. We fear nuclear war and chemical war and the fragility of our technological civilization. We fear artificial intelligence growing within our technology like a virus that is smarter than we are and that prefers itself and its concerns over what is human. We fear racism and sexism and ethnic cleansing. We fear cyber warfare. We fear robots and banking crises, the power of large institutions, private militias, and totalitarian states. We fear inequalities that undermine democracy and the engines of commerce that create them, inequities from hierarchies of power that break our dignity, our communities, and our mutuality of purpose, all executed by brilliant minds but in the absence of brilliant hearts.

It is time to change direction. It is time to people the earth with brilliant hearts even more than with brilliant minds, so that all actions that affect, now and for future generations, Mother Earth, other species, and humanity will be taken with kindness, compassion, and consideration for all.

A Golden Civilization: Principles and Ideals, Structures and Systems

The premise of A Golden Civilization is that it is time to focus on one critical question as we move inevitably from a warring-states mentality to a planetary culture: What are the structures and systems, the principles and ideals required to bring a Golden Civilization into being, a civilization that in all things models integrity and delivers freedom?[a]

We are very young as a complex civilization, a mere 250 years since the Industrial Revolution began. Bottlenose dolphins, the mammals with the largest brain to body ratio, have been on the planet for five million years, and gorillas, our close relatives and the largest living primates, have been around for 20 million. Yet neither species in all that time has so threatened the earth and its species as human beings have done in the last 250 years.

---

a. To model integrity and deliver freedom is a phrase used throughout the book as a descriptor for an essential action required throughout a Golden Civilization. If in these early pages of the book you require more grounding in economic or democratic structures to understand the term, please feel free to leap forward to the Seven Integrities chapter and, in particular, to the chart of The Seven Integrities and the Freedoms They Deliver at the heart of that chapter.

If we are to arrive at a Golden Civilization before the many threats to it overwhelm us, we must quickly and firmly establish its foundation. And we can only do this if, within each of us, we create the strongest basis for the best of our nature. For an organic system of democracy and economics to take root and flourish, our authenticity, our ideals, our virtues, and the most profound experiences of which we are capable must be the bedrock upon which that system is built and the soil from which it arises. It is our ideals and virtues that must be nourished by and become the focus of both our governance and our economics.

The Universe as a Brilliant Heart

*The greatest challenge of the day is: how to bring about a
revolution of the heart, a revolution which has to start
with each one of us?*

~ Dorothy Day

Our hearts have not been at the foundation of our civilization of
technological wonders and threats. Instead, we have imagined in our
brief scientific culture that the universe is a cold, dark place of twirling protons and planets governed by strict mathematical laws. Such
a governing principle to civilization casts a shadow over our hearts,
over what it means to be human, and over the possibility of freedom.
It is also not how many of our earliest ancestors for tens of thousands
of years before us understood the universe. They understood it as
alive, and the earth itself as their mother.

Imagine for a moment their world. Instead of a cold dark place of
formulas and abstractions, the universe is alive with being, already
a brilliant heart beating to the rhythm and melody of a miraculous
mind. And imagine that each of us is a microcosm of that ocean of
being within which all suns and planets swim. And each of us, in our
moments of light, our moments of awakening are, like the universe
itself, the Golden Civilization that we pursue. Consider then to what
extent our practical pursuit of a Golden Civilization is one of creating

and adhering to societal structures of integrity and wisdom, and to what extent it is simply to find and affirm our own nature, our authenticity from our experiences of freedom within ourselves.

Here, I intend to do both: identify the structures and systems of society that we need and explore the nature of the freedom we desire.

First, and more briefly, the nature of freedom, for if we are to create a Golden Civilization, it will be constructed more from moments of freedom than from rocks and atoms and abstract laws.

If we start with the world around us, how do we transform it and percolate it with great hearts, with freedom, and with life?

What Is Freedom and Where Is It?

In 2010, Daniel Gilbert and Matthew Killingsworth released a seminal study on the relationship of happiness to the present moment. With nearly a quarter of a million data points from 5,000 people in 83 countries they established that A Wandering Mind is an Unhappy Mind, which is the title of their study.[2] Participants were contacted by an iPhone application at random moments throughout their days to rate their happiness, and to identify whether they were distracted or fully engaged in what they were doing. The results were remarkable. Regardless of whether their task was pleasant or unpleasant, participants were happiest when they were completely present to the task at hand and unhappiest when they were distracted. It is these moments of happiness that percolate our days that I think of as freedom.

Most of my book is dedicated to the external structures of economics and politics that we call freedoms: freedoms of speech, freedoms of press, freedoms of assembly, and of markets. Flourishing markets give us choices. Democratic freedoms extend our individual range of freedom into the relationships and governance of civilization. It is the purpose of these external freedoms to deliver greater vitality to civilization and greater internal freedom to each of us, undistracted because unconflicted. We are given the freedom to be ourselves. If we want to secure this inner freedom at the very foundation of civilization we must know what it is, where it occurs, and how it relates to all of society's structures and systems.

> *For most of us, the experience of freedom is filled with both exhilaration and ease. They are moments in which we see the world and ourselves as they are, filled with light, free of self, momentary, uncertain, peaceful, but passionate and engaged. We feel awake, expansive, and alert. Our hearts are full. We feel happy.*

Completely present, we are aware of moments rushing by, and yet feel free of time and space. Throughout our lives we seek these moments out, more than any other. Whether we are with family, at work, in nature, singing, making love, eating, exercising, or at peace, it is from these moments of freedom as we engage with the world around us, that a Golden Civilization is created. And it is these same moments that a Golden Civilization delivers to all who come.

Most remarkably, for each of us, the location of freedom is the same and provides surprising insight for the construction of a Golden Civilization. As Killingsworth and Gilbert demonstrate, freedom is always experienced in the present moment. Freedom as the foundation of a Golden Civilization is right here and now!

> *Throw out the maps that you have seen of time and space— those oval grids of mathematical uniformity. Throw them out! They are all wrong. Reality is rooted in the present moment, rooted in our actual present experience, rooted in freedom. We have completely misunderstood time. Neither the past nor the future are larger than the present. Quite the reverse.*

> *Present moments are the most real things a being knows. In addition to being the location of freedom, they are all we have ever experienced. Present moments as moments of freedom are the foundation for a Golden Civilization. They are the basic units of its economics and democracy. Thus, the present moment appears boldly at the center of all the maps we will create.*

And as it is consciousness that experiences the present moment, states and transformations of consciousness are among the most significant elements of our maps, including transformations of freedom and consequences of kindness. Otherwise, our brilliant hearts remain hidden and opaque, inarticulate travelers across a sea of time and space.

Our task then, in these early pages, is to build new maps of reality, roadmaps that will deliver a Golden Civilization.

Although, aside from the Killingsworth and Gilbert study, there is little in science regarding the relationship of the present moment to freedom, mindfulness-based practitioners from spiritual and philosophic traditions have studied that relationship for thousands of years. Their descriptions are useful. We will borrow from both science and the practice of mindfulness to construct our maps of moments, of our brilliant hearts, and of freedom.

For some of you, the science in the next few pages may be challenging. It is not an easy question to answer, how to design a map that has present moments or moments of freedom as its basis. I think it is worth the challenge, but feel free to skim forward to the Mindfulness section a few pages hence, if you disagree.

Space-Time and Gravitational Collapse

The most unusual maps coming out of 20th century physics map a paradox. They reveal both space-time and an emptiness completely beyond space-time, a void crushed out of existence but filled with infinite possibility. These are maps of black holes, gravitationally collapsed suns, the most massive objects of our planetary systems, that have disappeared in an instant, obliterating all that was known. In their most massive states, black holes occupy the center of every galaxy in the universe. Although on the one hand we can imagine black holes as death stars, their geometry is a surprisingly apt model for how our moments of freedom escape from the universe of time and space. Using these paradoxical structures, we can begin to map a relationship that present moments have with time and space—not as units of Planck time[b] trapped upon the grid of time and space, but as experiences, completely free.

---

b. In physics, units of Planck time are the smallest units of time possible, 10^{-44} seconds in duration.

A Map of Black Holes

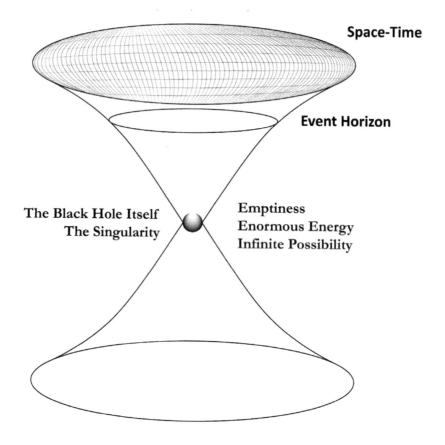

Space-Time

Event Horizon

The Black Hole Itself
The Singularity

Emptiness
Enormous Energy
Infinite Possibility

White Hole

There are two things to note on this map. First, the event horizon that actually surrounds the black hole in 3-dimensional space represents a point of no return. If, as you flew your spaceship around the universe, you were to cross the event horizon of a black hole, you would become lost forever to the universe of time and space as we know it. You could no longer resist gravity's relentless pull to the singularity[c] at the black hole's center. Not only would you become crushed out of existence, but in addition the universe you had lived in could no longer access anything about you.

Second, in this map I have added a bottom cone to represent a white hole to match the black hole up top. White holes are explosions of energy and matter out into universes from a singularity, rather than a collapsing of time and space into a black hole. They are quite speculative, but there is substantive mathematics behind the speculation. I've included a white hole here, as I find its geometry useful in understanding the relationship of present moments of freedom to the world of space-time in which we structure civilization, economics, and democracy, not to mention ourselves. They will help us understand the paradox of how moments of freedom can be experienced as both timeless and yet present within a structure of time and space, as both empty and engaged, and how they are free of self.

---

c.   A singularity is a one-dimensional point at the center of a black hole "which contains a huge mass in an infinitely small space, where density and gravity become infinite and space-time curves infinitely, and where the laws of physics as we know them cease to operate." From *The Physics of the Universe*, Luke Mastin, 2009. www.physicsoftheuniverse.com/topics_black-holes_singularities.html.

The Grid of Time and Space

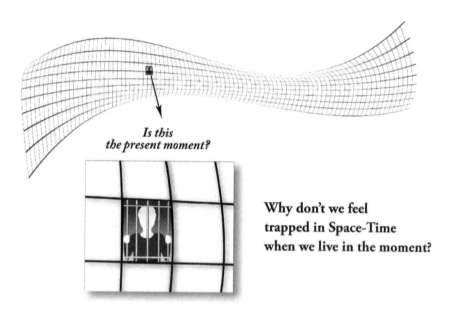

*Is this
the present moment?*

**Why don't we feel
trapped in Space-Time
when we live in the moment?**

Or this?

**It all has to do
with freedom.**

Science has chopped our universe up into individual units of time and space, constructing a grid that begins at the dawn of time and extends to the farthest reaches of space. So, when we experience a moment of time, why don't we feel trapped by the bars and cells that define it? Fundamentally, because these broken bits of time and space are only a small part of our actual experience. According to Killingsworth and Gilbert, when we are distracted in our moments, we feel unhappy indeed. But when we live in the present moment, fully engaged, we live in freedom, not in space-time. We discover who we are. We feel spacious and not confined by time. Our experience is profound. If we are to bring freedom systematically into civilization, its articulation must be recognizable on our maps, as it is in the maps that follow.

Human beings for thousands of years have described the inner workings of experiences of freedom and the pathways to it, arising systematically from contemplative or mindfulness practices focused on the present moment. Let's consider those experiences of freedom now by exploring mindfulness practice and mapping it as we have mapped black holes.

The Nature of Mindfulness and Its Benefits

Most of us know mindfulness whether we realize it or not. We experience mindfulness whenever we are present, whenever we are aware that we are here. Mindfulness practitioners are everywhere: in kitchens and in cars, on factory floors and in the marketplace, in forests and fields, in stadiums and in gardens. In all walks of life, wherever people are present, wherever there is happiness, wherever people are vital and alive, wherever they are kind, there is mindfulness. The aroma of fresh-baked bread and the touch of the ocean breeze make us mindful, as does the sound of someone dear to us sleeping in their room. Infants aware of their first breath are mindful just as the elderly are mindfully aware of their last.

When we talk about mindfulness, we include all of these experiences and in addition, and in particular, the many repetitive awareness practices which use mindfulness techniques to cultivate wisdom and depth. These practices come from both spiritual and secular traditions. They include repetitive prayer, Hindu chants, Sufi dancing, Christian contemplations, and Buddhist meditations. Secular versions can be found in philosophical inquiry, in training environments, listening-skill workshops, yoga and Tai Chi classes, and pain and sports clinics.

In addition to all these ways of mindfulness, when we talk of mindfulness as a discipline we will often be referring to a simple repetitive moment-by-moment practice of letting thoughts go and returning our attention to sensations in the body, most often to the sensations of breathing. This is the practice most studied in scientific literature and richly represented in contemplative history. Because of the very narrow and precise nature of the practice and the experiences of freedom that arise within it, it is possible to directly observe moments of freedom, how they arise, how they flourish, and what inhibits them. The relationship that virtue and authenticity have to freedom also becomes clear from observation. These observations have been made for thousands of years. It turns out that the more you practice mindfulness, the more you return in a dedicated and sustained way to the present moment, the more you experience freedom, and the more virtue develops within you.[d] As we return to the present moment, letting go of self-centered thinking, mindfulness deepens our hearts with emotional intelligence. It teaches us about ourselves and the nature of the mind. It empowers us and it connects us, through experiencing the present moment, with all the other time-bound creatures and processes in the universe.

Many of the practical benefits of mindfulness practice have been written about. Among them: greater focus, patience, kindness, health, energy, courage, selflessness, clarity, longevity, emotional intelligence, reduced anxiety, and less stress. Extraordinary as these all are,

---

d. See Daniel Goleman and Richard J. Davidson, *Altered Traits: Science Reveals How Meditation Changes Your Mind, Brain, and Body*, (New York: Avery, September 2017). Studies of meditators with thousands of hours of practice. This is an extraordinary book that surveys scientific studies of how mindfulness changes the brain, embedding individual virtues as character traits in mindfulness practitioners.

what interests us most particularly as we seek to design a Golden Civilization and its freedoms, are the articulations of freedom that arise as a consequence of mindfulness.

The discipline of mindfulness is hard work. Practitioners are humbled by the challenge of staying with or even returning to the present moment. For all of its benefits, the hard work might not seem worth it if it were not for experiences of freedom that take place within a dedicated practice. These have been variously described as including heightened sensations, greater moment-by-moment awareness, experiences of time slowing down or stopping, as an absence of self-centered thoughts and preoccupations, as energy and creativity, empowerment, happiness, and concentration. They can include experiences of virtue, of humility, compassion, awe, tranquility, and equanimity. The most profound experiences have been described as pure consciousness or as awakening, enlightenment, cosmic consciousness, being reborn, and a sense of being at one with all things.

> *It has been said that when one begins a mindfulness practice, mountains are just mountains. But when we find ourselves very deep in our practice, mountains are no longer mountains, but something far more extraordinary. Then at the end of our practice, mountains are once again mountains. I understand these "once again mountains" to be our true nature, our authenticity. Through mindfulness practice, we come to know who we are.*

As throughout this book we look at the structures of economics, democracy, and media required for a Golden Civilization, it is important to keep in mind that how we bring clarity, kindness, authenticity, and freedom into our world day by day and moment by moment determines how golden our civilization will be.

When I think back over the successes in my life, I attribute each one of them to my mindfulness practice. As wonderful as each success has been for me, it has arisen from this simple practice. The practice is so simple that it can be mapped against time and space to display how to bring vitality, meaning, and freedom into the universe, creating the road map for a Golden Civilization. In Appendix One, I describe this mindfulness practice if you would like to try it, and in our next chapter we explore The Map of Mindfulness.

The Map of Mindfulness: The Doorway to Freedom and Listening to the Origins of Things

The present moment is at the center of everything, in our lives, and on the Map of Mindfulness. Everything seems to move toward it or radiate from it but in fact it is all there is, all we experience. As you use the map, you realize that everything else is contained within it. All of time and space, all of rest or the Great Spirit,[e] and all action lies latent within it.

On the Map of Mindfulness, you can see the familiar black-hole/ white-hole structure looking like an hourglass with the singularity that escapes from the universe of time and space at its center.

> *Here the singularity represents that instantaneous and ungraspable explosion of energy we know as the present moment, as well as the spacious experience of freedom that is possible within it.*

e. In mindfulness practice, experiences of great peace are common. These can be explained by shifts in brain waves. Their causes can be traced to a simple change in cognitive habit away from a self-centered focus. For those of a secular mindset, these explanations may be enough, but for those religiously or spiritually inclined the experience is profound. I have included both secular terms and Great Spirit to describe it, and hopefully to be acceptable to both mindsets.

Here the grid of space-time outlines the way we navigate the world in our minds, so it also stands for the self, our histories, our anticipations, and our self-centered stories.

On the map, mindfulness is the process of letting go of the grid of space-time and self as we move, with focus, toward the present moment. The base of the hourglass no longer represents the explosion of white hole energy out into the universe. Instead those energetic engagements with the universe are represented by the right-hand arrow I call Entrepreneurial Spirit.[f] They represent our passionate engagements with the world that arise from the seed of enormous energy and power that is the present moment.

> *As much as the present moment can represent moments of freedom, it can also represent the opposite, moments of distraction and unhappiness. I call this experience, "the mirror of forgetfulness." The very nature of the present moment does not allow us to rest in it and explore it. Rather, it bounces us back, like a mirror, instantaneously to the world of time and space, so that when we are not awake, focused, or free, we forget that there even is such a thing as the present moment. Instead, distracted and unhappy, we get lost in the intricate designs and the addictive allure of self, of our stories and space-time as we fruitlessly try to create something stable within it.*

---

f. Rightly speaking each of our lives is an entrepreneurial engagement and each of us an entrepreneur. See my chapter, Entrepreneurial Spirit, on the relationship this energy inside each of us has to our experience of freedom.

The subtitle of the map is "Listening to the Origins of Things." That is what mindfulness teaches us. We listen, inside ourselves. It is through the experience of mindfulness that we understand the nature of things, of all things, and their origins inside ourselves.

The Map of Mindfulness becomes the doorway to freedom because it shows us how, by shifting our habits of thought, our world can naturally be free of attachments, free of our driven restless engagement with the world, and instead filled with clarity and joy.

How freedom arises within a mindfulness meditation is quite interesting. There is a moment that occurs in most meditations where we suddenly find ourselves peaceful, spacious, and at ease. Often, we are still in the midst of the same restless thoughts we began with, but we find great space between each of them. The peace arises mysteriously, but what has happened is at once momentous yet simple. We entered the meditation filled with habits of thought that all revolved around "me," filled with our "to-do" lists, wandering across the grid of time and space. Struggling to find peace, we find ourselves annoyed at the meditation and annoyed at the volatility of the present moment. Its nature as a mirror of forgetfulness keeps bouncing us back to the restless world we seek to escape.

But suddenly everything shifts, just as it does at the event horizon on our map of black holes. Here, we discover that we've replaced the habit of self with a habit of returning to simple sensations, a habit of listening to origins, of being present—all without the agency of self-stories. We find ourselves returning to moments of sensation rather than to thoughts of ourselves.

And as we continue to return to the sensations of breathing, peace gathers, deepens, and develops. Our attachments and aversions no longer compel us. On the map, I call this moment of peace "letting go of self." It is a moment in which we suddenly drop all the way down to the base of the hourglass, to the realm of virtue and Great Spirit.

As we open to this experience, virtues are gathered, purely through selflessness, including kindness, clarity, authenticity, patience, equanimity, joy, and many others. They are not gathered in the analytic world of time and space, but in the spacious, focused, and free world of Great Spirit and great rest. It is here we integrate and deepen our self-knowledge.

The Map of Mindfulness

Listening to the Origins of Things

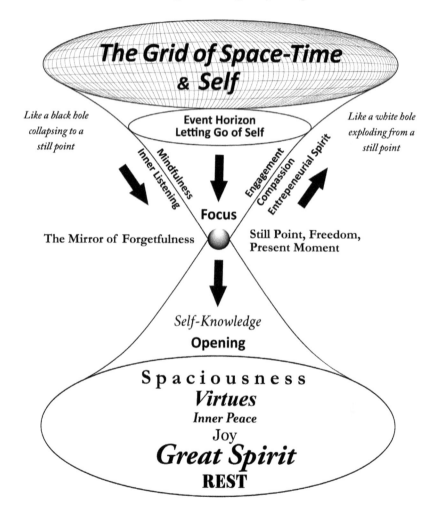

Mindfulness and Its Freedoms

> *Two remarkable freedoms arise from mindfulness practice.*
> *The first is great peace.*

As the mind meets moments without a thought of itself (of I, me, or mine), it experiences tranquility, emptiness, and other deep states of consciousness. It has access to all the virtues but especially the kindness and compassion that arise from selflessness. Here the mind can experience itself and realize its own nature.

> *The second freedom is the enormous energy that arises from*
> *our sustained engagement with the present moment.*

Awake and alert, we weave our present moments into the world of time and space. It is this energy that creates a Golden Civilization, that makes a paradise of Earth.

> *The present moment holds everything. It is the intensification and condensation of all of time and space, as well as of Great Spirit.*

As biological and historical creatures in a data-driven age, we tend to think of the present moment as ephemeral or as advancing in an arrow of time across the grid of time and space. It's the grid that we think of as real—the moments are mere flickering ephemera of little consequence. But that is not accurate, nor is it our immediate experience. At the present moment, it alone is real and the grid of space-time and self is a memory, a thought, an anticipation, a story. It is only the present moment that we ever authentically experience, and it is always and only in the present moment that we act. Our inability to stay present within the moment expresses its explosive nature as the most powerful and (nearly) unattainable object in the universe. It is our hidden jewel. Most of the time, the present moment is taken for granted as we pursue material things and experiences with our grasping natures out on the grid of time and space. We shrink from the immediacy of these explosive present moments that are most intimate to us, most powerful, and most true. Unsteady and fearful of these moments, we remain ignorant of them and unconscious.

Our relationship to the present moment and its freedoms is critical to the establishment of the sustainable structures and systems we seek to create in economics and democracy.

The difference between a conscious universe and an unconscious one, between one that is awake and one that is reactive, as we will see, is the difference between a Golden Civilization and one that is in chaos and confusion, one that is constantly failing.

An Unconscious Universe

Within an unconscious universe a Golden Civilization is not possible, and yet it is the unconscious universe in which we tend to live. It's the one we've been taught. It's the one on the grid. It's the mindless, automatic universe that just happens, unobserved by our brilliant heart and unappreciated. It can be crafted from numbers. It's the one we chaotically create for ourselves when we react to our world with stress or suffering, rather than proactively transforming the world with kindness, clarity, and wisdom. Because it is our habitual world, it is easy for us to rest in, but it is a fitful rest.

There are two versions of the unconscious universe that I have mapped: one analytic, based on ignorance; the other chaotic, based on fear. In both we cling to belief systems that are disconnected from and even unaware of our fullness of being: at times brilliant thought, but without a brilliant heart.

Of course, consciousness is relative. The question here is whether the consciousness that fills a moment is rudimentary, reactive, and relatively unconscious, or is it awake, concentrated, and filled with being and the experience of freedom, aware of itself? Are we bounced back to the world by the mirror of forgetfulness lost in abstractions, confused, disoriented, and unconscious, or do we come to the world fully awake?

If fully awake, we are not lost in stories of ourselves. Instead, we are clear in regard to all that we experience and to what we create in space-time. Our access to the realm of wisdom and Great Spirit is natural and organic.

When we are unawake, the worlds we create are broken, unsatisfactory, and incomplete. They are filled with longing. And that's the danger. Rather than waking up, learning to be present, we cling either to objects on the grid of space-time, or to Great Spirit, great rest. Neither Great Spirit nor the present moment can be accessed with a clinging mind. Great Spirit is too amorphous, and the present moment too quick. To a clinging mind, they are unattainable—distant imaginings. The danger to civilization arises then as space-time and Great Spirit become shrouded in beliefs that can be clung to, beliefs that justify war, fascism, racism, and other harms to humanity or to nature.

Whether we act from analysis and logic or from superstitions and beliefs, we become cut off from the nature of things and from our own nature, in a world unaware of itself, unaware of the present moment.

In the "Unconscious Universe Based on Fear," civilization is driven by hunger, fear, and delusion. It is a world of superstition and warring states, with no access to the present moment.

In the "Unconscious Universe Based on Ignorance," we find our world of materialism and analysis, but we are equally disconnected from the present moment, from our experiences of ourselves, and from spirit.

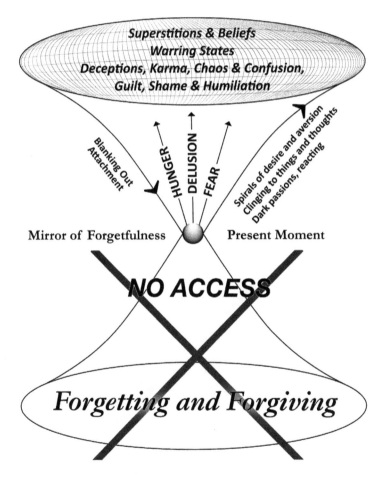

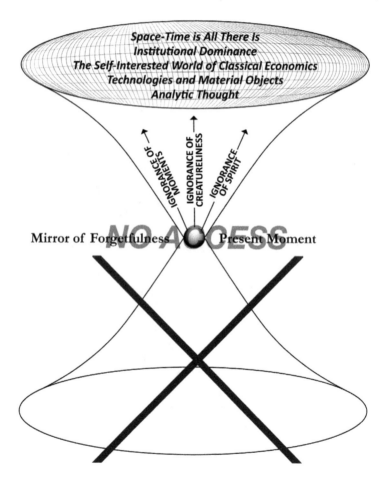

Unconscious Universe Based on Ignorance

Space-Time is All There Is
Institutional Dominance
The Self-Interested World of Classical Economics
Technologies and Material Objects
Analytic Thought

IGNORANCE OF MOMENTS

IGNORANCE OF CREATURELINESS

IGNORANCE OF SPIRIT

Mirror of Forgetfulness — Present Moment

The world of space-time can be unconscious or conscious,
much as science and institutions can be used for good or ill.

A Conscious Universe

> We rely heavily on our analytic thought and our science, but our depths of experience, our profound experiences, our child-like experiences, and our experiences of virtue tell us more.
>
> The Conscious Universe, and the Golden Civilization, are propelled in all directions by a mirror of awakening rather than a mirror of forgetfulness.

It was when I was three that I first asked myself, "Why is there something rather than nothing?"

The question would become the most formative question of my life, one that would haunt me for decades, and one that even now I relish returning to.

Asking the question always takes me into a quiet and deep place where thought stops and no one else can go. As a child I went there often. These were my first meditations.

Puzzled as to the answer to this evocative question, I nonetheless knew that something profound stood at the heart of things. Something profoundly quiet and yet growing like a great beast inside of me.

And then one spring morning, not long after I graduated from college, as I walked down Massachusetts Avenue between Harvard and Porter Squares, I plunged into the depths of the question as if it were a vacuum sucking out of me all of the knowledge and all of the life that I had come to know. Swirling in its eddies, deep in the question, suddenly my brain expanded and exploded in light. A surge of energy rushed through my body like nothing I'd ever experienced before. There was such vitality in it, I felt as if I could leap into the sky and stride across the tall buildings and even across the clouds.

What happened that spring morning is hard to describe, but the experience left me with an unshakable understanding of the universe as alive, that all things are alive. And if they're not alive by our scientific definition of life, they are something far more extraordinary than being alive could ever be.

The astonishment of that moment never left me. Deeper than visioning, I'd learned that to see reality clearly, one must keep the mind open, alert, focused, passionate, naïve, and engaged.

Even earlier I'd had inklings of this. In high school, my English teacher was struck by an essay I wrote about innocence. In it I asserted I would protect my innocence at all costs, that it was the most valuable thing I knew. I did not understand it then but I do now. By innocence, I meant my authenticity, what was true inside me and free. When we look to create a Golden Civilization, more than any other functions, the systems we employ will model integrity and truth and deliver freedom. To do this, they will with reverence protect our innocence and authenticity at all costs, for these are the essence of both truth and freedom.

Throughout my life I have more than anything else mined intently and unstintingly the experience of freedom in every moment.

Freedom is at the heart of a conscious universe. In fact, I see the map of the Conscious Universe as a brilliant heart, beating and breathing from space-time to Great Spirit and back again. A Conscious Universe constantly transforms itself, is always moving from suffering to wisdom and back to the material world again, endlessly and effortlessly, opening and closing, always moving through the present moment of freedom.

The map of the Conscious Universe is important. Without a conceptual understanding of the world that includes both our creatureliness and our consciousness, our secular space-time maps diminish our humanity. They deliver a flawed democracy and a self-interested economics, materialistic, and filled with limitations. As we navigate the world, we naturally think in spatial dimensions, and of past and future, but without a contemplative and kindly basis to our lives that thrives in the present moment, we lack a ready understanding of the consciousness within us and of creatures and life all around us. From that standpoint, we are neither particularly self-aware, nor aware of others. This causes us to undervalue ourselves, our spirits, and our capacity for transformation, as well as other creatures and the planet. And this leads to all our woes. It enables war and species extinction.

> *Society's current mapping, all boxed out by bars and cells into products and dimensions, is what I call refrigerator economics, valuable for those who seek monetary profit in their endeavors and things to put into their pockets or their refrigerators. It allows us to put a price tag on everything, which ironically overvalues everything material while undervaluing everything else. Freedom, consciousness, and life itself are not on our current map, and they are worth far more than all other things combined.*

As our myths have taught us from ancient times, whether Adam and Eve or Doctor Faustus, the kind of knowledge the human species has access to is dangerous. Without wisdom attached, it is self-destructive. The dead world of atoms and abstractions from which we assume we arose is the world we are destined to embrace and, without wisdom, in short order. The only human species that can exist into a Golden Civilization of thousands of generations is one that has tamed greed and hatred and diminished its outsized sense of self. People will not view themselves as conquerors or as owners of time and space. Their realms of freedom will be much larger than that, and they will understand that there is nothing to be conquered except themselves.

In a Conscious Universe, whenever we wake up to the present moment, that moment is transformed to a moment of freedom. There are no moments of freedom outside of these. As we move forward in our understanding of a Golden Civilization, we will see that moments of freedom are the essential units for both an economics of freedom and the politics of a Golden Civilization.

A Conscious Universe: The Golden Civilization

"Eternity is in love with the products of time"

~William Blake

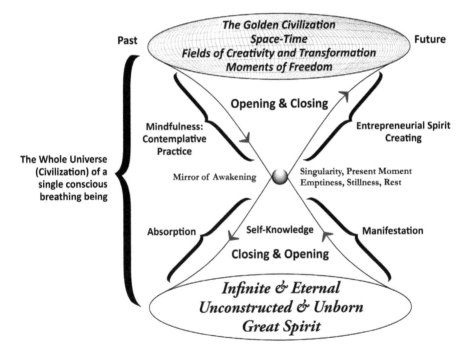

Part II

THE SEVEN INTEGRITIES

Essential Structures of Democracy and Economics

Human beings...have enough intelligence, goodwill, generosity and enterprise to turn Earth into a paradise...by the end of the present century.

[The problem is that] we seem unable to stabilize either economic policies or the means of governance higher than the level of a village.[3]

~*E.O. Wilson*

Introduction

It's time for the world to take up Wilson's challenge. It's time for us to answer these questions:

- What are the economic policies and the means of governance that would turn Earth into a paradise by the end of the century?

- What does a Golden Civilization look like?

- What are the structures and systems, policies and ideals that would ensure a Golden Civilization for a thousand generations to come? What are the integrities by which we must live?

We must address these questions; our alternative is untenable. Either we create a conscious civilization that models integrity and delivers freedom—or we will remain unconscious and instinctive and will live within the bars and cells of time and space, trapped in a world of ego, enslaved by disasters, and by the cruelty of others. Given the realms of knowledge to which human beings now have access, to live unconsciously courts disaster for the species and the planet.

If civilization is our creative act, it is time we wake up into it. It is time we understand how we choose to create civilization with each action we take in the world.

The essential practices of a Golden Civilization start within ourselves: practicing an inner listening that cultivates the present moment and develops authenticity and freedom. It is the way we gather virtue and build character. Each building block of character is a building block of civilization. But our freedoms require structures of integrity within society to support them and protect them—both economic and political. Given the flaws in human character, how do we ensure that integrity and freedom are embedded in the very structures of civilization? How do we ensure that civilization can handle the complexities and dark potentialities of knowledge without systematically or accidentally destroying humanity, other species, or Mother Earth? How do we make the combination of brilliant hearts and brilliant minds so dynamic and so organic that never again do we fail in our higher purpose? A Golden Civilization is a vibrant being, like the universe itself. It is not a separate thing, confined within space and time, dark and afraid—anymore than any citizen within it should be.

Our map of space-time is inadequate. It fails to tell the whole story. It leads naturally to the kinds of negative externalities civilization is flawed by, including war, famine, inequality, pollution, species extinction, corruption, banking crises, global warming, totalitarianism, materialism, cynicism, and distrust. All arise as a consequence of the dominant influence of self-interest rather than self-knowledge in economics and politics. What we require instead is for civilization's structures to model integrity in all things and to deliver freedom to all people. Our challenge is to bring self-knowledge to the place in civilization that self-interest has occupied.[g]

---

g.   See Appendices Three to Nine for studies and statistics that reflect the degree to which distrust, inequality, and corruption pervade civilization, rather than integrity. In particular, the surveys in Appendix Seven on how

Self-knowledge, in this sense, is experiential, not driven or broken by analysis. It has two elements. The first element is the depth of understanding I call the Great Spirit in our maps. And the second element is our calling, our passionate engagement with the world that explodes into time and space from the present moment. I call this Entrepreneurial Spirit. Throughout our chapters on the structures and systems of the Seven Integrities we will weave these twin threads of self-knowledge — depth of understanding and passionate engagement.

Model Integrity, Deliver Freedom

The purpose of each system in society is to model integrity and deliver freedom. Nearly all of the problems we face have arisen because so many of our systems have not reliably done either. In the following chapters, I will explore seven systems or Integrities critical for a Golden Civilization. Before we look at those Integrities, let's consider what it means for an Integrity to deliver freedom.

In our Mindfulness section, we explored the deeper realms of freedom, of being awake, of virtues, of energy, and clarity. While these realms can be delivered internally through a contemplative practice, they can also be delivered by the kindness, intelligence, and grace of people

---

widespread is our distrust of media, business, finance, and politics, all keys to the Seven Integrities of a Golden Civilization.

within society, and by society's structures, systems, and institutions. They can be delivered by the modeling of these qualities throughout an institution. They can be delivered by the intentional reduction of the stresses and suffering of an institution's stakeholders, or by providing products and services that make lives easier or more purposeful. Within each structure of integrity, freedom can be delivered by delivering empathy and compassion wherever a person is suffering, or words of inspiration and encouragement when a person longs for freedom. Freedom can also be delivered across the Seven Integrities by commitments to democratic and economic freedoms for all. They can be delivered by the rule of law.

For a Golden Civilization to take root, we each require the freedoms of self-esteem, confidence, and self-respect if we are to speak truth to power or to resist bullying, and to confront, challenge, and change hierarchical structures of power around us. If we are to know ourselves, we require freedom from institutional mindsets, freedom from corporate and government propaganda. If we are to navigate the world with self-knowledge and wisdom, we require both freedom from and of religion, as well as freedom from and of belief, the freedom to choose to think and believe as we like. We need the freedoms to participate in markets and in democracy. These are all freedoms that can be modeled, respected, inspired, and delivered through the structures and systems of civilization, throughout its institutions, through its education, through its rules and regulations, and through its people.

And we need other freedoms: freedoms of speech and assembly, freedoms of information, freedoms from corruption, hunger, and war. Each of these freedoms can be delivered by appropriate institutional structures, structures of integrity as I call them, and by an ethos throughout civilization and its education that delivers freedom to each of us along with a desire to share that freedom with others.

Integrity here means freedom from corruption, and the impeccability of society's structures and systems to deliver freedom to all.

The Seven Integrities

I have divided the systems (or Integrities) required for our purpose into seven areas. I think of them as the seven essential organizing principles of a Golden Civilization. No doubt other organizations or systems are possible. I can imagine many arising and contributing to the creation of our Golden Civilization.

Freedom itself is the first of the "Seven Integrities." It is at their core. Here I think of freedom as not only happiness but primarily as the passionate engagement with the world that we will call Entrepreneurial Spirit. Two Integrities are primarily political: Democracy and Media. Three Integrities are economic: Advice, Products, and Markets. The final Integrity is Leadership. There is significant overlap amongst the Seven Integrities. Entrepreneurial Spirit (as an expression of freedom in the world) is the cornerstone of both democracy and economics, so it arises throughout the Integrities. And leaders can guide them all, even democracy, which is the governing Integrity.

Here is an outline of the seven areas we will explore. Note the dominant themes of economics and democracy within which five of the Seven Integrities are held.

Entrepreneurial Spirit: Freedom itself, our vital spirit, our passion to engage in the world, from cradle to grave. The spirit that sends our green shoots up out of Earth's dark soil to flower and bear fruit into the world.

Democracy:

Democracy (itself): Our community of freedom, our guarantor of freedoms of speech, assembly, press, and belief. The governing integrity that each of us belongs to, that secures each of the integrities with standards, systems, and obligations to deliver freedom everywhere.

Media: Cultural artifacts meant to illuminate freedom and what is true, AND what is rotten and false. Without its accuracy, independence, and wisdom, democracy is unsustainable.

Economics:

Advice: A mentor/mentee relationship that supports and inspires each of us to live our life of greatest freedom and authenticity. The incubator of freedom.

Products: Things and services for sale, extending our freedoms in time and space.

Markets: Settings for relationship transactions designed to most efficiently maximize freedom for all. Settings for freedom's emergence. The market places of engagement for the work of our lives—the practical requirements, the daily needs, and the personal passions.

Leaders: Inspirers of freedom, models of integrity. Leadership represents not merely our vitality and the natural maturity of our Entrepreneurial Spirit, but the very best of us in both the democratic and economic worlds, and in our families and communities.

When I use the term Integrity, for the Seven Integrities, I think of it as including both the freedoms to be guaranteed within each of the seven, and the structures and systems by which those freedoms are guaranteed. Thus the "Integrity" of Entrepreneurial Spirit includes both its passionate (or compassionate) nature within each of us, the quality of its spirit, and also the systems in society that guarantee that each of us lives with Entrepreneurial Spirit or has access to it. Consider this table that breaks each Integrity into the qualities of freedom inherent in it, and the structures and systems required to establish, protect, or sustain it.

The Seven Integrities
and the Freedoms They Deliver

	FREEDOMS	INTEGRITY
Entrepreneurial Spirit	• The rush of freedom itself. • The freedom of each individual to live in authenticity and within that to find the passionate purpose they are meant to live by, and then live it!	A Golden Civilization is dedicated to delivering this freedom to every person in it, a dedication that permeates all the Integrities. The Integrity of Entrepreneurial Spirit includes the structures of civilization by which each of our authenticities thrives and finds place in civilization.
Democracy	• Freedom to participate equally with all other human beings on the planet in the decision-making that establishes the rules by which we live and the structures that preserve our freedoms for thousands of generations. • Freedom of speech. • Freedom of assembly. • Freedom of belief. • Freedom from famine and war. • Freedom from corruption and deceit. • Freedom of transparency. • Freedoms of Mother Earth and her creatures. • Freedom to determine in democracy the rules by which all the other Integrities and freedoms best flourish. • Freedom to trust the unbiased wisdom and trustworthiness of political representatives.	The systems and structures, rules, and laws of democracy that are impeccable in their dedication to these freedoms, and most of all to the Integrity of democracy itself, without which all our other freedoms are threatened. The systems and structures that guarantee that money and power can never diminish our democratic freedoms and that figures of wisdom are always our political representatives.

	FREEDOMS	INTEGRITY
Media	• Freedom of the press. • Freedom of speech. • Freedom of transparency, truth, and accuracy	The structures and systems that guarantee our ability to trust that the press is not dominated by government or corporations or other wealthy and powerful interests. Scientific, investigative, and reporting standards are in place for the accuracy and unbiased nature of its news. We can rely on the media to inform our best lives, and for our democracy to make the best decisions. The Integrity of media includes our ability to trust its dedication to the integrities, values, freedoms, and principles of a Golden Civilization.
Advice	• Freedom to trust advice: • Freedom to trust advice we are given to navigate the economic and other complexities of civilization so that we can maximize our potential to live in freedom and live our life plans of greatest meaning. • Freedom to trust the accuracy of the advice. • Freedom to trust the unbiased nature of the advice. • Freedom to trust that the adviser is dedicated to who we are and to whom we aspire to be and to deliver us onto the most efficient path to accomplish those ends.	Structures and systems that guarantee no conflicts of interest for an adviser. Their entire dedication is to the clients' well-being. Structures and systems that guarantee that the underserved are secure in the availability of advice and that the advice given to them is as helpful as the advice given to the well-to-do.

	FREEDOMS	INTEGRITY
Products	• Freedom to trust products and services.	Clear distinction and unbridgeable wall between profit-seeking products and advice. The highest standards for truth in advertising—comprehensive.
Markets	Free markets: • Freedom to enter markets and to exit and to participate in markets so as to maximize one's ability to live one's life plan of freedom. • Markets are not dominated by governments, corporations, non-profits, the wealthy, or other powerful forces. • Freedom for the best products and services to rise to the top of markets and become available to all. • Freedom to trust that the sales, power, and profits of institutions never allow them to violate the freedoms of individuals established in the other six integrities. • Freedom to trust the fiduciary nature of institutional power. • Freedom for self-knowledge to flourish throughout economics as the container for self-interest.	The structures and systems devised by the people in democracy to guarantee the trustworthiness and freedom of markets, to maximize the likelihood of all human beings living in freedom for a thousand generations, and to maximize the most efficient allocation of human resources which are our lives, our self-knowledge, our authenticity, our capacity to love, and our passionate purposes.
Leaders	• The freedom to lead as we are called to do so. • The freedom to trust that our leaders, as well as ourselves and our children, are grounded in wisdom. • The freedom to trust in the leadership skills of others.	The systems, structures, and standards that guarantee that leadership and figures of wisdom are developed throughout civilization from early childhood on, and that the standards for leaders become more rigorous based on the more powerful the institutions that they lead.

What Drives the Seven Integrities, Self-Interest or Self-Knowledge? Money, or Integrity and Freedom?

Clearly, money and self-interest have dominated each of the Seven Integrities in the recent past. During that time, we have accrued many benefits. Much of humanity has moved from a feudal society to a technological one with longer lifespans, ease of travel, global communication, and access to all realms of knowledge literally at its fingertips. But we have come to a time where the future seems to be hurtling forward beyond our control, and those who have the greatest power of direction within it are the most driven by self-interest and money, rather than the interests of others or of Mother Earth. In addition, the costs, implications, and dangers of the way forward are beyond our comprehension. We require instead a world of greater wisdom in its people, vibrant in their freedom, with trusted structures of integrity throughout the world's institutions.

I am writing *A Golden Civilization* as a cry of concern and a vision of freedom for all people, for the earth itself, and for its species, but I can speak only for myself. My hope is that my message resonates with people from many parts of the world, and that it contributes energy and ideas to conversations about what a Golden Civilization looks like. My greater hope is that these conversations lead to sustained actions to accomplish a Golden Civilization.

Not only am I a solitary voice, but I have limited perspective as well. While I have been fortunate to travel to many countries throughout the world over my seventy years, to countries rich and poor, I have lived most of my life in America. I have taken for granted its great freedoms, but as those freedoms have become threatened I have become fierce to protect them and, moreover, to enhance them for all.

Much of my experience is with "first world" cultures, and in particular, America. As you read the book, there will be times when its detail and some of its action steps will be aimed at these cultures most familiar to me and many others where I aim to reach a more universal audience. Regardless of our perspectives, there are few places on this earth that do not cry out for freedom and integrity and with love and concern for our planet that would not be bettered by the establishment of a Golden Civilization. I hope you will find sufficient resonance between my perspective and your own experience to find value in my message.

Let us look at how each of the Seven Integrities might function in a Golden Civilization and at what we require to put the architecture of a Golden Civilization in place.

Entrepreneurial Spirit: Freedom

*The spirit that links them all, the experience of freedom
and of compassion.*

*Energy is Eternal Delight,
Exuberance is Beauty.*

~William Blake

The Seven Integrities start with Entrepreneurial Spirit. Entrepreneurial Spirit, as we intend it here, is not limited to shopkeepers or the self-employed. Not even economic, in the traditional sense of the word, it is more organic than that. It belongs to everyone. Entrepreneurial Spirit is our vitality, as basic as breathing, fundamental to our well-being, and to the well-being of civilization. Entrepreneurial Spirit is freedom itself and the passion for freedom that we experience and express in creative action and acts of compassion throughout our days.

We have grown so accustomed to hierarchically-driven growth from corporations and governments that we have trouble imagining any other way growth could occur. But hierarchically-driven growth is one of the least efficient ways to drive growth, because it is least organic. It lacks subtlety and complexity. It lacks humanity.

Hierarchically-driven growth is appropriate if you are a war machine, driving relentlessly toward a single purpose, but in a Golden Civilization, war is obsolete. Such controlling hierarchies are unnecessary. Such reins of power are shackles to the rest of us.

"War is Energy Enslaved," said William Blake. It wastes resources, breaks the human spirit, and desecrates the earth. What we want instead in an ideal world is the freedom of every human being to bring the best of themselves and their Entrepreneurial Spirit into being—along with the systems that guarantee it.

> *It is time, as we establish our Golden Civilization, to end our war and factory machine of a society and instead to fully emerge from the Industrial Revolution and its hierarchies of power. It is time to democratize Entrepreneurial Spirit and deliver freedom everywhere.*

Part of the problem is the continued use of the map we've grown accustomed to, of time and space.

On the maps we've created of mindfulness and civilization, Entrepreneurial Spirit bounces off the mirrors of forgetfulness and awakening with unimaginable force into the architecture of space-time. It has the power to stimulate tremendous growth, but also war. If we are unconscious, not awake, we instantaneously forget ourselves and the present moment. We lose touch with the Great Spirit. Instead, the present moment sends us spiraling chaotically back into time and space, grasping at things or pushing them away to gain stability, to undermine chaos. Even as infants, we created boundaries of Self to cling to, fitting neatly into the grids of time and space, selves that were flawed with incompleteness and longing, selves that were distracted and confined. We have all spent endless moments cascading back and forth between the power of the present moment and our self-centered worlds, lost in whirlpools of forgetfulness. But if we are awake, the energy that thrusts us back from the present moment is the energy of freedom, not of entrapment. It builds Golden Civilizations. There is no energy in the world more powerful. The question is: are we driven by it, or are we masters of it?

The key to Entrepreneurial Spirit is our relationship with the present moment, finding both our passion and our presence there—cultivating at once both its explosive power and the quiet depth of Great Spirit.

It is natural in busy lives to seek peace, driven as we are by the chaos of present moments. Peace is often part of our dream of freedom. We may think of it as letting go of our driven nature, and losing ourselves in a familiar pastime, a habit in which we have become comfortable, and to which we do not need to bring much awareness. We think of peace, in this way, as a break from being awake. But peace itself is unstable. It is not nearly as much the nature of things as changing moments are. The most powerful, practical, and most resilient way to find peace is paradoxically to become more awake through mindfulness, developing the selflessness that delivers Great Spirit into every one of our moments.

When we are awake, the present moment is both an intensification of Great Spirit and of space-time.

Each present moment is like a seed or an egg cracking open. Like children racing to recess, present moments stream from the singularity of ourselves into the worlds of time and space.

A Golden Civilization

Singularity of Ourselves

Present Moment

Great Spirit

Entrepreneurial Spirit as
The Dynamo of the Universe

Space Time
Civilization

Entrepreneurial

Spirit

Singularity of Ourselves
Present Moment
Mirror of Awakening

Democracy Delivers Entrepreneurial Spirit, and Entrepreneurial Spirit Optimizes Economic Growth

We are born to be free. A Golden Civilization recognizes that and, through democracy, delivers it. A Golden Civilization is dedicated to everyone's freedom. Within an economy, there is no more efficient allocation of human resources than that derived from our individual passions for freedom unleashed. In democracy, since freedom is what we seek, maintain, and fight for, lack of freedom causes chaos and invites war.

In the economics that Adam Smith outlined for us, Entrepreneurial Spirit arises from self-interest. But we can see how the self-interest of large institutions and the very wealthy can crush the Entrepreneurial Spirit of ordinary people with power and negative externalities. This is not the universal freedom of a Golden Civilization.

> *Entrepreneurial Spirit must not be bottled up like drugs and confined to the warehouses of the rich and powerful, sequestered by business school elites or available only to those with access to the private equity or venture capital machines. Entrepreneurial Spirit is meant for each and every one of us.*

In a Golden Civilization, we all share its possibility equally as our power in the world. But as things currently stand, we have surrendered our power to money-forces. We have confused Entrepreneurial

Spirit with a relentless drive for profit that is product-focused and factory-like, not nourished in the ground of self-knowledge and authenticity.

> *If money, rather than Entrepreneurial Spirit, is the measure of freedom, then one man or an oligopoly can accumulate all the freedom in the world. And then where will our freedom be? Where is the Golden Civilization? And where is democracy?*

It is said that innovation drives economic growth, but in truth the driver of growth and innovation is Entrepreneurial Spirit. Only when Entrepreneurial Spirit is released everywhere and in everyone, will we maximize economic growth, fulfilling our human potential. As we unleash Entrepreneurial Spirit, and it pops up everywhere, we will require new definitions of growth that take into account all manner of human and planetary flourishing.[h] And that's what really counts. That's what we should be measuring in society. And we should be measuring it as moments of freedom, rather than the hierarchically-driven economic activity measured only by money.

While Entrepreneurial Spirit can be launched individually, it can be supported by government policy, inspired by media and leadership, and facilitated throughout society by proper personal financial advice. In a Golden Civilization, a major purpose of each of these Integrities is to inspire or facilitate Entrepreneurial Spirit in every human being.

---

h.   This movement has already begun in Bhutan and other locations where Gross National Happiness has replaced Gross National Product. It is in its bare beginnings and we have far to go. We must learn as well how to measure moments of freedom, the development of virtue, and models of integrity.

Advice is the most personal and direct way to accomplish this, but it is democracy that aims to govern all the Integrities so as to maximize our freedom across society. So we will start there, with democracy, in the next chapter.

Action Steps and Basic Principles for Entrepreneurial Spirit

1. Make yourself free. Live your dream of freedom. Find it. Mine it. Do it every day. If you can't do it every day, then give yourself a whole day of freedom each week. If you can't do it each week, then each month. Implement a plan that will in short order lead you to your life of freedom. You are meant to be free. You are meant to live in freedom, not merely someday (at best) to retire into freedom.

2. Deepen with mindfulness your experience of the most profound regions of freedom while simultaneously increasing your mastery of the present moment.

3. In each moment of your life, seek to live with authenticity, be who you are meant to be. There is nothing more important than this. If you make a mistake, learn from it. Don't hide or rationalize it. Your growth as a human being is the engine for the growth of a Golden Civilization.

4. Lend support to each person you meet for their dreams of freedom.

5. Politically and in your communities, support all efforts to democratize Entrepreneurial Spirit and to spread the freedom of Entrepreneurial Spirit everywhere. Challenge large institutions, business schools, financial services companies, governments, billionaires, private equity, venture capital, and the elites to distribute Entrepreneurial Spirit equally to all people rather than, like misers, to hoard it just for themselves.

DEMOCRACY

The Democracy section of A Golden Civilization *includes a chapter on democracy and one on media. Standards for truth and transparency in both of these Integrities are critical if democracy is to be sustainable.*

Democracy can take many shapes. When I speak of democracy I am calling to its essence, to its ideal. In America, the form democracy takes is called a republic, distinguished by elective representatives and the rule of law. Often, when I speak of democracy I am thinking of it in its republican form. But my purpose is not to contrast the definitions of democracy and republic, nor to favor one system of democracy over another. My purpose, rather, is to inspire us to action by contrasting the form contemporary democracies take, dominated as they are by institutional power, with the form they would take in a Golden Civilization.

The democracy of a Golden Civilization is not for institutions or the wealthy. It is diverse, widely participative, infused with wisdom and equally accessible to all.

Democracy

Although there are Seven Integrities,
the one that guides them all is Democracy.

Let me start with a vision. What if instead of lobbyists and politicians, as we have come to know them, scurrying through the great halls of democracy—deal-makers, war-makers, financiers, arbitragers, weapons manufacturers, climate-change deniers, billionaires and the acolytes of billionaires,[i] for-profit and one-issue criers with narrow objectives on their minds and all the power of money or raucous voices behind them—instead of these imagine there are only figures of wisdom in the hallowed halls, people you instantly recognize and respect and feel respected by. Everywhere, in every hall, in every

---

i. I have met a few billionaires, at least one of whom I had the privilege to spend real time with. I say privilege because I found him a man of grace, compassion, concern, dedication to his communities and to democracy. He wore his responsibilities with great care, and I learned much from his bearing—a successful, creative man, a visionary and yet a common man, working tirelessly to make the world a better place. I am sure not all are as concerned or as compassionate.

When I refer to "billionaires," I do not intend to be derogatory to them as people. I wish for nothing but freedom and authenticity and great hearts for each of them. Rather, I am referring to their institutional power which gives them more freedoms than a democracy or a free market can sustain if it is dedicated to all of our freedoms not just the wealthy. So, billionaire refers to the *power* of the extremely wealthy in our society. Billionaire is an easy, convenient term to use.

office, in every lobby, in every room, figures of wisdom, attentive listeners, thoughtful people of great heart, who, when you come by, pull up a couple of chairs, sit down with you and listen. People who respect you and want to hear from you. Not people making decisions for businesses (or for themselves) and too busy to talk with you, so much as people making decisions for you, with you, and with you in mind. How would that be?

Impossible? Implausible? Quixotic as it may seem, I think it could be accomplished almost overnight, with the insistent passion of a democratic people and with leadership.

A true democracy requires internal qualities, a particular spirit within each of us, as well as external systems and supports. Let me outline the requirements as I see them for democracy in a Golden Civilization, along with its values and standards. Using the outline as a container, we will then dive into greater depths.

Internally, for a democracy to thrive each of us requires the inner resources to be prepared to lead, to act, and to care. Among those resources:

1. Virtue and Integrity

Corruption kills democracy. Without virtue and integrity, democracy fails. Virtue starts inside each of us, but in a Golden Civilization, virtue is institutionalized through experiential education and training. We learn to value virtue above everything, above even our own self-interest. Larger than self-interest, virtue is part of the self-knowledge that is cultivated at the base of our maps.

2. Freedom

For democracy to flourish in a Golden Civilization, we must understand the experience of freedom within ourselves and the value of it for all people. We care for it for everyone as if wherever it manifests it were our child or our breath.

3. A Common Spirit

We will know, respect, and experience our brotherhood and sisterhood across genders, races, ages, countries, beliefs, education, and wealth. We will understand our common creaturehood (our common breath) with all species, and with the unfolding, breathing nature of the universe. In a Golden Civilization for democracy to unfold, it will be in kindness and with respect for all being.

4. Leadership

Leadership skills are developed by all of us, because if others can't immediately step up to the plate, then in a democracy, we must.

These are learned behaviors and must be nurtured.

Externally, here are some things we must do to deliver the democracy of a Golden Civilization.

1. The passion for democracy must be a movement that never ends, employing social media and the freedoms of assembly, speech, and press across all of civilization, calling out for and establishing democracy everywhere.

2. Beyond that, it is time to establish true democracy in those nations that claim to have one:[j]

---

j.   See Appendix Six: Declining Democracy. The V-Dem Institute from the University of Gothenburg presents in its Annual Democracy Report 2018

a. To ensure <u>one person, one vote,</u> each of us, in the heart of democracy, equal and free.

b. To <u>eliminate institutional dominance,</u> including the dominance of political parties as well as corporations and money in politics.

c. To be always <u>open to new forms of democratic participation,</u> including proportional representation and other forms of democracy as our technology develops and as we learn from our communities what works best, to ensure that everyone has a voice, and that no one is purposefully excluded for political reasons.

d. To systematically bring our <u>figures of greatest wisdom to the very center and heart of democracy</u> and all its branches, including the judiciary and the press.

"Democracy for All?" a comparison of the states of democracy of 178 countries between 2007 and 2017. It is a remarkable study from which we have included its signature chart with score and confidence intervals based on the following indicators: suffrage, elected officials, clean elections, freedom of association, freedom of expression and alternative sources of information, rule of law, judicial constraints on the executive, legislative constraints on the executive, an egalitarian component, a participatory component, and a deliberative component. The chart included in Appendix Six demonstrates the advances and backslides of countries from 2007 (just prior to the US banking crisis) to the first year of Donald Trump's presidency. It calls attention to the countries that have made significant advances and those that have regressed. Not surprisingly, the United States has experienced a significant backslide in the state of its democracy. What is alarming is how fragile our democratic institutions are and how rapid that decline has been in the most powerful leading democracy in the world. The US is not alone. The study concludes that both "Western Europe and North America are back to levels of liberal democracy last seen nearly 40 years ago." Notice also how the other two superpowers, China and Russia, are near the bottom of the chart. Clearly economic liberalism and trade with western democracies has delivered very little democratic freedom to their populations.

e. To protect (or establish) the <u>freedoms of speech, assembly, press, and belief,</u> and establish new <u>freedoms from war, famine, environmental devastation, and corruption</u> everywhere.

For all of this it is time to:

i. Take <u>money out of politics</u> and media.

ii. <u>Reduce inequality</u> so that our economic differences do not stand in the way of our being in community with each other.

iii. Deliver <u>basic income and life plans of freedom for all</u>[k] so that each one of us contributes to civilization at our highest capacity.

iv. <u>Educate everyone:</u> deliver universal college education and more than that— wisdom throughout education. Bring into being everywhere a genuine global community capable of making complex decisions and filled with respect for one another.

3. <u>Establish,</u> by governing, <u>the systems and structures for the Seven Integrities that will guarantee the sustainability of integrity and freedom for a 1,000 generations.</u> Pay attention continually to the structures of each of the Seven Integrities: Entrepreneurial Spirit, Democracy, Media, Advice, Products, Markets, and Leadership. Each must model integrity and deliver freedom to all.

4. <u>Secure Mother Earth.</u> Nothing must threaten our mother, our home, our base.

---

k. Life Planning as a means to freedom and entrepreneurial energy is explored further in the Advice chapter and in Appendix Two. It is an approach to financial advice that I pioneered and taught for over thirty years. Life Planning puts the primary focus on a client's dreams of freedom and on their living lives of greatest meaning and purpose. Among its mottos: Model Integrity, Deliver Freedom.

> **5. _End War._** *We must bring to an end the institutionalized and sanctioned systems of murder and violence that keep us all in thrall to government and to the violence within our own natures. Ultimately even police shouldn't have guns.*

6. Establish leaders across all layers of society as figures of wisdom rather than as managers of avarice and power.

Maps of Democracy

> *Moments of freedom are the essential units of both democracy and economics.*

And so, on our map of Conscious Democracy, where the present moment is at its center, so is freedom. Both a Golden Civilization and Great Spirit radiate from and coalesce toward moments of freedom. The maps reveal the human pathways that gather virtue and wisdom and that forge democracy into space-time as a Golden Civilization.

Contrast a map of a democracy that is filled with unconscious actions with one that is conscious:

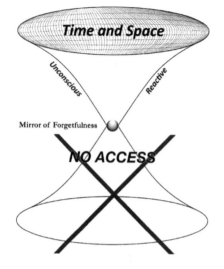

Unconscious Democracy
Hierarchical and Analytic • Reactive and Polarized

Time and Space

Unconscious   *Reactive*

Mirror of Forgetfulness

NO ACCESS

Conscious Democracy

A Golden Civilization

Mindfulness Listening   *Active Creative Engagement*

Mirror of Awakening   Present Moment
Moments of Freedom

Gathering
Virtues

*Great Spirit
Gathering Wisdom*

If freedom is on our maps and we know that it is our goal, nothing stands in our way. Here, the freedom of the present moment and the wisdom of Great Spirit are recognized as essential to democracy and as part of our very nature.

We need wise leaders for a democracy to thrive, but because it is a democracy we need that same wisdom in each of us. We think of wisdom often as wise action, as a quality of engagement with the world around us. But its essence is a quality of understanding inside us.

> *The simplest and most practical definition I know of wisdom is that it is the selfless understanding of the present moment and the impermanence that surrounds it.*

As such, while centered on the present moment, wisdom includes the whole map, incorporating space-time and the selflessness of Great Spirit.

> *As sensitive as a tuning fork, within its vulnerability to impermanence, wisdom is the force of stability and understanding that permeates a Golden Civilization.*

Wisdom is the glue that holds a Golden Civilization together. And it is awake. Most exciting, wisdom is something we can study, deepen, and develop inside ourselves in our education systems and with practices like mindfulness.

> *Embedded inside each of us, wisdom becomes the foundation of participatory democracy.*
>
> *Self-knowledge, or personal wisdom, includes this universal wisdom along with the clarity (also selfless) of one's own mission and the passion and determination to make it happen, to live one's life of greatest meaning.*

This is the passion of Life Planning and of freedom in democracy.

Markets and Democracy

Although we have had an enthusiasm over the past several decades for market-based solutions to social problems, there are important differences between markets and democracy, and we must not confuse them.

In democracy there is an essential equality and compassion that balances the meritocracy and competition of markets. They were born to balance each other, not for one to defeat the other.

> *Markets flourish with innovation, while democracy thrives with collaboration. Markets keep spinning off into new creations, democracy keeps bringing us back together into deeper and more diverse levels of community. They are the centrifugal and centripetal forces of civilization.*

But they are not equal. For markets and democracy to thrive with freedom, democracy must deliberate and determine the structures by which markets most efficiently deliver freedom to all.

Markets maximize the efficiencies upon which democracy places its values. Since the primary value of democracy is on freedom, the primary focus of economics must be: to maximize human freedom now and for a thousand generations into our future.

In markets, success brings you to the top. In democracy, we are equally free, and we celebrate our equality.

Democracy gives everyone a voice in how to maximize freedom across civilization through its rules, principles, regulations, and policies. Markets, on the other hand, facilitate the efficiency of exchanges that deliver us into our unique dreams of freedom. Democracy represents the commitment that we all have to work together to make sure freedom is delivered sustainably, forever, and to all. Democracy is the chalice of freedom. It sees the spark of freedom in everyone, equally.

The freedom of markets fosters and rewards our unique freedoms as they deliver the details of our individual life plans into the structures of civilization.

When institutionalized market thinking dominates democracy, as lobbyists and paid politicians encourage, arguing that without giving way to corporate self-interest we won't be able to compete with other countries, we lose the big picture. We fail to see what's important about democracy and civilization. In a Golden Civilization, it is not money that we are in competition for; it is not traditional economic development. Perhaps for some of us the difference is only slight, but in a Golden Civilization it is freedom that is our passion.

> *A Golden Civilization maximizes the efficient allocation of human resources by maximizing our access to, and passion for, freedom. In cultures of greatest freedom, "productivity" is measured as much by virtue, kindness, generosity, creativity, wisdom, vitality, and compassion as it is by material well-being.*[1]

When we feed on spreadsheets and focus too narrowly on financial profits (particularly those of corporations), we lose sight of our purpose. Society becomes inefficient. Money's relationship to freedom becomes unclear.

---

1. See earlier note on Bhutan where Gross National Happiness has replaced Gross National Product.

The Challenge of Inequality in Democracy

Inequality...is not only morally wrong,
but practically also a source of problems.[4]

Wherever it occurs, poverty is a significant contributor to social
disharmony, ill health, suffering and armed conflict. If we continue
along our present path, the situation could become irreparable.
This constantly increasing gap between the 'haves' and 'have-nots'
creates suffering for everyone.[5]

~Tenzin Gyatso, 14th Dalai Lama

All men are created equal.
~The Declaration of Independence

Poverty is the worst form of violence.
~Mahatma Gandhi

Want to Make Money Like a C.E.O.? Work for 275 Years [6]

The more people possess, the greater their losses; so the rich are not as carefree as the poor. The higher people rise, the faster they fall, so the upper classes are not as secure as the common people.

Association with city people is not as good as friendship with elderly peasants. Calling on upper-class mansions is not as good as getting to know peasant homes.[7]

~Huanchu Daoren

Inequality is the Enemy of Democracy

The biggest threat to democracy is the concentration of wealth in the hands of the few, and therefore the concentration of power.

~Uruguay's Pepe Mujica, called "the world's poorest president" and "the world's most humble president" [8]

The least I can do is speak out for those who cannot speak for themselves. The greatest danger to our future is apathy.

~ Jane Goodall

> *In a democracy, there is no political inequality; money doesn't buy elections or political privilege. One person one vote is the law of the land. A great democracy both inspires and humbles us as it asks us to model equality amongst each other. There is no discrimination by race, sex, age, occupation, belief, disability, wealth, or income. To establish a Golden Civilization such discriminations must cease.*

And yet, in the market portion of civilization, there are clear advantages for a democracy to find just the degree of financial inequality that will most efficiently stimulate innovation. But there is no advantage, and only great danger to all of us, from the degree of financial inequality we experience today.

Democracy does not thrive in gated-community cultures. In such communities, people are separated from each other, and politics becomes polarized and angry. Who among us wants to live next door to someone who makes $20 million a year? If we could get to know them, they may be wonderful people, but if we get into a dispute with them, would any of us have an equal chance in a court of law or a political battle? It is no wonder that society is cynical.

When, as is now the case, 42 wealthy people own as much as 3.7 billion others[9]—as half the world's population——something is very wrong. If democracy has facilitated this, then what we currently call democracy is immoral. In truth this inequality was not facilitated by democracy. It was facilitated by the taint of money in politics. In a democracy money has no vote, and it is up to the people to ensure that is so and to decide the optimal degrees of inequality to be allowed in society.

No democracy would ever decide to give the wealth of 3.7 billion people to just 42. We have been tricked, hacked, hoodwinked, and deceived. It is our moral responsibility to reclaim democracy. For a Golden Civilization to come into being, inequality must be dramatically reduced.

In a Golden Civilization, the levels of inequality are such that none of us feel threatened by the wealth of the person next to us, or by their poverty, but rather we celebrate each other's freedoms and our equality as human beings and citizens.

Certainly, we need strong economic incentives for entrepreneurial businesses. In the 1950s and 60s, the average CEO of a listed company would take home 20-30 times what his lowest-paid employee would take. Now we see that number has mushroomed to the hundreds and occasionally thousands. Returning to 20-30 times will bring a much stronger participatory democracy into being and increase innovation by creating more entrepreneurial endeavor across civilization. Plato suggested that the income of the wealthiest in a society should never exceed five times the income of the poorest. Perhaps in a Golden Civilization we will settle somewhere closer to that ratio.

At present, it is not unusual in any year to see salaries of $10 million to $120 million among the elite.[m] Such inflated salaries do not create leaders, as they increase division and inauthenticity in society. They create bosses often fawned after or resented by their employees and neighbors. Such overpaid executives are rejected by their communities and feared and separated from the people. How can they be leaders?

---

m. See Appendix Three: Income Inequality for sample range of income inequality.

When there are extreme inequalities of income or wealth, how can democracy be effective? Do each of those 3.7 billion people wield as much political power as the 42 billionaires who control as much wealth as all of them put together? Of course not. But that's how it would be in a true democracy. Market power is one thing but democratic power is something else. It belongs equally to each of us.

> *Inequality is not a failure of capitalism, it is a failure of democracy.*

Extremes of inequality arise wherever markets (including political markets) are allowed to be dominated by the rich and powerful. They arise when we confuse "free" markets with the "freedom" of companies (or governments) to limit markets through their power. The people, and not the markets, should determine, through democratic means, the limits to inequality in our society.

Great profits should go to the creators of new products and services and systems. But not forever. And not at the expense of a Golden Civilization or Mother Earth. The rewards for innovators and creators should be determined not by them or their paid henchmen in corrupt political systems, nor by media owned by themselves or others of similar fortune, and certainly not by a market unleashed from democracy. Rather, the rewards should be determined by markets governed by democracy where all votes are equal, and where we choose with our votes figures of wisdom to debate and determine the structures of markets and of society that will maximize freedom for all.

Here are two policy solutions to inequality, both simple and elegant, that could be quickly implemented. One solution taxes only the rich to ensure that inequality never gets out of hand from above. The other uses a basic (guaranteed) income to eliminate poverty and reduce inequality from below.

Taxes

Among the many ways to reduce inequality, the simplest and most direct is through taxation. The problem has been that with the ever-increasing influence of money in politics, taxation as a policy has been toxic to the political class who owe their elections to the wealthy. All of us would prefer to be richer, and so can be convinced to vote for lower taxes. But since in our current model the rich control the politicians and paid lobbyists write the legislation, the rich get richer from these policies and the rest of us get relatively poorer. The most recent "tax cut" was an example of this, where Warren Buffett announced that his company made $29 billion from the tax cut while the Speaker of the US House of Representatives, Paul Ryan, touted a secretary gaining an extra $1.50 per week from the bill.

There is a simple solution to this:

> *Instead of constantly giving the rich more benefits, tax only the rich. Remove "taxes" from political debate by limiting taxation to the top 10% of society, or perhaps the top 5%. Very simple to do.*
>
> *• First, determine what is the optimal level of income inequality for our democracy.*
> *• Second, eliminate taxes on the bottom 90%-95%.*
> *• Third, reduce taxes on all but the top 1%.*
> *• Fourth, put a steeply graduated tax on the 1% only.*
>
> *That will do it!*

Consider the following charts of income levels and share of income taxes.

Annual Income[10]

Year	Top 0.1%	Top 1%	Top 5%	Top 10%	Top 25%	Bottom 50%
2014	$2,136,762. and above	$465,626. and above	$188,996. and above	$133,445. and above	$77,714 and above	$0-$38,173.

Total Income Tax Shares, 1980-2013[11]
(Share of Federal Income Tax Paid by Each Group)

Year	Total	Top 0.1%	Top 1%	Top 5%	Between 5%-10%	Top 10%	Between 10%-25%	Top 25%	Between 25%-50%	Top 50%	Bottom 50%
2014	100%	19.85%	39.48%	59.97%	10.91%	70.88%	15.90%	86.78%	10.47%	97.25%	2.75%

Here are tables expressing the two possibilities I mentioned (from among many other possibilities that would bring inequality to levels that would stimulate a Golden Civilization.)

Eliminate Income Taxes for the Bottom 90%

99-100%	Graduated Tax increase paying the rest of income taxes necessary
95-99%	10% Tax Reduction
90-95%	20% Tax Reduction
0-90%	No Tax

Eliminate Income Taxes for the Bottom 95%

99-100%	Steeply gratuated tax increase paying the rest of income taxes necessary
95-99%	10% Tax Reduction
0-95%	No Tax

Tax policy solutions should not be limited to income taxes. After all, inequality is measured as much by wealth as by income. For 2017, Oxfam reported that 82% of the global increase in wealth went to the richest 1% of the world's population.[12]

Thomas Piketty in his book *Capital in the Twenty-First Century* argues persuasively for a global tax on wealth. There are many reasons for such a tax. One is that the rate of return on wealth outpaces the growth of economies and of wages. So the rich with their investments get richer and the poor who work in the economy get poorer, and the gap between them eats away at democracy, delivering freedoms more and more just to the rich.

In addition, given tax havens, only a global tax would catch all the wealth. This is important if we are to become a global society and take proper care of Mother Earth and become a Golden Civilization. No one should be able to escape into their own private world of money-laundering, tax havens, and riches at the expense of the rest of us.

A steeply graduated annual tax on the wealth of the most wealthy 1% in society would go a long way to establish our democratic intention for greater equality in society. It might start at a nominal amount for those right at the threshold of wealth but increase substantially for those worth more than $100 million, and even more so for billionaires. We can calibrate it precisely to achieve a specific wealth distribution over time, balancing rewards for innovation with the benefits of a Golden Civilization and the aim of freedom for all.

Estate taxes are another area where the extreme inequalities of the top 1% can and should be generationally reduced. Democracies are incompatible with aristocracies.

For inequality to be reduced, we must know its extent. There must be an open book, complete transparency of wealth, income, and taxation. Tax havens, tax evasion, and money laundering are a theft from civilized society. For such crimes, the assets hidden should be confiscated and jail time imposed. The larger the amount, the longer the jail time. Corporate charters should be revoked and future corporate charters forbidden. The severity of the punishment should match its dollar amount. Raiding the Treasury for one's own benefit is a crime against each of us individually, a crime against democracy, a crime against humanity, and a crime against Mother Earth.

Basic Income

While an equitable tax structure can do much to reduce levels of income inequality from the top of the income spectrum, a negative income tax, or a system of basic guaranteed income, can adjust it from the bottom. A basic income for all benefits democracy, stimulates the economy, and brings higher levels of freedom, well-being, and happiness across civilization.

> *There are many reasons to implement a basic income. The most persuasive one for a democracy is that poverty is filled with suffering and those lost in suffering can't see clearly, can't experience the world as it is, and can't be counted on to function in a healthy way. Poverty burdens our world with inefficiencies of health, unwelcome dependencies, and widespread dissatisfaction.*
>
> *It prevents the flourishing of freedom, adding unnecessary greed, lethargy, and aversion to the world. Even voting, the most essential function in a democracy, loses its vitality and credibility. Those who suffer often don't have the energy necessary to vote, and furthermore may have difficulty knowing how best to vote, as fear, anger, lethargy, or poverty obscure their clarity and ability to accumulate the knowledge and self-knowledge essential for a great democracy to function.*

Arguments for a basic income go back hundreds of years to Thomas More's *Utopia*. Among those early arguments was the recognition that the onset of private land ownership deprived many of their ability to be productively self-employed. The argument was made that we all have a right from birth to participate in civilization. Without that participation, it was argued that land owners had stolen from us the God-given rights we were born with.

> *Some argue, on the other side, that a basic income will encourage laziness, drug use, and other deleterious behaviors, but studies don't bear this out. In fact, studies have shown higher productivity, healthier lifestyles, lower medical costs, better nutrition, stronger families, better childhoods, less crime, and lower dependencies on alcohol and drugs.*[13]

Among the many institutional benefits cited is the possibility of simplifying government by coordinating a basic income with other transfer systems. Most agree that eliminating poverty would bring huge benefits. As a consequence, some argue a universal basic income (UBI) should be set just above the poverty level. Others argue for much higher benefits so that UBI could completely replace other income-transfer programs.[n]

For years, I have advocated incorporating Life Planning into any basic income program, giving free hour-long annual life plans to all in need. Life Planning, as we've noted, is the term for a kind of coaching that financial advisers do that is dedicated to discovering and delivering their clients into their dreams of freedom regardless of their means.

---

n.   From a practical standpoint, with the vast disparities of wealth, incomes, and purchasing power, not only among people, but also among nations, basic income should first be applied in each nation individually before tackling global issues.

Life Planning turbocharges the benefits of basic income by helping each person clarify their most passionate purposes, inspiring them to deliver them, and providing them with the financial knowledge and architecture to do so. The combination of basic income and Life Planning will increase economic growth and stimulate entrepreneurial endeavor much more than a plain vanilla approach to basic income. The combined energy is optimistic and infectious. It enhances both traditional measures of growth and the deeper measures of meaning and happiness.

Much of our traditional focus in economic policy has been directed toward jobs (e.g., unemployment levels) and the products that jobs produce (Gross Domestic Product). The truth is, people want freedom, not jobs and not products, although there is a relationship—people want to work, to be productive, to be part of what makes civilization thrive. For most of us, work is an aspect of freedom. But working is different from "jobs." Jobs is part of an institutional industrial mindset of civilization as filled with factories, not freedom. A life of work, in contrast, is filled with freedom as work is freely chosen. The focus on jobs and profits by politicians surrenders our democratic power to large institutions. They then become the arbiters and decision makers. As a consequence, they dominate innovation, creativity, and freedom. Basic income returns that creative power to the people. It delivers to us the individual freedom to make economic decisions that maximize our humanity and thus our contributions to society throughout life. Through the mix of Life Planning and basic income, society maximizes the efficient allocation of human resources in a democracy that thrives with innovation and freedom.

Money in Politics? Or Wisdom?

Just an oligarchy with unlimited political bribery. [14]

~Jimmy Carter on the United States of America

Substantial numbers of legislators sell out the public interest in exchange for political money.

~Fifty Shades of Green: High Finance, Political Money and the U.S. Congress, by Ferguson, Jorgensen and Chen. The Roosevelt Institute, May 2017 [15]

One should not enter in among the power brokers. If one does so the stain will last all one's life.[16]

~Huanchu Daoren

By most definitions of the word, the subverting and selling of democracy to the highest bidders is treason.

Welcome to the world of campaign finance in America, the most powerful democracy on the planet.

There has been much great work done on the topic of money in politics, particularly in America. I refer you to two of the best resources. First, the Center for Responsive Politics, whose website Opensecrets. org tracks sources of political money and its movement from donors to politicians in America. If you are curious who buys the elections and how their money is then represented in key committees in Washington, you need go no further. Opensecrets.org is an eye-opener. You cannot emerge from that site without questioning the very foundations of our democracy. If you're reading this from another country, you will find Opensecrets.org a model of transparency for what should be available to every culture in the world.

The second resource is the report *Fifty Shades of Green* by Ferguson, Jorgensen, and Chen from the Roosevelt Institute.[17] Read it to see how directly political money influences members of Congress as they vote on the floor.

There have been a number of attempts at campaign finance reform in America, each of them greeted with great public enthusiasm, but each attempt so far has created more problems than it has solved. It's time we addressed this issue thoroughly, no loopholes permitted, to create a political system that will allow a Golden Civilization of integrity and freedom to emerge.

The latest blow to integrity in campaign finance and thus to the viability of our democracy was delivered in the Supreme Court's 2010 decision Citizens United. You can grasp some of its consequences from this testimony by Sheila Krumholz, Executive Director of the Center for Responsive Politics, before the Senate Democratic Policy and Communications Committee on July 19, 2017:

"I can attest to the fact that the work of unveiling the sources of money spent to shape U.S. elections has now become extremely challenging. As always, it comes down to transparency."

"In particular, the Citizens United decision threw the door wide open to unlimited contributions from unlimited and secret sources giving to supposedly independent outside groups interested in shaping electoral outcomes."

In addition, regarding "foreign corporations, individuals and governments...foreign donations can be given easily, legally and secretly to nonprofits that are now allowed to be highly politically active."

"We have found:

• Politically active nonprofits that report to the IRS political spending that contradicts their FEC° reports covering the same period;
• Entities that raise and spend tens of millions of dollars but have no employees, no volunteers, nor even a bricks-and-mortar presence, but exist only as a UPS box—raising the specter of money laundering organizations whose sole function is to act as intermediaries, obscuring money's source and pathways;
• Purported "social welfare" and "business league" nonprofits whose financial activity spikes in election years and then plummets in non-election years to far lower levels reflecting

---

o. Federal Election Commission

their pre-Citizens United activity—a pattern more typical of political campaign committees than organizations devoted to social uplift.

"Voters quite logically evaluate campaign communications differently when they have information about who is promoting the message, which is why political operatives and donors seek anonymity—to take away the ability of people to think critically about and possibly discount their message.

"Unfamiliar and innocuous-sounding names used by politically active nondisclosing nonprofits may actually lead voters to find their claims to be more credible than those from organizations with which they are already familiar."

From democracy's perspective, institutions have been awarded a "freedom of speech" that only the very wealthy in our country can actually afford. Democracy is no longer about our equality; it is about our subservience to the proclamations of billionaires and the most powerful corporations in not only America, but the whole world.

Ferguson, Jorgensen, and Chen in *Fifty Shades of Green* identify seven broad areas where political money and influence can enter democracy, often in the dark. They include payments to lawyers, political figures, charitable causes and foundations, think tanks, traditional campaign spending, stock tips, and public relations. Other avenues include mortgages and other loans, money going to spouses and family, and even the ability of the rich and powerful to have lunch, or a phone call with anyone on the planet, simply by making the contact. Government responds by doing favors back. If we are going to create a

Golden Civilization, we need to address in detail how money corrupts our political system and undermines democracy, and it must all be stopped. The penalties for the misuse of money in politics must be enormous. They must threaten liberty as well as financial fortune. It must never happen again.

There can be no deliberative democracy but only obstructionism, and polarization, if our politicians are bought. A politician's constituency becomes one person, their political contributor who is their boss, and the politician is not hired to make the best decision, but to obey. Political boss donors don't care a lot about your wisdom, your ethics, or your morality, as long as you do their bidding.

It is important that we keep reflecting on this. Large institutions don't breathe. They have no life, no heart, no contemplative depth, no access to genuine freedom. They should have no political standing in a democracy, none at all. But we've let these institutions (and billionaires who act not as free individuals, but as dominating institutions) elect our politicians and our judiciary sworn to uphold our democracy. They own the media by which we form our opinions. Their lobbyists dominate the regulatory processes and the writing of legislation. If we are to have a Golden Civilization, we must end all of this.

Wisdom

When a prince's personal conduct is correct, his government is effective without the issuing of orders. If his personal conduct is not correct, he may issue orders, but they will not be followed.

~Confucius

As a society, we have emphasized knowledge in civilization, a knowledge-based economy, knowledge-based systems. But for democracy to thrive in a Golden Civilization, we need hearts and brains together. We need wisdom-based systems and a wisdom-based democracy. We need great listeners all the way through. If there is no wisdom, expedience and self-interest rule. Half-truths and the influences of marketing take over. Before you know it, we have been conditioned to expect lies and deceit in office. Hypocrisy, manipulation, and money talk instead of sincerity and authenticity.

We require two things to achieve wisdom in democracy: structures and systems to support and perpetuate wisdom, and we need to build wisdom into the character of our politicians and ourselves. In a Golden Civilization, the value of wisdom in the populace and its leaders is deeper and stronger than the values of the marketplace or institutions.

In a Golden Civilization, our politicians are great listeners, both inside themselves and to others. They bring empathy and inspiration to the dreams of freedom of everyone they meet. Clearly, we need standards for leaders. As mindfulness and self-knowledge practices spread throughout society, will standards of ethical leadership naturally take root? We will reflect more deeply on the training and standards of leaders in our chapter on leadership.

Our deliberation as to the actual structures of democracy will evolve as technology evolves and as we get money out of politics. Our principles are clear nonetheless.

> *Democracy is for us, not for our institutions. Institutions are meant to serve us and all of our freedoms, not to be our masters.*

Institutions have no right to a freedom of speech if, by their power, they diminish one democratic citizen of the right to express their freedom of speech. Again, we must get money out of politics and out of media.

Solutions to Money in Politics

Several things could be done, a number of them right away, to reduce the influence of money in politics.

First, and most controversially, our top-level politicians must choose between money in the marketplace and service to all citizens. If we don't restrict the profit-making ability of our politicians, we are in danger of having one emperor after another, tweaking a regulation here, eliminating one over there, making deals with corporations, changing the tax rules. With each change, hundreds of millions of dollars pour into their coffers.

What would inspire a Golden Civilization instead? What actions would convince the people of their leaders' wisdom and of their dedication to each one of us and to the system's integrity?

Pepe Mujica, former president of Uruguay, recently retired with a 70% approval rating. Instead of a big limousine, he drove a VW Beetle while in office, and he lived very modestly, giving his income to charity. Gandhi and Pope Francis, though great and powerful leaders, inspired their followers by their humble lifestyles. At times, we have asked high office-holders to put their assets in a blind trust during their time in office. Enforcement of blind trusts would be a great step. How much more inspiring for all of us it would be if they gave away their fortunes entirely (with the possible exception of their homes) in order to serve the people. The government has always been generous with pensions for high office-holders after service. Doesn't it make sense that politicians have to choose whether they serve their own profit, or the people? In a Golden Civilization, our leaders would inspire us by being a leader amongst us, not a ruler hobnobbing with the rich and powerful and lording over us.

Second, politicians must never serve those who paid for their elections by voting for issues that will pad the pockets of their wealthy contributors. That is not democracy but indenture and hire. Until we get money out of politics, politicians should recuse themselves from voting on their own interests or the interests of primary campaign contributors and other sources of money for themselves or family members.

As long as money remains in politics, in every correspondence, on every business card, website, and advertisement, an office-holder's 10 top donors should be prominently displayed and dark money fully identified. A law requiring recusal could support the principles of campaign finance that honors democracy. Let the lawyers, academics, and ethics specialists fashion a law that allows no ambiguity. If even the spirit of the law is violated, there would be fierce consequences.

Third, and in any case, it is time to finish the work of campaign finance reform—with no loopholes possible. Since thwarting the donor class and their subservients has proved most difficult to date, perhaps the American people (the voters) should demand formation of a commission with all the powers necessary to completely take money out of politics, including the personal fortunes of those who are running. There must be strict enforcement provisions to act quickly wherever the intent of the law is taken advantage of.

Fourth, ban all political advertising. From the beginning, political advertising has lacked thoughtful discussion, much less wisdom. More often than not, it reflects who can spend the most money to put up slick, animated visual messaging appealing to our basic instincts, often laced with innuendo and inaccuracies. And in the elections, money rather than wisdom most always wins. (See Opensecrets.org for details.) If our goal is to have politicians of wisdom who excel at thoughtful deliberation, then that is what we should look for in our media. Would figures of wisdom advertise? How would they like to be elected? What about half hour talks on each of the major issues of the day? An hour to present their grand strategic vision? Political debates that have more depth and time for discussion, with time for follow-up? News analysis on the facts, and statistics that support or refute the opinion expressed? We need a process designed to call upon each of us to deliberate with our better natures. The process itself should inspire wisdom, strengthen confidence, and deliver knowledge into the country. Political advertising as it now exists should be banned.

Fifth, vet politicians thoroughly. All politicians' finances should be an open book. They must, in addition, subject themselves to investigative journalism. Tax havens and failures to disclose should result in loss of position, voided elections, and jail time.

Sixth, for a President, a cabinet member, or senior adviser in the executive branch, and for a Senator or Congressman or our judiciary, corruption (as we see in our campaign finance of today) should be seen as treason and punished as such.

Seventh, until we get fundraising completely out of politics, which is our goal, there should be a maximum annual campaign/political contribution amount that is set for all donors, billionaires included. Ten percent of the minimum basic income in society makes sense (currently perhaps $1,000 - $4,000), so that even the poor can tithe to politics if they want and have as much political influence as a billionaire. Rather than what we've seen in recent decades from financial services, where banks and billionaires can raid the corporate treasury for billions and then give a cut to politicians for their political campaigns as their tithe.

These seven actions may seem like a lot, in our political climate, but we must stop asking what is possible in the midst of such corruption and ask instead what is necessary for a Golden Civilization to thrive with freedom. It is no time to compromise on what is necessary. Compromises have led us to the plight we are in.

Institutions

Those who live virtuously may be desolate for a time, but those who depend on flattering the powerful are destitute forever.[18]

~Huanchu Daoren

Special interests dominate the debates in Washington

**~Barack Obama, Community Organizer
and President of the United States**

Institutions provide a great service to democracy. In addition to manufacturing and delivering products and services, they gather data, analyze, and disseminate knowledge. They are masters of the grid, and so are useful resources in all decision-making.

Both for-profits and non-profits often possess detailed and comprehensive knowledge of issues that others do not. But the knowledge comes with a singleness of purpose—whether profits or point of view—that makes them suspect. These organizations will argue their position rather than view a situation holistically or empathically or with wisdom. And their economic clout makes them unfair adversaries rather than welcome collaborators in a democratic process. They use their money to get their point across in ways that none but the richest human beings possibly can, dominating speech and press as well as democracy, and thus robbing us of our freedoms.

In democracy, we must determine what mix of institutional knowledge, outside consultants, outside-the-box thinking, and engaged listening to citizens politicians require to make wise decisions as fiduciaries for millions of people and a thousand generations. We must make those decisions without the undue influence of institutions.

> *Government in a Golden Civilization, in a democracy, is meant to facilitate, protect, and maximize human freedom. It is not meant to be the center of corporate economic power or decision making. In order to protect our freedoms, democracy has a responsibility to care for our planet for as much of eternity as we can claim; this responsibility far exceeds that of maximizing quarterly profits or short-term jobs. Democracy has a greater responsibility to be compassionate toward a people's suffering and their dreams of freedom than to be responsive to the cash-flow requirements of billionaires and their institutions, although at times it must weigh each. The integrity of democracy must never be sacrificed to, or tainted by, institutional self-interest if a Golden Civilization is to be sustainable.*

Institutional scandals of fraud, hypocrisy, corruption, and cheating fill our media pages, weakening and undermining trust in both capitalism and democracy. They are inevitable in systems where money is the measure of freedom rather than wisdom. It is democracy's responsibility to ensure integrity throughout our institutions. In the democracy of a Golden Civilization, even more than integrity, wisdom and authenticity thrive everywhere—all the way to the highest office.

In a Golden Civilization there is a rigorous separation of institutions and the state, much as there is of church and state. The "state" is meant to be ours and ours alone. It is meant to become ever more human, not parceled out to interest groups and corporations. Democracy is for the people.

For wisdom to gather, institutional dominance in democracy must end. For democracy to work, for us to trust its structures and systems, our representatives must be sages, kind hearts, figures of wisdom and intelligence, with open arms.

If lobbyists are allowed into government at any level, they must be invited, not hover like birds of prey wherever democratic decisions are made. Government is not for them but for us. They have corporate, not democratic agendas.

In a Golden Civilization, there is no revolving door between government and corporations, between politicians and lobbyists. If you are born to serve, then you are sworn to serve, or in sharp contrast, profit is your passion. There must be significant firewalls of years, dollars, and laws between the two poles.

How do we weigh the relative merits of a competitive business marketplace against human meaning and freedom? What do you say when it is argued that government interference in business will make business inefficient? That's why we elect persons of wisdom, not purchased politicians, in a democracy. Where there are concerns for humanity and Earth, literally life and death concerns, business may look inefficient from a for-profit corporate standpoint.

> *But efficiency in a society is not primarily about profits and money. It is about the sustainability of freedom for thousands of generations.*
>
> *And who should make those decisions? Figures of wisdom. Everywhere. A Golden Civilization is filled with wisdom.*

Democracy, Listening, and Our Open Hearts

The government of a great democracy acts with wisdom, constantly breaking through institutional rigidity. It is possible only if we break through our own rigidities, open our hearts and learn to listen.

> *The greater our capacity to listen, the more vast the reaches of civilization.*

That should be obvious in regard to our openness to cultures that are different from our own, but it is also true deep within ourselves, where listening is learned. When we are quiet in meditation, we naturally bring kindness and comfort to our sensations, which are also the sensations of life itself and of all creatures. The more we know ourselves in this way, the more we experience our kinship with life and the world around us and the more present we become for democracy.

Education

I am not of the industrial/institutional camp that believes the purpose of education is to get a job, as if we were slaves to our institutional culture. Rather, education is meant to give us the capacity to navigate the world with curiosity, to make it a better place in ways that we choose, as we deliver freedom to ourselves and those we love.

In a Golden Civilization, for democracy to thrive, our first step must be to know ourselves.

And then, as democrats, as educated citizens we must be prepared to deal with the ethical dilemmas of our day. Today they include surveillance, pollution, inequality, artificial intelligence, robots, cloning, species extinction, war, as well as the nature, purpose, and structures of democracy itself. All involve decisions, strategy, and direction that should be made in the wisdom of democracy, not in the competitive surges of the marketplace where the glories of short-term profits can obscure negative externalities that might last for centuries or millennia.

> *In a complex civilization, in order to vote intelligently and for democracy to be strong, we must equip all citizens with the strength of self-knowledge, with a capacity for leadership and the ability to address the ethical dilemmas most likely to present themselves to society. Free, comprehensive, and universal college education available to all who want it would go a long way to accomplish this.*

For self-knowledge and wisdom to flourish, we must start their education much earlier, in primary school or before.

A strictly competitive, skill-based education system places unnatural and unsustainable hierarchies over authenticity and the heart and the passion for freedom. Instead we must intermingle the two. As long as our education is aimed at technology rather than wisdom, we will remain warriors rather than democrats. Our governance will be dominated by autocrats and hierarchical forces rather than ourselves.

In a Golden Civilization, wherever we go, people are supportive, empathic, and enthusiastic for our dreams of freedom. This is the democratic soil in which Entrepreneurial Spirit takes root, where each of us learns to be free, ethical, and wise.

Here is my outline of
Education Requirements for a Golden Civilization:

1. Experiential:
    A. Internal. Objectives and practices: self-knowledge, authenticity, leadership, contemplative freedom, emotional intelligence, vitality, flexibility, creativity, mindfulness, and virtues.

    B. External, creaturely. Nature and survival programs such as Outward Bound, including basic understanding of health, food, and water systems. Understanding our bodies, our roots, and planet Earth: for our survival if our technological structures fail us, and to sustain Mother Earth.

2. Communication: nonviolent communication skills essential for the functioning of democracy, markets, leadership, and media.

> **A.** General skills. Building upon mindfulness with experiential learning, so that everywhere we support and are inspired by each other's dreams and pursuit of freedom. Building upon the natural understanding that all of us are born equal. Learning speech habits that continually affirm these understandings. Developing non-institutional practices of listening and engagement along with respectful inter-communication processes (group, personal, and technological.)
>
> **B.** For resistance to tyranny, non-violent resistance training, watchfulness, active citizenry, wisdom, and engagement processes. Learning how to speak truth to power.

3. Traditional:

> **A.** Multi-cultural, liberal arts, culture, science, and economics. Understanding who we are in the context of our history and the great actions and thoughts of those who came before us.
>
> **B.** Practical money skills incorporating our dreams of freedom, so we can navigate the economic world and create the structures that will maximize our own Entrepreneurial Spirit.
>
> **C.** Politics:
>> **i.** Teach the all-inclusive nature of democracy, where each one of us is created equal.
>> **ii.** Understand the strengths and weaknesses of all systems of democratic government, including the less used and more speculative forms (e.g., proportional representation). Understand the critical nature of the rule of law to identify and protect our free-

doms, without which democracy could not exist, including our participatory right as equal citizens and the freedoms of speech, assembly, press, and belief.

iii. Study how to protect democracy when it is threatened and how to guard and strengthen it when it is not. Require courses in how authoritarian regimes, ethnic cleansings, and genocides came about and what citizens should do in the face of such evil. Suggest approaches to ensure that democracy, integrity, and freedom thrive in the midst of challenges from the complexities of technology as well as ethical dilemmas.

D. Planet Earth—study the science so we are always watchful protectors of the planet and shepherds of its species.

Mother Earth and All Her Creatures

For as long as space endures,
And for as long as sentient beings remain,
Until then may I, too, abide
To dispel the misery of the world.[19]

~Shantideva

As crude a weapon as the cave man's club, the chemical barrage has been hurled against the fabric of life.

~Rachel Carson

How do you know but ev'ry Bird that cuts the airy way,
Is an immense world of delight.

~William Blake

> **The joy that mindfulness brings comes from the simplest act**
> **of consciousness, from bare attention. Who's to say that that**
> **simple act cannot be accomplished in every creature in the**
> **universe or in every molecule? Who's to say that mindfulness**
> **is not the nature of the universe itself?**

A dystopian world view can easily be drawn from today's news. A barren earth, ancient glaciers slipping to the sea, coastal cities flooding, insects and birds disappearing. First their music is lost and then the earth itself.

A Vision for a Golden Civilization

If I were to look back 200 years from now at this time, my greatest delight would be that we quickly ended famine and war and then stopped global warming before its extremes flooded the coasts, extinguished numerous species, forced mass migrations of humans, destabilized democracies, and spread human misery and violence across a desperate planet.

I would instead be heartened to find clean Earth, air, and water, and find our institutional and factory cultures in harmony with all creatures and with Mother Earth.

The Mission

As we lay the foundation for a Golden Civilization, if we want to be sustainable for a thousand generations, if not for the natural life-span of the human species, surely our first objective must be to secure the health, safety, and longevity of planet Earth.

Among the systems most critical to our mission are those of knowledge and science, our trust in them and our ability to use them with wisdom. We have learned a great deal about how to create new products for humanity and how to analyze and improve many mundane details of our lives. We have generated and discovered an enormous quantity and quality of information. But from this information, we have also gained the ability to extinguish species, including our own, and to diminish the health, vitality, and joy of our descendants for all future years by our thoughtless interference with natural systems of air and water, climate, environmental ecosystems, and biology. And with our hierarchies of power, we can destroy very quickly, almost instantaneously in terms of the life of the planet. If we are to become a Golden Civilization and better use our ever-increasing knowledge we must employ a wisdom we have not yet gained.

If we were more wise, whenever our institutions of science detect danger to our planet, we would recall all the knowledge we possess and act to protect our home base. When cries of warning come from the majority of our best scientists, we would act immediately with vigor to end the danger, at all costs. We would never sacrifice our children's planet for short-term pleasure or gain.

If, as is happening now, we ignore the near unanimity of our voices of science, then shame on us for the great and inevitable loss of life and habitat to occur. Shame on us for allowing villains and fools to thwart democracy for their own pleasure and profit. We must take back our power as equal citizens. We must act with wisdom. If we do not take the time and make the effort now, there may be no time left and the effort required may surpass our means.

We must end the explicit murders that arise from the arrogance of our institutional culture and its coveted hierarchies of power. These murders sweep across all of Mother Earth and her species, not just as pollution, but also as war, oppression, ethnic cleansing, and other atrocities. With billionaire money and institutional self-interest dominating our media and our democracy, we legitimize murder and suffering for the sake of power and the interests of owners.

The saddest thing I know is that the human species is either thoughtlessly or intentionally killing its own species and other species, all over the planet each day. These threats to species and the earth may have arisen through economic activity as negative externalities. But as knowledgeable democratic citizens, it is our collusion that enables their continuation. Our cynicism, lethargy, ennui—our own banality of evil—must be recognized as feeding the problem.

"But what can I alone do about it?" is no longer an acceptable response. Each of us must do everything we can.

These murders threaten the earth itself. They arise from a failure of democracy, and of its leadership to ground us in values and principles deeper than self-interest. We must address these failures first within ourselves and then politically, by addressing pollution and our debt to other creatures and war and our debt to other people. These are the province of democratic—not corporate—decision making. They call out for immediate action and for new structures of democracy that replace self-interest with wisdom.

The World Wildlife Fund reports that in just the 42 years from 1970 to 2012, 58% of the global population of wild vertebrate species has been lost.[20] Scientists say the rate of species extinction in the 20th century has been conservatively estimated at 100 times the norm of prior periods, and many argue that the rate of loss is factors higher than that.

These lost species were adapted and fine-tuned over millions of years to live on Mother Earth, with biological wisdom beyond our ken, all lost essentially in our time through our carelessness, our corruption, and our collusion. These are the highest rates of species extinctions in millions of years, and many scientists believe that by our actions (and inaction) we may be creating, and in the midst of, the sixth mass extinction of species in the history of the earth.

We have colluded in this by allowing our "democratic" government to be elected by a few billionaires and for-profit institutions whose interest is not for the earth, its people, and its species, but is for maintaining and increasing their personal wealth and power over a tiny span of time in Earth's 4.5-billion-year history. As we live in a democracy, we can choose with our votes not to countenance this behavior any longer.

As the Golden Civilization arrives, democracy shifts from a band of brothers and sisters gathering together to counter tyranny and institutional dominance, to our gathering as a community that is caring and compassionate for all the world's creatures and for creation itself.

Creatures can't see clearly if they are suffering. In our terminology, they can't experience freedom. Just as human beings suffer in the face of war, famine, or of mass migrations, the stresses and sufferings of global warming, pollution, and species extinctions mean creatures act inefficiently in their environments. They make poor decisions. They have less clarity, more panic. They are more selfish. They are less conscious.

Imagine all of us for a moment as the shepherds of our planet and its creatures, perhaps of other life-giving planets and moons in our solar system and across the universe—shepherds, not exploiters for profit condoning the casual slaughter of our cousinly creatures, but shepherds.

In a democracy, it is our choice.

War

War is Energy Enslaved
Energy is Eternal Delight

~William Blake

Of course, war and the large military establishments are the greatest sources of violence in the world. Whether their purpose is defensive or offensive, these vast powerful organizations exist solely to kill human beings. We should think carefully about the reality of war. Most of us have been conditioned to regard military combat as exciting and glamorous—an opportunity for men to prove their competence and courage.

War is neither glamorous nor attractive. It is monstrous. Its very nature is one of tragedy and suffering.[21]

Peace can only last where human rights are respected, where people are fed, and where individuals and nations are free.[22]

However, there can be no peace as long as there is grinding poverty, social injustice, inequality, oppression, environmental degradation, and as long as the weak and small continue to be trodden by the mighty and powerful.[23]

~Tenzin Gyatso, 14th Dalai Lama

The first step in the direction of a world rule of law is the recognition that peace no longer is an unobtainable ideal but a necessary condition of continued human existence.

~Margaret Mead

A civilization of warriors is not a civilization at all. It is based on murder. Today's world is in a constant state of war. From the vantage of the Golden Civilization, our descendants will look back on our time as primitive, cruel, and destructive.

There are two ways to end war. One of them is temporary. The other way leads to a Golden Civilization.

One way to end war temporarily is to fight it out, which is what we do now. May the strongest nation (or alliance) win. This ends in totalitarianism or in destruction. Where the greatest power wins, it is not necessarily the wisest or most democratic. The totalitarian state that survives may disguise itself as democratic (or even as something "better," as China now does without providing its citizens even the basic human freedoms of speech, press, assembly, or belief.) It will pretend it is peaceful. It will pretend it is dedicated to freedom. It will call itself America or China or Europe. Or it will call itself the United Nations or the New World Order.

The other way to end war requires a sustained approach and a commitment, not merely to peace but, pointedly, to end war.

It involves imbuing our systems and structures themselves with wisdom, and the commitment to develop inner peace in our leaders and in ourselves.

The challenge is great. Look around you. Is there anywhere on the planet greater arrogance and ego than in our leaders? Given this, how can war not be inevitable? How can greed not flourish? We require a generation of wisdom in our leaders, of humility, of dedication to peace, if we are to build a sustainable civilization rather than bring our species along with millions of others, closer to extinction.

When we engage in war, psychologists call it projection. We are trying to kill off our own dark natures, projecting them on others. Far better to go directly to our darkness and transform it into wisdom. Our endless wars will never succeed and will cause endless harm, until we end the violence possible inside ourselves. And that is only half the story. We must also claim our power in democracy and bring to an end all of the engines of war within the systems and structures of society. In a democracy, we have that choice and that responsibility.

> *War is murder, plain and simple.*

We are brainwashed when we think otherwise. Brainwashed by the ease with which our passions can be pulled into murderous or righteous or revengeful fantasies. We are brainwashed by the media and by our governments and by the most powerful forces of institutional life so that they may maintain their power, and so that they may profit.

Even if people see wastelands in the wake of war, they still take pride in their weapons. [24]

~Huanchu Daoren

Over 100 million people were killed in wars in the 20th century alone, 20 million of those by America. That is 20 million and 100 million too many. Some cite statistics to show that wars have diminished over time.

> *But no one questions that our capacity to slaughter billions in war is many times greater than it's ever been and getting greater by the day. And our capacity to put fools and dictators in office has not diminished, even in a world awash with what we call democracy.*

Without structures of wisdom, the likelihood exists that we will continue to put such fools in office with mass destruction at their fingertips and that they will act on it long before our 20 million years or our thousand generations or even this century is ended. That is unacceptable.

> *To the extent that we are passive citizens, we are all culpable.*

The Vision

The world is at peace. Not because we have battled through a great war, but because we have decided, collectively, in our democracy, it must be so. And we have taken all of the steps necessary to make it so.

> *It is ridiculous that we have allowed a proliferation of weapons in America and all over the world. They make violence so easy and war inevitable.*

Of course, it is not weapons alone that cause war. Arrogance, covetousness, cruelty, unkindness, and "playing hardball" cause war. Imposition by powerful forces on cultures that want to continue in their ways causes war.

> *Institutions on a mission, or out for profit, have little compassion for those who stand in their way.*
>
> *Ending war has a great advantage for democracy. It stabilizes democracy because we don't need a command and control system to protect us—and no need for hierarchies of power to rule us. It enables democracy to flourish all over the planet. Ending war is the single greatest thing we could do for the flourishing of democracy.*

Moreover, as William Blake points out: to all of civilization ending war brings great energy, it brings great delight.

A planetary culture is the only culture that can fully honor Mother Earth, but for a planetary culture to safely emerge, war must become obsolete. It must be recognized as a desecration. It destroys valuable resources that can never be replaced. Each murder takes away an entirely unique civilization of being. We cannot afford the resource depletion of military expenditures or the more serious depletion of creatures, cultures, and species.

> *It doesn't matter what the cause is. If it is, as some argue, the depredations of poverty that cause war, then we must eliminate poverty. If it is the arrogance of power and wealth, then it is time to diminish arrogance, wealth, and power across society.*

If war is a manifestation of capitalism it is because we have allowed and cultivated more self-interest in society than self-knowledge. It is false that war is inevitable. We have both the power and the responsibility to end it.

Justifying War

In leadership circles there is talk of the just war, but, with rare exception, there is no justification for war. There is only the fear-based passion for it stirred up inside our minds or by government and media.

We may think that war serves a grand cause, or protects our country, that it defends our families or our way of life. Whichever side we are on, the "just war" defense is made, which makes a mockery of the concept.

As Bob Dylan has warned us, we never ask questions when God's on our side.

God is never on the side of war.

Framed by images of courage, justice, and Great Spirit, the world of war is the most monstrous of all. It hides its leviathan, its cold icy mountain of death just beneath the surface. Far from noble, war is murder.

It is wrong to throw our financial and scientific resources, the vibrancy of our youth, and our whole cultural milieu into war-making when these resources could be used for far greater and more humane purposes. It is wrong for institutional powers to stir up passions for war, encouraging people to cling to naive beliefs, and then manipulating them to throw their lives away for the benefit of billionaires' profit or politicians' power. Yes, in some situations, war has been necessary to end tyranny. The holocaust comes to mind. But as we become a planetary society and a Golden Civilization, there must be no place for war.

Without the transparency that comes from global democracy we will continue to go to war seeking to deliver ourselves into freedom. It is time to deliver that freedom to all people now. Not by war, but by bringing war to its end.

Strategies

A leader may chart the way, may point out the road to lasting
peace, but many leaders and many peoples must do the building.

~Eleanor Roosevelt

You cannot shake hands with a clenched fist.

~Indira Gandhi

If we are serious about ending war, we must recognize two things. First, we must recognize it is we who create war, by allowing ourselves to be prompted to fight and kill to achieve peace. We must seriously study and control our own reactivity to curb this and to not be driven by rage.

Second, we must become active citizens to end the external causes of war. In a democracy, we are each responsible for the systems and structures of society that lead us to war. Government is ours—we are responsible for its decisions. The media we allow and consume is our media—we are responsible for how it stirs us up, for what it reports, how it reports, for its standards. The economic system is our economic system. We are responsible for its systems of rewards, its inequalities and equalities, its products, and its services. In a democracy, the people, not powerful individuals and not institutions, have the power and the responsibility to make the laws and to craft our culture as we would like it to be. Why would we not choose to end war? Why would we not choose to create a Golden Civilization?

A Question for Each of Us

Here is a question I have asked of groups in many settings:

> *In a global civilization, war is obsolete. A great leader emerges and sets in motion the forces to establish the structures and systems to end war within a generation. You are that leader. What will you do?*

We should all ponder this question, if we are not to be complicit in the wars of our times. Try actually creating a list of actions you would take.

> *Here's what I would do:*
> *I am the head of the UN, or the President of one of the most powerful democracies in the world, or the head of an influential non-profit, or the CEO of a global media empire. I intend to dedicate every moment of my life to inspire humanity to achieve its most glorious mission—the establishment of a Golden Civilization and democracy across the globe, preservation of Mother Earth, and an end to war in this generation.*

My first step to end war is to gather all like-minded leaders and strategize with them how to most quickly accomplish our common goal. I would engage with all anti-violence and anti-war organizations.

A key constituency, ironically, is the world's military organizations. While many nations continue to need protection from violence it is vital that "the military" share our goals of peace. Those in uniform are among the most brilliant strategists and tacticians in the world;

they also know first-hand the abhorrent effects of war. We need their passion and their brilliance to end war within a generation.

Then, as a society, we identify each cause for violence or war and over a 20-year time frame we engage methodically and energetically to reduce each cause by 80%-90%. The likelihood of war should diminish dramatically. Then, we could address the remaining 10%-20% with even more resolve and resources to reach our ultimate goal.

Both carrots and sticks will be necessary in this approach.

To achieve peace within twenty years, we must address each of the following:

A. Decision makers: Imagine if, in a crisis, decision-makers were 80% more likely to choose peace rather than war, nonviolence over violence, and transparency and authenticity over deception. We must train decision-makers and leaders everywhere to be peace-makers. Train them in inner peace, self-knowledge, and processes of forgiveness and reconciliation. Across forms of governments, leaders range from dictators to elected leaders to wise leaders. We must transform dictators into democratically-elected leaders and transform elected leaders into figures of wisdom and thus extinguish the cynicism and distrust within society that leads to war. We must also train leaders in corporations and non-profits and create a leadership community of decision-makers and truth tellers who can collectively constrain bullies who choose to employ violence and deception.

B. Societal Structures of Suffering: When suffering is great and we are tempted to wage war, leaders trained in peace may not, by themselves, be enough to avoid the temptation. Our goal, therefore, must be to lessen, by at least 80% over the next twenty years, the external structures of suffering that build anger and cause war. These structures include the deleterious use of drugs, poverty, inequality, environmental degradation, historical animosity, invasions of privacy, famine, discriminations of every kind, and oppressions of the freedoms of democracy, speech, press, assembly, markets, and beliefs.

Diminishing or eliminating these negative structures requires a new understanding of Entrepreneurial Spirit. Rather than just venture capital and private equity machines restricted to institutional markets, we need to mobilize ourselves. We need a democratization of Entrepreneurial Spirit to tackle these problems at the grassroots. Our understanding of markets and of financial advice must shift to accomplish this, as we will see in the section on economics. A basic income, universal college education, Life Planning, and genuine democracy will bring the community and Entrepreneurial Spirit necessary to accomplish these ends.

C. The Engines of War, Contributors to War, and its Instigators: Our twin engines of war are the hierarchies of power and the weapons they use. We must bring peace to both. Hierarchies of power contribute to war through an institutional dominance that facilitates intentional deception, mass mobilizations, and aggression. They include governments, defense establishments, media, for-profit and non-profit corporations, private militia, religious organizations, ethnic groups, weapons manufacturers, and other hierarchies of wealth flush with the arrogance of money and power. Approaching each hierarchy individually as well as collectively, we must reduce their means to instigate war by 80% in this next generation.

Weapons range from nuclear bombs and missiles to knives and handguns. Over time, weapons of war must be abolished. In a democracy, the rule of law and democratic freedoms provide our greatest protection from abuses of power and the use of weapons against us. If they don't, then it is our responsibility as democratic citizens to make the laws stronger. We must mobilize institutions and the citizenry to develop strategy and tactics that will permanently reduce the engines of war. For the military, the grandest mission of all must be to bring a permanent end to war.

D. All Kinds of War: War's range is vast, from traditional, cyber, and hybrid to terrorism, and from nuclear, biological, and chemical to robotic. Even extreme movements like gang rumbles and cartel narco violence are forms of warfare. The institutional structures that foster such warfare must be reigned in, diminished, or abolished altogether. By the end of this 20-year period, I would make the punishment for war between states so severe, on both sides, that it is unthinkable for either.

E. Ranges of Behavior: Concerned citizens, organizations, and figures of wisdom must work tirelessly to reduce (by 80% in the short term) murder, maiming, rape, theft, spying, and breach of privacy, domestic violence, and child abuse. We must likewise closely examine the cultural values and media business models that idealize, encourage, or stir up violence.

We should also address how we speak to each other, how we conduct adversarial discussions and arguments in our communities and in our halls of education. We must look at and learn to diminish bullying, threats, mean speech, hate speech, and speech that is rageful, paranoid, seductive, arrogant, or patronizing. We must work to replace these abrasive and un-useful behaviors with nonviolent communications and actions, and with presence, kindness, empathy, and wisdom.

We must foster inner peace and self-knowledge, and their supporting systems at the foundation of society rather than pure self-interest.

F. Internal Structures of Suffering: Structures of suffering are diminished by mindfulness and transformed into wisdom by emotional intelligence. Specific, individual categories of suffering can also be addressed with community support structures and with cognitive psychology. To end war, we must first change ourselves. We must learn to employ strategies to minimize the negative impact of clinging to belief systems that exclude others. And we must minimize the impact of ignorance and of our darker and conflicted emotions including greed, craving, aversion, fear, envy, jealousy, anger, shame, guilt, humiliation, anxiety, festering resentment, blame, and complaint.

> *Practices of emotional intelligence, including mindfulness, help us deepen and transform these difficult feelings into reservoirs of wisdom and self-knowing. These experiential practices can be institutionalized throughout our education, as can experiential practices of selfless listening, compassion, forgiveness, kindness, authenticity, equanimity, patience, generosity, integrity, and courage. In a hierarchically driven world, we need all of these virtues accessible within us if we are to speak truth to power with words rather than with weapons.*

The key here is to match our institutional culture as closely as possible with the virtues, wisdom, and authenticity that bring out the best, most generous, and inspired actions from each of us.

While there will be much skepticism about the plausibility of ending war in one generation, it is valuable. If we do not explore our skepticism, we will not adequately prepare ourselves for the challenges of the endeavor. For instance,

1. What if a powerful country escalates its military development?
2. What if a powerful country seeks to exploit peaceful countries and take advantage of them?
3. What if a destabilized country goes rogue and brandishes weapons?
4. What do we do if a vicious dictator takes over a country?
5. What do we do if a nation, people, religious faction, or ethnic group undertakes to perpetrate a genocide?
6. How do we address the spread of violent ideas?

We certainly don't want to be foolish or endanger lives or enlightened democracies. There will be times when we need to use strength. I would want the military establishment to help us plan for these emergencies as part of our larger objective to steadily diminish the threat of war, murder, and violence. Keep in mind, the bobbies in the UK rarely carry guns and never used to. We must steadily reduce and remove risks, while protecting people from a world awash in weapons and violence.

To avoid tyranny, we will want to allow less and less power in the hands of any one person or institution. To emerge as a global culture (or better, multi-culture) we need the strongest safeguards against any and all government corruption and abuse of power. Modeling integrity is key to every aspect of a Golden Civilization.

Who will enforce peace? I imagine something extremely limited, mostly tactical and perhaps like the US Coast Guard. The rule of law is an important consideration, but peace is more about ethos than it is about laws. It's about what we learn as children and come to embody and expect in adulthood.

We ourselves are the key—our own deliberations in anger, outrage, or fear in the face of escalation of conflicts and violence, and our own deliberate actions that follow.

Media plays a huge role. Stories are important. If we are to change ethos, the stories of brave people who stand against violence, reported regularly in the media, would help shape ethos. Highlighting the wise sayings of the great teachers and leaders of our religions, philosophies and, occasionally, states will provide not only models for action but also perhaps instruction in next steps, guidance on a way forward that does not rely on fear and anger.

The end of war will arise from alliances of democracy with sustainable structures of freedom strong within them. Conversely, the end of war will never arise from totalitarian regimes, as war or the constant threat of war is essential to their existence. So, it is paramount that all peoples and all nations build upon and strengthen movements toward democracy. In trade, our most favorable agreements and deals should go, by far, to those countries with the most sustainable democratic freedoms.

Thus, until a Golden Civilization is established, democratic nations must reduce trade with autocratic countries, including the most powerful, China and Russia. Since the days of perestroika, the movement toward freedom in Russia has suffered greatly. We thought, wrongly as it turns out, as we opened up our markets to Russia at the end of the 20th century, that democracy and markets were equivalent. We allowed the Russians to think that free markets were those that could be dominated by the most powerful forces in the marketplace. Control could be given to billionaire cronies in exchange for political support. Free speech, democracy, and freedom of assembly, press, and belief, our highest values, were undersold, and wisdom was never sold at all. Through free trade we gave Russia and China great power they would not otherwise have found, and decades later they continue to use that power to stifle the basic freedoms of democracy in their societies and elsewhere.

Our forefathers protected our right to bear arms because of their justifiable distrust of institutional power and its threats to a fragile democracy. But in our day, we see how guns have made America into the most murderous of all developed countries in the world. As reported by multiple news agencies, 1,516,863 people died from guns in American from 1968 to 2017. There is a way to reduce that number toward zero going forward.

> *Where there are no weapons, no one dies from them. Clearly, the answer to protecting democracy and creating a Golden Civilization is not in more weapons, but rather in creating a stronger democracy.*

How do we diminish weapons everywhere, including in government hands? The most clear and present dangers we face are hierarchies of power, which can only be tamed by great democracy.

Ultimately, without a reliable way to bring war to peace inside ourselves, war in the world will never end. Johann Sebastian Bach, in his "St. Matthew Passion" takes us deep inside our own violence. It is a very wise work of art. In it we not only witness the innocence of Jesus, the depravity and remorse of his betrayers, and the viciousness of his accusers and murderers, we become them all. We recognize that we have been each of these characters. Most poignantly, we experience the simplicity and truth of Jesus as if it were our own purest nature, our innocence, and we betray it and murder it. I have seen the "Passion" many times—I can no longer witness institutional arrogance and covetousness around money without recalling Judas' terrified remorse and the lines, "See the money, the wages of murder." Our governments and institutions overflow with such covetousness. But we, citizens and voters, are the ones who perform the murder. By condoning war and violence in our society, we murder our own innocence, and in doing so spread that murder across the globe. Bach emphasizes this with the passion of his brilliant music. We feel our responsibility for the murders of all innocent souls. We recognize that we are the ones who must end violence.

In his music, Bach calls on us to make our hearts pure, to first realize and then tame our covetous, murderous nature. Only in such realization, as individuals and as a society, do we end conflict and war.

One thought to close with:

> *In Tibet, for a thousand years, instead of an army and weapons, they gave young men the inspiring experience of profound states of mind, experiences of freedom.*

As a consequence, they chose contemplative practice as their version of being warriors. Their intense focus was as ideal for profound spiritual practice as it was for war. Such spiritual practice is far more rewarding than is war for the person and for society as well. The loss of ego has value, whereas loss of life has none. The Tibetans transformed warlike instincts into compassion and wisdom. Instead of becoming soldiers, 20%-30% of Tibetan men became monks. We can do something equally extraordinary with mindfulness practices, wisdom, self-knowledge, and compassion. Perhaps we could settle if 20%-30% of our young people became wise.

Concluding Thoughts

I consider human rights work or activism to be a kind of spiritual practice. By defending those people who are persecuted for their race, religion, ethnicity, or ideology, you are actually contributing to guiding our human family to peace, justice, and dignity.

Human rights are of universal interest because it is the inherent nature of all human beings to yearn for freedom, equality and dignity and they have the right to achieve them. [25]

~Tenzin Gyatso, 14th Dalai Lama

We must come to see that the end we seek is a society at peace with itself.

~Martin Luther King Jr.

The tasks ahead may seem overwhelming but remember how young we are as an industrialized and complex society, barely 250 years, and how many millions of years successful species live. If we are to be a successful species, it is time to reset our bearings and act together. The most recent archeological studies suggest that the Bushmen of South Africa, hunters and gatherers, were stable and at peace for 150,000 years.[26] Our task at this moment of history is to design the systems and freedoms of democracy that will enable us to likewise thrive for 150,000 years, or for a million, or for as long as Earth is inhabitable and beyond.

> *To model integrity in democracy requires that all citizens live in freedom. Therefore, all citizens require the best of education, a basic income, and a life plan of freedom that is their own. All citizens require respect and a life of dignity. They require an equal voice in the political system. They require the freedoms of speech and assembly, of belief, and of a free press. They require freedom from war and discrimination, and an organic relationship with Mother Earth. Regardless of race, religion, gender, opinions, or ability, we all require these things.*
>
> *An engaged democracy means an active citizenry where none of us is afraid to call out institutional abuses of power.*

Democracy calls to all of us. One person, one vote is not only the law of the land; it expresses our love for and commitment to each other.

Democracy is the one integrity worth fighting for. While I hope we never again have to kill to protect it, democracy is worth all of our passion. It is worth risking our bodies and our beings. It is the supreme integrity, as it holds our freedom in its hand.

We must demand dedication to our freedom, and the highest standards of transparency and integrity, from our governments. Our present mandate is to generate a movement far greater than the movement that brought down the Berlin Wall, greater than all democratic movements of the past. Democracy is only as secure as its weakest link. All across the globe we must claim our freedom and support all others as they claim theirs.

Action Steps and Basic Principles for Democracy

Democracy: Top Actions for a True Democracy

1. Get money out of politics. Nothing is more important than this.

2. Secure a basic income—remove poverty—by ensuring 20%- 50% of average income for all.

3. Eliminate discrimination of all kinds. There is no democracy where discrimination exists.

4. Establish a universal right to a college education.

5. Establish tax policies without loopholes to reduce inequality globally and permanently. Establish confiscatory tax policies at tax havens with complete global transparency everywhere and for everyone.

6. End war on all levels, including within ourselves.

7. Foster wisdom in everything—make ethical and mindfulness training universal throughout society.

8. Throughout democracy, replace money and institutional self-interest with wisdom and self-knowledge.

9. Protect planet Earth. For the 21st century: restore fresh air and water everywhere, end species extinction, and stop global warming.

10. Support free speech, democracy, free press, freedom of assembly, and freedom of belief. Make global democracy the movement of our time to end war, end racism, end famine, and bring freedom to everyone.

Basic Principles of Democracy

1. We are all equal and citizens. We must be eternally vigilant to reclaim political power that is taken from us.

2. We are all born to be free—not as any institution might define it, but as we ourselves understand it. The first task of democracy is to maximize the delivery of freedom to all.

3. Democracy is our home. It may be boisterous at times, but in a Golden Civilization it is not cantankerous, patronizing, arrogant, bullying, or mean. It is welcoming and compassionate. Its elected figures are figures of wisdom.

4. Democracy consists of magnificent, inspiring, and compassionate listeners, believing in and supporting each person's dream of freedom.

5. Democracy models integrity in all things fostering authenticity and freedom. No hypocrisy in democracy. It is fierce against the abuses of power that threaten it.

6. Citizens are educated to be leaders and decision-makers with a global liberal arts, experiential, and multi-cultural education for all, so that we can all trust democracy, so that we can tackle the most complex issues with knowledge and compassion, and so that we can understand each other in all our differences.

7. Democracy is transparent. In a democracy, lies are frauds against the people.

8. As we once separated church and state, the time has come to separate all institutions from the state. Democracy is meant to be our home. It is not rigid, not even a state, but rather a community of equal human beings in action.

Media

A blade of golden light
Streams across the ice
With perfect aim
Wherever I go it follows
Piercing my heart
A message of morning
Direct from the sun
Breaking the earth in two
From one great beast to another
It penetrates my heart
And this is my response
I trust the sun to tell the truth
I love its morning news
Where do you find yours, great friend
Where do you find yours?

~George Kinder

What Is Media?

As are your repeated imaginings so will your mind be, for the soul is dyed by its imaginations.[27]

~Marcus Aurelius

The breath, with its streams of present moments, was our first news, our first media, at the moment we were born. It told us, in a completely new language, "You're alive." Soon other media arrived teaching us hunger, thirst, delight, anger, joy, sadness, fear, putting us to work, connecting us with others, and reminding us of those we loved and things we had to do. We continue to look to media, now abstracted into symbols of thought, to give us these things and more. Media can deliver us into a Golden Civilization by shining its light on the world, and by imagining with us how the world is meant to be. In a Golden Civilization, media will be as authentic, clear, and transparent as its origins, as important to our life as breath.

It already is that important. And like breath, it gives us nourishment, delivers us peace, tells us we're alive, stirs us to action. Its impactfulness elects leaders. It warns us of dangers. It links all of humanity and Mother Earth.

At the same time, media are marquees, flat boards. If media are truthful, at their best they are works of art that inspire us with the beauty and alertness of the world. They deliver wisdom. At their worst, they are advertisements or falsehoods. In a Golden Civilization, media points to the truth. It makes the world transparent. Media that is intentionally deceptive, manipulative, or which arises from conflicts of interest destroys Golden Civilizations. Transparency and trustworthiness must be at its heart.

Where media touches the deeper layers of freedom, of authenticity and of our being, of the present moment and Great Spirit, it brings those freedoms to us.

> *Media dominates our conversations. One could say that our culture and our media are our civilization. Media makes citizens of us, global and informed. As we create a Golden Civilization, it is important that we become conscious of what we expect from media. As democratic citizens we must be aware of its standards, and of our responsibility to safeguard, monitor, and set those standards so that the freedoms of all people thrive now and for a thousand generations.*

In a Golden Civilization, media is not strictly neutral in its reporting, nor driven by self-interest. If it is to be free it will be free of influence, dedicated to our freedom and the freedoms of democracy. As it reveals freedoms to us, it challenges all power structures that hide or diminish them.

Today, at the advent of social media, we consume media more as passive listeners to institutional culture than as active creators of a Golden Civilization. In a Golden Civilization, the media is ours. As we engage culturally in the world, we create media, and through it, we bring people to freedom.

In a Golden Civilization, media challenges us to find what is right speech and right action. It challenges us, as it challenges itself, to speak the truth. It inspires us to cultivate authenticity within ourselves and to engage authentically in the world.

As we engage with media in our private and reflective time, it also comforts us. It impacts us on deep and visceral levels. As media tells us stories, it brings us, with opinions or with actions, into community.

Here is the paradox, and the challenge. As we know, institutions cannot breathe, and therefore they cannot know themselves. They cannot break bread with us and eat. They cannot sing a hymn or hear a song of protest; and yet we give them enormous power over every aspect of our lives, over our bodies and our brains and our hearts and our votes. Where media is driven by institutional self-interest rather than a dedication to our wellbeing, we are taken advantage of by its power. We are driven by its objectives rather than our own mindful passion. It sows distrust and spreads the disease of cynicism and worse. It can spread poverty, autocracy, and war. We must only relinquish power to loved ones and figures of wisdom on our behalf. How do we create a media that deserves such trust?

The Range of Media

In a sophisticated culture there is quite a range of media, including sources of information, arbiters of ideas, and varieties of creative expression. Often, we think of "the media" as being predominantly journalistic, including the function of reporting events as they occur, the deeper investigative reporting, and media's interpretive and editorial functions. In a broader context, we include culture, advertising, and the distribution centers of media, as well as its individual units: smart phone apps, smart phones themselves, movies, books, art, drama, newspapers, web-pages, journals, single-purpose media including messages of non-profits and advocacy groups, advertisements, podcasts, radio broadcasts, political ads, media companies, bookstores, libraries, universities, marquees, placards, flyers, poems, photographs, and many other sources of information and interpretation.

No doubt the range of media will continue to increase as time goes on, as it has so much in our own time, unless it is that in a Golden Civilization we eschew cultural artifacts, preferring the solace and the authenticity of nature, of community, and of our inner natures.

Recently, social media has popped onto the scene. For a significant portion of the world, social media has become a constant cultural milieu. In addition to the many efficiencies that such rapid dissemination of information brings, social media is providing an enormous boost to the democratization of both media at large and society. It is exciting to think of each of us and all of us as commentators, journalists, reporters, and editorial writers chronicling and interpreting the life around us.

In these early days of social media, two things stand as warning signs. One is the ease with which inaccurate information has entered the mainstream, including fake political news, too often arising from calculated and malicious intent. The second is the monopoly powers of new media owners. Social media is another example of how quickly developing technical knowledge can mushroom into hierarchies of power that benefit the powerful and wealthy elites. Overnight they have gained the ability to control the content and distribution of news, which can either establish or destroy democratic freedoms.

> *For media to support democracy, it must never selectively benefit those in power.*

We must address permanently and sustainably the hierarchies of power arising from our technical advances.

Free speech and free press are key issues for the full range of media from journalism to advertising to culture and the arts. Journalism and advertising impact both democracy and markets and require the highest possible standards of truth. Intentional violations are criminal acts. In contrast, art and culture must have the greatest freedom of expression, within community standards governing expressions of violence and obscenity. Markets for speech or press or belief are not free when they are dominated by the self-interest of institutions.

Freedom of the press is a lynchpin for civilization. It is critical to both the freedom of markets and of democracy. The press plays a crucial role in the election of political leaders. Investigative journalism reveals corruption and the wounds of society that require healing. Without press freedom, we do not have the informed capacity to vote or participate in a democracy. Markets likewise will be uninformed and unfree. Media, and a free press, requires as much attention, dedication, and support as do democracy and markets if we are to be free.

From the whole range of media, I will focus on three overarching categories: journalism, advertising (or single-issue media), and culture.

Journalism

Journalism provides the basis for much of our decision-making in society. Among the Seven Integrities,[p] journalistic media in general and investigative journalism in particular have the most impact on democracy and leadership. Without journalism, democracy cannot function, and leaders are poorly chosen and ill-informed. Journalism is also critical for the other Integrities; it reveals the strengths and weaknesses of each. Journalism searches out new ideas with the potential to revolutionize our lives, enhancing our self-knowledge, our wisdom, and our freedom.

Advertising

Among the Seven Integrities, the use of advertising in media most impacts markets, products, and advice. In a Golden Civilization, it helps facilitate the efficient allocation of resources, particularly those meant to deliver us into our dreams of freedom. Its influence on politics is large and has often been insidious. Its influence in media has kept billionaires, aging institutions, and undemocratic forces in power at the expense of many layers and qualities of freedom, including trans-parency, depth, flexibility, community, generativity, Entrepreneurial Spirit, truth, and creativity.

Culture

Among the Seven Integrities, media as cultural expression has the most influence on the range of our individual Entrepreneurial Spirits, on our understanding of who we are, our self-knowledge.

---

p.   Entrepreneurial Spirit, Democracy, Media, Advice, Products, Markets, and Leadership.

> *The purpose of the arts is to deliver us into our greatest authenticity, paradoxically through artifice. Culture teaches us new ways to think, refines our ability to feel, educates us toward action, creativity, and engagement. It strengthens our virtues, including courage and kindness. It shocks and delights, makes us laugh and moves us to tears. It brings us back to ourselves. It tells us who we are and what our civilization is. It reveals who we have been and who we might become. It inspires us, as a great leader might, to be better people than we are, and to be more of who we are.*

Cultural media includes all cultural artifacts. As and when it is produced by individual human beings, it comes from a deeper place in our democratic freedoms than freedom of the press; it comes from freedom of speech. In culture as in life, we require freedom of speech to reveal that which was heretofore hidden.

Objectives in a Golden Civilization

Listening to the talk of the streets and alleys is not as good as hearing the songs of the woodcutters and shepherds.

Talking about the moral failures and professional blunders of people today is not as good as retelling the fine words and noble deeds of people of old.[28]

~Huanchu Daoren

The overarching standard for media to be a transparent window on our world must be to model integrity and deliver freedom, all the while seeing into the cutting-edge of what is required for civilization to flourish.

In a Golden Civilization, all people have access to media. Media embodies the highest standards of truth-telling. Investigative journalists are stars. Scientific discovery, self-knowledge, and great hearts are norms, inspiringly so. The best of journalism approaches works of art. In a Golden Civilization, we think of media as figures or expressions or experiences of wisdom, with authenticity flourishing on all levels.

Media warns us and keeps us alert to our greatest dangers, as well as our great opportunities. In a Golden Civilization, media articulates, promotes, supports, and sustains the basic freedoms of democracy, the health of the species and of the planet. It lets us know wherever there are concerns, so that we may act as needed to maintain civilization as our home, and act upon ourselves to grow ever more wise and free.

There are long-held standards for investigative journalism that the best news media already follow. In a Golden Civilization, we will all know those standards. We will know who follows them and who doesn't. There will be no place for false news, nor for information concealed or manipulated by institutions.

In a Golden Civilization, the media's values and standards for integrity are not some abstract independent code. They have a purpose. They are there to deliver us into freedom. Media is a perpetual window on a Golden Civilization as we imagine it, and on actions we need to take to get there. As such, media must accurately reveal to us the world as it is. If we citizens give media the freedom to impact us with their voice, we should expect media to adhere to the highest standards.

Among media's values and standards:

1. The overarching values of freedom and integrity.

2. Accuracy, truth, relevance, transparency, and respect.

3. The democratic values of free speech, free press, free assembly, freedom of belief, and their sustainability within the rule of law.

4. Other democratic values, including equality of all human beings, freedom within democracy from money's influence and corruption, freedom from war and violence, and the honoring of Mother Earth.

5. Free markets as opposed to market dominance; the expectation of financial information and advice that delivers freedom rather than sells products.

6. The value of the depths of individual freedom, of self-knowledge, wisdom, and human virtue. The ongoing value of the development of great hearts within us.

7. Ongoing and thorough investigative journalism to root out corruption and transgressions of our values. Journalism that is insightful and sustained until the threats to our freedom have subsided.

8. Freedom within media from conflicts of interest and from the influence of money and power over its judgments and expression.

In a Golden Civilization, the media's adherence to these standards is demonstrated in its stories, its actions, and its structures.

Stories, Actions, Structures, and Standards

> *The content (or stories) that the media presents to us repre-*
> *sent choices they have made from a nearly infinite range of*
> *possibilities. These choices are neither random nor neutral.*
> *In a Golden Civilization, these choices support our values*
> *and activities in three ways: they inform us, inspire us, and*
> *when needed they warn us. The consequence of media's stories*
> *is a strengthened civilization. Media by itself can deliver a*
> *Golden Civilization.*

For example, if freedom from war is a right of all human beings, then media as envisioned would publish until that right is secure. If you say media already tells us these stories, then my response is, why do we still have war? I do not mean to undermine, disrespect, or disregard the courageous and brilliant journalism that takes place all over the world every day—journalism that reveals the horror or the profiteers of war, journalists that at great personal risk reveal corruption in high places. I savor that journalism and admire the journalists and media that report it. This book depends on such journalism. But considering media as a whole, embedded as it is in structures of institutional power, as long as war exists media hasn't finished its job, and possibly hasn't even done its work. When accurately exposed by media, the horrors of war spur the human race to act to stop war.

Stories that help end war would accomplish the following. They would:

- Undercut the glory of war and demonstrate its monstrosity.

- Question institutionalized murder, tracing its sources.

- Display facts on murders in war, resources wasted, environmental and cultural damage.

- Touch the heart of war's brutality and its tragedies with non-stop, personal interest stories.

- Expose merchants of war, its profiteers. Who is making the money? Who is gaining power? How do they promote it? What lies do they tell? Who are the purchased politicians and who owns their media? Make transparent the profiteers. Detail their avenues of profit. Make the money explicit.

- Focus stories on those who have courageously stood against violence, and those who modeled non-violence.

- Provide comprehensive and ongoing reporting on challenges and strategies to end all war, to diminish our inclinations toward violence, to end threats of war between powerful nations with fierce attachments to opposing beliefs, and to eliminate terrorism. Look for comprehensive solutions to the seeming intractable problems.

- In movies, television series, and stage drama emphasize stories of peace rather than those of vengeance and war.

Inspiring us all to band together to bring an end to war isn't the only area where media hasn't completed its work. Below are some democracy stories media might include to help deliver sustainable democracy into a Golden Civilization. Yes, media does now report these stories, but democracy is uncertain, troubled, and bought. What self-reflection and action are required by media and our democracy to better their ability to guarantee a Golden Civilization?

Here are some stories that will strengthen our movement toward democracy:

- How basic income supports and inequality hampers democratic communities.

- The necessity of access to universal college education for democracy to function in a complex society.

- A constant focus on dark money and corruption and getting money permanently out of politics and media. Constantly identifying and shaming politicians (including the judiciary) and their contributors, their owners. Calling for recusals from those with material conflicts. Trumpeting our standards for fighting corruption. Offering comprehensive solutions.

- Front page stories of inspiring people from all walks of life.

- Concern regarding Mother Earth's dangers and the requirements for its protection for thousands of years. Calling out both government and corporate actions that endanger our children's future. Presenting solutions. Demanding environmental justice.

- Making sure financial advice leads to freedom, rather than profit-seeking financial products. Identifying advisers with integrity who are dedicated to consumer dreams of freedom and who help them to realize those dreams.

- Stories on ending racism and sexism and belief systems that belittle or demean other human beings, simply because they are different.

- Revealing and helping to diminish or democratize monopolies and hierarchies of power. Articulating alternatives.

Outside of the influence of the press, movies have perhaps the most impact on popular culture. They communicate the most popular stories. Yet, so many movies today are violent. Even in "heroic" movies, their advertisements are filled with violence, as if violence were a virtue or the only means to end violence. These stories are often created by money interests that we are unaware of, whose values are not transparent and where profits outweigh wisdom.

In a Golden Civilization, rather than arising from money and power, media's stories start with great listening. Media's integrity is not modeled by blaring marquees of advertising, but by listening so well to the community that media unfailingly informs us with accuracy, respect, and truth.

Map of Media

Media

On the Map of Media, listening is at the heart of the discovery process. Ever approaching truth, media's lens is the present moment, from which it reveals what is hidden, the 'new's. At the same time, media gathers comfort, virtue, and freedom from the bottom half of the map, and through truth-telling, distributes these as inspiration, outrage, and compassion in an endless series of present moments into a Golden Civilization.

One can easily imagine a media map that instead deludes us with what has been termed "fake news." This type of media, if we allow, can pull us into false and destructive responses.

Transparency is the key. Without transparency extending all the way down through present moments to wisdom and self-knowledge, media can destroy civilization.

But the space-time grid is tricky. How can we tell the difference between an outrage that arises from wisdom and one that arises from fake news? Unfortunately, we can't always. This is where the structures and standards of media, including transparency, are so important. While we can judge the source of the news, determine if there are multiple credible witnesses, our most convenient reliance will be on those media providers which we know to have the highest standards of integrity, and on those reporters with the deepest reach to wisdom. We must learn to rely on ourselves as well to be able to temper our impulsive and ravenous responses with wisdom.

What Blocks a Healthy Media?

What blocks a healthy media from functioning? Primarily, conflicts of interest. Transparency helps here, but it's not sufficient. Money still talks, even where it's revealed. It's time to understand and end debilitating conflicts permanently.

> *If the press is not first and foremost dedicated to democratic and personal freedoms, but is instead dedicated to garnering power for owners, their friends, and advertisers, then that press is not free and not to be trusted. It does not belong in a Golden Civilization. Freedom of the press means free of the undue influence of hierarchical power—whether government, corporate, non-profit, or billionaire. Beyond being transparent, in a Golden Civilization, a free press is dedicated to our freedoms and to our self-knowledge, not our servitude.*

Today, journalists are nearly as distrusted as politicians and financial advisers. When all three professions are met with disrespect, civilization teeters on the brink.[q] In a Golden Civilization, each of those professions and the institutions that hold them incorporate the highest standards for wisdom, integrity, and dedication to freedom. They inspire all of us to be the best we can be.

Censorship can be explicit or it can be subtle. A single word allowed or deleted can change the course of civilization. A Golden Civilization is

---

q. See Appendix Four: Corruption, Appendix Five: Freedom of the Press Worldwide, and Appendix Seven: Distrust of Professions.

throttled every time an investigative journalist is killed or imprisoned, and every time free speech or a free press is quashed or dominated by institutional power.

The Owner Class: Conflicts of Interest

The most significant problems for a free press arise from conflicts of interest with the hierarchical powers of government, corporations, and billionaires. For a media to function and to be of service, it must be independent and dedicated to the values of a Golden Civilization. Instead, what is "newsworthy" is too often driven by profit, sales, or self-interest rather than wisdom.

The issue of ownership of media is huge. How could it not be in a society that requires freedom of the press to elect its democratic leaders, but that also has misvalued money as the measure of freedom and allowed the media to be owned by the wealthy? In a Golden Civilization freedom goes far deeper. It belongs to everyone.

As things presently stand, we are all brainwashed. While you can find daily excellent journalism, just six companies and a handful of billionaires control 90% of media.[29] How can we not acknowledge that we live very much in their culture? It is even worse in countries of the world where the media is controlled by dictators. Humankind requires a free press for both democracy and a Golden Civilization. Instead we have been hoodwinked to hand over democracy to these institutional powerhouses. How else could media have kept us in thrall to war, massive inequality, purchased politicians, lobbyist legislation, and to denial of climate change?

Again, to see clearly, we must take money out of media as we take it out of politics.

Although we may think our media to be among the freest in the world, with power residing in so few hands, a simple inimical shift in institutional attitudes could spell disaster. In a recent survey by Reporters Without Borders, the US ranked 43rd out of 186 countries for press freedom, and the UK placed 40th. The US and UK could learn much from the countries that lead in this survey.[r]

We remain unaware of the money interests that dominate media. Ownership information is not transparent, nor the economic interests of owners, or when and how they interfere. And they return favors to our Senators and politicians, simply by not revealing who has bought their interests and their votes.

> *In every culture there is a huge institutional bias in the media. It's time that ended. Whenever a Congressional representative is quoted, we should see a citation as to major donors, such as "whose campaign was financed largely by the oil and gas industry" or "financial services industry" or "pharmaceutical industry." This way we can see and understand the influence of money in politics and measure its conflict with our democratic values.*

But in most cases, media ownership is aligned with the values of the elites and the owner class. They do not fiercely report these fundamental transparency issues, front page and daily. The media must be

---

r. "2017 World Press Freedom Index," Reporters without Borders, www.rsf. org. See Appendix Five: Freedom of the Press Worldwide.

transparent about their own institutional biases, including the extent of the perks they receive from powerful friends.

The failure of media is a failure of democracy. As citizens of a democracy, the media's standards, values, and ownership structure are all up to us, the voters.

Murders, Violence, Imprisonment, and Other Forms of Censorship

I am grieved and outraged whenever I hear of a journalist killed, a whistle-blower imprisoned, or an activist abused. These are martyrs of democracy, courageous truth-tellers, telling us what we need to know to not live in despotism. At the UN and in every country in the world, people should take to the streets and leaders undertake significant response actions. Our society must not tolerate heinous acts against journalists and others meant to suppress their revelatory or investigative freedom. Such acts must bring swift and significant consequences from free societies. Only the wisest of people are as important to a civil and free society. Among presidents and prime ministers in the world, only a handful are as courageous, honest, or important to a Golden Civilization as these truth-tellers.

When journalists are killed or imprisoned in an autocratic country, we should stop trade, quarantine assets, and pass resolutions to immediately brand the perpetrators and diminish their power through international tribunals that prescribe fierce consequences until the harms end.

Inadequate Resources

Recently, we have approached both the funding and the operation of media in society as if it were an issue for markets to determine, rather than an issue critical for the functioning of democracy. Thus, we have diminished publicly funded media and moved from subscription-funded toward corporate-funded using various forms of advertisement and ownership. In other words, we have increased the conflicts of interest between media and the private sector, undermining the trustworthiness and credibility of media.

We need a strong, investigative media, independent from both government and corporate interests, if we are to cast our democratic votes with confidence and intelligence. We must design a system where the funding of media has no strings attached.

For centuries the press has been called the Fourth Estate, as the fourth branch of government. In a Golden Civilization, media is honored for that position and funded for it, much as the independent judiciary is funded, but not owned or beholden, as a crucial branch of government.

In a Golden Civilization, media is known for its wisdom and passion for justice not just in the ranks of principled journalists, but throughout all aspects of media, including its management level. Its personnel and very structure maintain the highest standards of transparency, and conflicts of interest are fastidiously avoided. Media is independent from hierarchies of power, including both government and corporate. Its dedication is to serve the people and a Golden Civilization. Leaders in media must be chosen for their wisdom and skill, not for connections to money or power.

If we are to rely on media for our democracy to function, then corruption in news media is tantamount to treason and other high crimes. For journalistic media to support democracy in a Golden Civilization, ownership of the media must belong to the journalists, where it doesn't belong to all of us as part of our democracy. Some combinations thereof democratizes the news so that it is not primarily hierarchical, not arising from or accumulating power at the top.

On the other hand, if we hold media to such high standards, rather than merely allow market forces to steer their activities, how is discipline and efficiency maintained? How do we get competition and diversity if it's not market driven? How do we know media is meeting the needs of the people? Clearly, there must be some competition, whether between regions, organizations, journalists, specialties, or points of view. Competition to succeed in truth, to exceed expectations for news that is clear and illuminating, is worthy competition.

Democracy requires not only national, but also local investigative journalism and in-depth coverage in every corner, but if media decays, through ownership structures or other powerful influencers to being a mere mouthpiece, civilization is at risk.

Single-Purpose Media

Advertising and other single-purpose media have consistently blocked a healthy media and the emergence of a Golden Civilization. Single-purpose media includes not only advertising but also propaganda, non-profit mouthpieces for corporations and owners, and legislation written by lobbyists. Single-purpose media narrows the values of media from those of a Golden Civilization to a single strain, most often the profits or power of its owners. Steady, expensive advertising can overwhelm the wisdom in solid reporting, as it has in fields as diverse as financial services, fast food, the environment, and drugs. How are these advertisements different from the propaganda of autocratic regimes? Why have we allowed corporate-funded non-profit entities to create doubt around matters of urgent public health and safety such as species extinction, the sustainability of Mother Earth, fast food nutrition, tobacco, guns, and drugs? This is inimical. The press is meant for our freedom, not for the freedom of the rich and powerful to profit at our expense.

Free markets and free speech require a free press that does not surrender control to market-dominating institutions.

Advertising

What kind of advertising would support the values of a Golden Civilization, and thus be acceptable for media? Truthful, certainly. Transparent, of course. But what would be included in transparent advertising? How can advertising model integrity and deliver freedom?

Let's use a hypothetical example of a new burger chain, Golden Sunset Burgers. It could be truthful to say that the restaurant just opened on the corner of Southern and Main. And truthful as well to show an image of a mouth-watering burger and fries, implying tastiness and a filling meal. But would it be completely true, would it be transparent? Would truth be better served by including the calorie, salt, and sugar content of the meal? Should the ad state the significant breast cancer risk over a lifetime from eating fries? Would truth and transparency require statistics on the dramatic rise of obesity in cultures that eat such fast foods? Would it require revealing the risks of obesity and heart disease? Should loss of income, longevity, happiness, vitality, and life be listed as possible consequences? Would the ad stand up to the media's standards for a Golden Civilization, of modeling integrity and delivering freedom to its consumers?

What else should be in a truthful ad? What about the company's profits, CEO salary (in contrast to worker salary), the owner's wealth and record of contributions to entities that "independently" tout the great nutritional benefits of fast food, or who spout climate-change denials? What about the working conditions of third-world employees? Use of tax havens? Contributions to PACs and others revealing captive politicians, the friendly legislation they've favored, and the pertinent committees they've sat on?

Perhaps only investigative reporters could tell us these things in rare exposés at best a few times a year. But money buys the ads daily, in the case of audio and video, hourly, and on websites they can be up all the time. Money determines that what we get instead of truth and transparency dedicated to our well-being are beautiful smiles and mouth-watering images.

What is truth? For a quick meal, the only truth we may need is a business address. But for a media that will create and sustain a Golden Civilization, with free markets and democracy, all of these things are important. And more. The transparency we want most to maximize in civilization goes not only across but all the way down our map, into its depths, through the present moment and into the realm of virtue. It delivers freedom for every human being and models integrity. Given that, would it not be a violation of the standards in a Golden Civilization for either news media or cultural media to accept advertisements at all?

And should not corporations, on their signs and webpages, be held to the highest standards of truth? Even higher perhaps than news media, since they have an obvious conflict of interest? They should not be allowed to delude us or to hide anything from us when selling something to us for profit. Dominant advertisers give the impression of authority and honesty and imply a "truth" that the media itself cannot possibly justify or believe.

Clearly, by selling advertising space, the media today colludes in presenting false surfaces to us. What would it be like in a Golden Civilization? No falsehoods. Rather, complete transparency that models integrity and delivers freedom. Advertising would present simple facts of product features and benefits, and if ads failed to reveal important truths or did not support societal values, they could not be used.

If we redefine advertising, how do consumers find products, including new and innovative solutions? I suspect we need new venues, new media sources like electronic yellow pages and search engines that are solely dedicated to advertising, fully revealing, comprehensive, truthful, transparent, and not dominated by the influence of the richest and most powerful organizations.

Are we in danger of burdensome regulations? Clearly, we require truth from media, corporations, and government. If we espouse higher societal standards and demanded integrity in that context, perhaps we'd need even fewer regulations. Regardless, we must never be deluded by the power of advertising to ignore our freedom, our health, and Mother Earth. But these are in fact places where great profits have been taken, made at the expense of our freedom, health, and home.

Good journalism informs those with adequate time to read and consider. In our busy lives, the rest of us may rely on ads to direct us—on marquees, branding jingles, video and radio ads, web pop-ups, and elevator speeches that fill our airwaves and our bandwidth. Money creates buzz that supports profit-structures rather than true value. It distorts truth and undermines the value of media to society.

Too often advertisements, false and misleading language, brand enhancement, and political power have overwhelmed the power and function of media and investigative journalism to reveal truth and deliver freedom.

TV and radio advertising, and now social media advertising have given institutions overwhelming power and influence over individuals. We see this in the power of financial services advertising (as will be discussed in the Advice and Product chapters) and in the tasteless ads of pharmaceuticals and violent movies, shaping cultural norms and values. We allow advertisers essentially to be privileged owners of the press and our culture, exchanging human virtues for their profit and making mockery of the press' freedom, and of our freedom to speak as well.

Worst of all, and most tasteless, are the political ads. They undermine our values as well as the seriousness and reverence our democracy deserves. More than anywhere in our communal lives, the issues we confront in democracy require us all to think. Political ads should be banned across all media. Instead, let's insist the media educate us in depth regarding candidates and issues in forums that express and support the values of our democracy, of a free press, and of a Golden Civilization. Money and media at present buy our votes. This is shameful. The combination wastes resources and destroys democracy. It's time for media to recognize and claim its higher calling.

Corporate-Front Groups

With vast inequalities in society already, it is not appropriate for billionaires or corporations to undermine democracy through third-party, non-profit advocacy groups. Yet, the non-profit world is filled with corporate-front groups presenting self-serving arguments to increase corporate profits. For instance, such money is funding non-profits to bring climate change denial into the mainstream, despite overwhelming scientific evidence to its existence. Such non-profits kept tobacco thriving much longer than was appropriate for public health. There are such groups, often posing as consumer-based organizations, targeting many issues of public concern, including taxes, markets, guns, politics, pollution, global warming, tobacco, drugs, health and safety, finance, nutrition, immigrants, globalization, and many others. These organizations diminish democracy and increase inequality by allowing, in essence, wealthy individuals and corporations greater access to the freedoms of speech and of the press than common citizens, learned scientists, or wise figures have.

At the very least, the media should vigilantly "out" these groups and their contributors, limit their usage of the press, and insist upon transparency. Once we identify these "corporate fronts," we should ban them.

Similarly, when we identify cases where these non-profits undermine a free press and diminish the free speech of others, we should ban them, or ban those practices. In a Golden Civilization, where a non-profit's or corporation's purpose is to communicate, it should be held to the highest standards of journalism. As to accuracy and respect, their standards must be even higher than for individuals. Currently, there are tax benefits for billionaires to fund these mouthpieces. Where freedom of speech is involved, tax deductions and donations should be limited to what an average citizen can afford to give. But, in truth

> *money should never have the power to dominate a free press or the democratic freedom of speech.*

In a Golden Civilization we want all points of view, but there would not be great disparities of wealth, allowing the purchase of inordinate quantities of speech by the wealthy. Speech from all organizations would be accurate and follow journalistic or scientific standards, except in poetry and the arts. Media would have a fiduciary obligation to all of us and to Earth.

What of "revealed" truths—poetic and spiritual truths? If they were public advocacy groups and their opinions directly contradicted consensus science, then just as for media, their speech would be subject to reporting standards. The public should never be deceived, even artfully. At the same time, opinions should not be censored. All voices participate. Though we may have strong opinions about denial of climate change, we must remember that Galileo, St. Francis, and Van Gogh threatened the orthodoxies of their time. Orthodoxy can be as oppressive to transformational ideas as deceit and money can be. In a Golden Civilization, all ideas are considered, debated, represented. A Golden Civilization fosters a great flourishing of ideas, experimentation, research, and debate. Media in a Golden Civilization is transparent. It reveals the whole of the world to us.

Lobbyists and Propaganda

Lobbyists can also diminish healthy media and thus hinder the progress of a Golden Civilization. They press single and narrow points of view with all the strength of the funding behind them, which can be considerable. Pressure from lobbyists can warp the deliberations and actions of our elected officials and blunt the democratic input of the rest of us. Lobbyists can dominate the thinking in our legislative committees and often compose the media of legislation for our legislatures.

We have witnessed how false news can diminish democracy. It erodes our understanding of culture, economics, science, planetary concerns, war, and peace. Whether propaganda (false news) arises from governments, or private sources, it is inimical and should be fiercely punished. We must insist on standards and adhere to them. If the intent behind a message is to subvert democracy, then it approaches treason. The parties and/or nations that foster cultures of propaganda must be shunned and diminished—and educated in the tenets of freedom.

Culture

One purpose of a Golden Civilization is to free the genius of human thought, artistic expression, spiritual depth, and invention from the deprivations of extreme poverty, famine, illness, institutional bondage, and war. When we consider the histories of such figures as Galileo, St. Francis, and Van Gogh, we see how close we can come to losing great genius, individual expression, and discovery to orthodoxies of the academies and institutional powers of a given time.

This is likely to prove even more true going forward as the complexities of knowledge become embedded in institutional structures that spread hierarchies of power across civilization. How do we protect, inspire, and enable individual strokes of genius to light our way?

In a Golden Civilization, Universal Basic Income together with a society that consistently democratizes and delivers wisdom into hierarchies of power will bring explosions of cultural richness, simply by expanding human freedom.

The most important areas for freedom, for the development of our wisdom, our self-knowledge, and our great hearts are always jeopardized by institutional power. In culture, wisdom and creativity must predominate over institutional and even market forces.

Although revolutions in social media and communication technologies have democratized opportunities for artists to share their work, technologically based hierarchies of power can still control both the distribution and the means to produce new work.

Movies and television shows are the most obvious institutional art forms at present, but more forms will arise, raising similar questions to the following.

Do movies reflect the values:

Of their owners and markets? Or of the emerging Golden Civilization?

Of profits, or freedom?

Of institutions, or of figures of wisdom?

Of cleverness, or of authenticity?

Of money, or of self-knowing?

Of individual creativity, or of committee?

How much is creativity stifled by dominating powers? How much are self-knowledge or great hearts held back? If movies were produced by figures of wisdom, how would our culture shift? Can we facilitate that outcome?

For a Golden Civilization, we must free movies, television, and other mass media from institutional bias in all aspects, including the means and tools of production, the resources needed to produce the movies, promotions and advertisements, marketing and distribution, and of course decision-making as to final product. Social media helps by providing more avenues for cultural expression. Technological innovation and basic income can help. Increased government funding for the arts will help, but government can be as biased and ignorant as corporations in artistic judgment. Groundbreaking art is, by its very nature, often unrecognizable at first. It challenges both our authority and our sensibility. Creating opportunities for art to emerge may be tricky but art is necessary for a Golden Civilization to flourish.

Freedom of speech is important here. We have argued for holding corporate freedom of speech to journalistic or scientific standards, truth, and accuracy. But what of art? Compared to a corporation, what level of freedom of expression should movies have? Who is responsible for (who owns) the freedoms exercised—the producers, the artist, or the institutions? Or the consumers or decision committees? Who owns the freedom when only the wealthy run things? Or the government? There is tremendous value when individual freedom of speech flourishes. Much less so when the freedom exercised is institutional.

Whenever culture is held in the grip of institutional forces, we must work to democratize those forces. Even the power we surrender to figures of wisdom or persons of great creativity must be challenged by new ideas and new art. Democratic structures including associations, elections, lotteries, etc., can help ensure vibrancy. In a Golden Civilization, media delivers enormous freedom of expression across all populations, making transparent the deepest levels of human understanding and delivering endless moments of self-knowledge to all its citizens.

Ourselves: How We Block a Healthy Media

Unless (until) we develop the ability to clear our own minds, we can be brainwashed by media. Media can make us ravenous—make us fierce believers in untrue things. Media can blur our ability to think clearly, without the attachments of "self," without obsession, clinging, craving, or aversion. Without the ability to clear our own minds, we block a Golden Civilization and a healthy media. We block again when we cannot take clear action. Developing our own wisdom and self-knowledge is critical here as elsewhere.

Final Thoughts

In a democracy, the people decide the structures and contexts of media, not billionaires or institutions. Institutions are our servants in the decisions we must arrive at. The media itself is our servant. It serves the values of a Golden Civilization.

Domination of the political media market by parochial interests undermines democracy. Dominating the cultural media diminishes our self-knowing. While large organizations may most efficiently spread news and maintain the greatest stores of information, they also can be biased, and as we've pointed out, democracy sold to the highest bidder is an equation for treason. It is up to democracy to manage and diminish that bias. Standards of journalism, restricted ownership, no advertising, and ownership by journalists themselves can all be part of the solution.

There must be figures of wisdom and ongoing democratic oversight and even revolution wherever large institutions have a tendency to dominate markets of ideas. We require systems to distribute hierarchies of power into democracy, and recusal of that power from further influence. We must address all categories of media including movies, publishing, social media, advertising, and politics. There will be less of an issue if less inequality is built into society and more free markets, as well as free speech, stronger democracy, and universal dedication to the values of a Golden Civilization.

The Markets chapter outlines a principle of large power. That is, the larger the power, the greater its fiduciary responsibilities to the rest of us, to our freedom, to democracy, to future generations, and to Mother Earth. How can that fiduciary duty be ensured? For media, beyond the structures, systems, principles, and laws required, we return to our earlier question. How can we create a media of figures of wisdom that we trust? Journalists, just as politicians, must be trained to be wise.

Training and Standards

Journalists are the great arbiters of culture, presenting for our delight what is remarkable or inspiring, and for our chagrin, what is deplorable and what must change.

Standards and education for journalists must match those of leaders. Their great task is to make the world completely transparent for us, so that we may navigate it with greatest freedom and efficiency. In a Golden Civilization, through media, the grid of time and space becomes as transparent as a moment of freedom.

The training for a journalist in a Golden Civilization includes both freedom and the grid. Here are some thoughts on basic and ongoing training for journalists in a Golden Civilization

Training for Journalists

I. Basic Level of Training

    A. Experiential

        1. Listening skills, empathy, the experience of one's own freedom, and strengthening belief in the freedom of all others.

        2. Experience in business and government, non-profits, and the arts.

    B. Study

        1. The study of historical change agents (including whistle-blowers) such as Confucius, St. Francis, Galileo, Van Gogh, Dorothy Day, Helen Keller, Rachel Carson, Gandhi, Martin Luther King Jr., Daniel Ellsberg, and Steve Jobs.

        2. The study of how dictators, autocrats, oligarchs, and destroyers of democracy rise up.

        3. The histories of free press, free speech, freedom of assembly, freedom of belief, and civil rights movements—and the dangers that can threaten them.

        4. Freedoms that would be beneficial or necessary to humanity in the future.

II. Ongoing Training

    A. Experiential

        1. Annual week-long mindfulness retreats and self-knowing trainings for understanding the deeper nature of freedom.

        2. Annual week in poverty experience.

3. Study of ethics in media, including ongoing support groups for journalists.

4. Experiences among groups and communities of those who suffer discrimination in society.

B. Study

1. Liberal arts education.

2. Periodic discussions around the health and fitness of the structures and systems that sustain a Golden Civilization and which are meant to protect and encourage our freedoms.

Action Steps and Basic Principles for Media

A. Basic Principles

Journalistic media must be a completely independent branch of democracy. Its function is to make the world transparent so that we, in our democracy, and as we navigate the world, can make decisions of greatest wisdom. The basis of that transparency is threefold: science, investigative journalism (through stories), and wisdom arising from experiences of self-knowledge, freedom, virtue, and the present moment. Transparency reveals truth. Journalists are revealers of truth. That truth must be unbiased from influences of power and money.

> *Just as unbiased and transparent media are essential for our functioning as a Golden Civilization and as a democracy, we must fund them as an essential branch of government. We must design their structures so that they are always preserved from bias or influence, so that they always serve the values of a Golden Civilization.*

B. Action Steps

1. Remove money and power from media and politics. Media serves democracy. Vigorously oppose government, corporate, and billionaire dominance of speech, whether through advertising, single-purpose non-profits, or other forms.

2. Disallow advertising in journalistic and cultural media. Ban political advertising everywhere.

3. Until money is shamed out of politics, with every quote of a political figure provide details of who owns them, who funded their election, and the nature of their own investments and where they are housed.

4. Incorporate figures of wisdom and self-knowledge into media as we remove the influence of money and institutional self-interest.

5. Support a free press and insist upon media as a Fourth Estate or a fourth, publicly funded and independent, branch of government, alongside the executive, legislative, and judicial branches.

6. Support (and insist upon) free speech, freedom of the press, and vigorous and extensive investigative reporting.

7. Support the highest standards for journalists, embracing the values of a Golden Civilization. Identify when and where those standards are not met and hold transgressors accountable.

8. Challenge the media where it is riddled with conflicts of interest, hypocrisy, or lies.

9. Even as a branch of government, media must model a competitive free market of ideas and viewpoints, holding to the highest journalistic standards and providing ease of access for small participants and fierce consequences for false news at any and all levels.

10. We must, as leaders and as citizens, each be willing to use social media to be journalists and whistleblowers in society when institutions fail to serve a Golden Civilization.

11. Treat murder of journalists as treason or, if instigated by foreign powers, as an act of war. Criticize, boycott, and diminish the power of governments that limit a free and investigative press.

12. Clear your media mind. Use mindfulness and other wisdom practices to lessen your capacity to become reactive to judgments, opinions, and beliefs, so you can search out what is truthful, know it from inside yourself and know as well what is right action and right speech for yourself in each situation. Media crafts culture and informs democratic decision-making, but by itself it is not wise. Wisdom comes from inside. Never sacrifice or taint your wisdom in reaction to media.

ECONOMICS

It is time for something radically new in economics. It is time to replace the product and transaction orientation of classical economics with an explicit focus on freedom. I will apply that focus in the following three chapters on Advice, Products, and Markets.

Economics articulates the territory where each of us daily engages with the world to maximize our Entrepreneurial Spirit. It is where we make the choices and take the actions that bring us to freedom. Markets provide settings for the transactions that deliver to us experiences of freedom and the Products that support those experiences. But it is Advice that aims directly at freedom. Great Advice identifies the most efficient route to the flourishing of freedom and a Golden Civilization.

Advice

In my professional life I have been a fee-only financial adviser,
a life planner, and a trainer of advisers all over the world. My
goal has been to establish an economic system that, through
Life Planning (Advice), democratizes Entrepreneurial Spirit.
I will touch upon this briefly here. If you are interested in more
detail on Life Planning, seek out my books on money.[s]

I would like to call this chapter "Financial Advice" but I cannot as the term is so badly abused. Many squirm hearing it. It can feel particularly disturbing in a book dedicated to freedom, integrity, and the ideals of a Golden Civilization. But in a Golden Civilization, where money has continued to evolve in complex and organic ways, financial advice is often necessary to help us navigate the world and find freedom. In such a world, financial advice is a basic right of every human being, not just for the rich and powerful. Financial advice as I understand it, teach, and practice it, is explicitly designed to deliver individual dreams of freedom and Entrepreneurial Spirit into the world. That is its purpose, and even more for the poor than for the rich.

---

s. See Appendix Eleven for books by George Kinder.

But for generations financial advice has meant "Product Sales" and consumers know it. They sense something's fishy. Financial advisers occupy one of the least trusted professions.[t] For my purposes, Financial Advice, much as the term might make us shudder, is key to a Golden Civilization.

How so? Proper financial advice ensures everyone is supported and inspired toward their dream of freedom by maximizing their passionate engagement in the world. Lives are not curtailed by foolish or tragic money mistakes. The great complexities of finance, insurance, investments, taxes, and retirement are put to the service of freedom for each person.

> *Five things are required if Advice is to deliver freedom across all levels of society and thus maximize the most efficient allocation of human resources:*
>
> *1. Advice must be personal, completely trustworthy, and aimed entirely at delivering a client into their dream of freedom.*
>
> *2. There must be no product ties and no conflicts of interest in financial advice. The integrity of advice must be unquestionable and impeccable.*
>
> *3. Across society our individual dreams of freedom, our Entrepreneurial Spirit, and our authenticity must have the highest value, more than any corporate or government objective.*

---

t. See Appendix Seven: Distrust of Professions

> *4. Advice must never be seen as the province of only the rich. If we are to live in freedom, then the ability to navigate the money world with confidence is a basic right for each human being, as basic as education, food, fresh air, and water. In a Golden Civilization great advice is an essential element of education. It is available (and affordable) everywhere, for everyone.*
>
> *5. The skills of advice that inspire people to live with authenticity and passion must be deeply rooted and second nature at all levels of society. We must all become great listeners and support each other's pursuit of freedom. It is just how we live.*

A society flourishing with advice has strong families, enormous creativity, is rooted in Great Spirit and profound values, innovates continuously to support its communities, and cares for Mother Earth, all arising from these dedicated human relationships that unleash entrepreneurial energy everywhere.

Great financial advice is personal. It requires great listening, an authentic relationship, and inspirational insight to identify and then link our dreams of freedom to the financial architecture that makes those dreams happen.

Yes, great advice depends on listening, even more than on providing solutions. A person who is listened to will often find means to resolve issues on their own, discover dreams of freedom, overcome obstacles, and take significant action. In Advice, only after a process of listening do the practical elements of finance come into play.

A great listener is empathic, at ease, supportive, and kind in the midst of difficult emotions. They are non-judgmental, open-hearted, and appreciative toward aspirations and dreams of freedom.

Great listening is key to the trustworthiness of an adviser. It is the selflessness of that listening that makes the relationship work.

In the following graphic, I've adapted the Map of Mindfulness to show how advice is delivered into the world. Recall how when we practice mindfulness, selflessness develops as well. Modeling selflessness and empathy as they listen, advisers provide space for clients to experience the present moment as a place of personal exploration, without being drawn by anxiety to grids of financial complexity.

It is at the present moment that all the power of advice and all the energy of freedom reside. The present moment is the key to listening and to the inspired actions that come from listening. Mindful mastery of the present moment is the single most important skill of great advice.

Here is the map of the advice process that delivers freedom: On the map, you can see the gathering of virtue at the base, the awakening at the present moment, and the world of authenticity that is created in time and space.

Advice

Moments of Freedom
Economics of Freedom

A Created World
of
Authenticity and Freedom

Listening
Mindfulness

Entrepreneurial
Engagement

Singularity
Mirror of Awakening

Present Moment
Advice Moments

Selflessness
Gathering Virtue

Empathy
Ease
Compassion
Spirit
Joy

Life Planning is the term that is most widely used for the financial advice process dedicated to delivering clients into freedom. It is a generic term with a number of approaches. My own contribution to this field is known as EVOKE®. Its focus is both on listening skills (including inner listening or mindfulness) and on the delivery of a moment of inspiration and self-knowledge for a client where they recognize their dream of freedom. It is typically a moment of great energy that unleashes Entrepreneurial Spirit in each client who experiences it. It drives the planning process forward. The EVOKE methodology is active in many countries. I describe it briefly in Appendix Two.

The dreams of freedom realized through advice vary greatly, but five themes stand out, as part and parcel of a Golden Civilization. Although we do not think of them as involving money, a life planner recognizes how they do, and how money excuses can get in the way of accomplishing them. I call them the Five Pursuits:

1. Family (or relationship) is by far the most common. Securing and strengthening these relationships provides meaning and enables all our other pursuits.

2. Spirit or Values is the second most common. Sometimes secular, sometimes explicitly religious, with spiritual practice, ethics, or community as its basis, it can provide a foundation for everything else we do.

3. Creativity is third, whether in business or the arts. When it is present, it often contains the greatest energy among the Five Pursuits.

4. Community or giving back is fourth.

5. Environment, or a sense of place, is fifth. It could manifest as wanting to live in the city or in the country or designing a home or yard, or as a passion to protect Mother Earth.

Skilled life planners inspire clients to live into their dreams of freedom. The passion that is ignited often bursts through obstacles that we thought stood in the way. Most often we realize that our main obstacle has been ourselves and money excuses, even more than money's practicalities.

The kind of advice that delivers freedom and is dedicated to the client is a staple of a Golden Civilization, accessible to all. Accomplishing dreams of freedom is the primary purpose of advice. But a major obstacle to great advice in today's financial advice industry at large is the way it is delivered as part of a sales process, where profit from the products is more important to an adviser (or firm) than freedom for the client.

But to both society and ourselves our dreams of freedom are far more important than either product or advice. Moreover, the vitality, as well as the tenderness of our dreams are quite dependent on the financial adviser's ability to listen and the degree to which they are dedicated to our freedom.

Advice is a delivery system for freedom. Advisers in a Golden Civilization are profound listeners, inspiring engagers, energized coaches, and empathic mentors filled with financial acumen. Advisers believe unconditionally in each client's dream of freedom and are determined to deliver it. They don't sell products. They have no ties to financial product companies.

This is what advice is meant to be, not what it is or has been. Product companies have often systematically undermined advisers who follow best practices. Company-controlled, product-based advisers water down or eschew providing holistic advice (the Certified Financial Planner designation); fee-only advice (no commissions, no products for sale); advice that meets the fiduciary-standard (codified in the Investment Advisors Act of 1940, which guarantees that client interests come first); and Life Planning, with its goal of helping clients realize dreams of freedom. Product company profits have taken precedence over ethics, robbing consumers of perspective and choice. Instead of ever-expanding realms of freedom derived from such financial services, we find increasing levels of distrust. Billion-dollar corporate settlements for fraud, grotesque disparities in equality, and cheating scandals spread corrosive attitudes in our society.[u] Rather than supporting individual dreams of freedom, we suffer the systematic buying of political votes and subversion of regulatory power to stifle that freedom. And rather than ensuring Entrepreneurial Spirit is available to everyone, it is made available only to the elite.

I wish this were just a question that could be resolved by the proper functioning of free markets for the consumer's benefit, but far from it. Certainly, a proper, functioning, free, and competitive market would bring the best advice to consumers because that is what they need and demand. But we don't have free markets. Our markets for advice are dominated by product companies, their quarterly objectives, advertisements, and power over regulation. The simplest solution is to serve all consumers and to get product companies permanently out of the advice business. Call it what it is: Sales. Criminalize corporate attempts to buy political power to protect their profits and malfeasance. Liberate markets from institutional dominance and bring the influence of consumers and wise advisers to the fore; bring trust back into financial advice.

---

u. See Appendix Eight and Nine for summaries of financial industry scandals arising from the recent banking crisis.

> *Financial advice is destined to be among the most noble of professions, because it delivers freedom. But when financial advice fails to model integrity, it undermines both markets and democracy.*

In a time of growing financial complexity and rising inequality, the norm should be financial advice that is widely respected, fee-only, dedicated to freedom for its clients, fiduciary in all aspects, comprehensive and available to all, rich or poor alike.

Action Steps and Basic Principles for Advice

First, value advice so highly that we all learn to be advisers:

    1. Learn to listen:

        a) Deeply to yourself—inside yourself—without thought but with mindfulness.

        b) Deeply to others.

            i. With emotional sensitivity, compassion, and empathy to sorrows or upset.

            ii. With excitement, appreciation, encouragement, and support to the slightest nuance of inspiration or a dream of freedom.

    2. Encourage the learning of listening skills among your family (spouse, children, others). The result will be a stronger and happier marriage and stronger families and, in turn, stronger democracies.

3. Support all dreams of freedom wherever you can.

4. Get life planned. Engage with a practiced life planner and then live your life plan; wait no longer.

5. Insist there be no conflicts of interest from financial advisers or anyone else listening professionally to your dreams of freedom, fears, or sorrows. You want all attention on you and your objectives, not on their objectives of selling products.

6. Seek out fiduciary advice where the focus is entirely on your freedom. This advice maximizes the most efficient allocation of human capital. It creates Golden Civilizations. Insist upon it for yourself, and for everyone in society.

7. Champion great financial advice as an essential element of universal education, as it delivers freedom.

8. Seek and recommend fee-only advice (no commissions, no companies (banks, brokerages, or insurance companies) that push product). Get product companies out of the business of providing advice.

9. Support movements to professionalize all forms of advice, freeing them from institutional bias. In our complex civilization, we need pervasive and unbiased fiduciary advice in many professions, such as in regard to health and to our many interfaces with technology. Doctors, for example, should be held free from the influence of product companies—no allowing of Big Pharma to buy up endorsements of their drug products to enrich themselves, or their agents in health care. In a Golden Civilization there would be no such kickback schemes.

10. Give the gift of freedom—listening with empathy and inspiration—to everyone you meet. Or, at least, to one new person a day. Let's make this kind of listening the hallmark of our civilization.

Products

If you want money more than anything,
you'll be bought and sold.[30]

~Rumi

To the eyes of a miser a guinea[v] is more beautiful than the sun.

~William Blake

Financial Products are essential building blocks in the architecture that supports our dreams of freedom. When they overstep that role or they pretend to be something they are not, as occurred in recent financial crises, distrust and cynicism spread. Dreams of freedom are lost.

Financial products include savings accounts, money market accounts, insurance policies, mortgages, and investments in stocks and bonds. A hodge-podge of budgeting, saving, or investment decisions uncoordinated with our life plan can jeopardize years of freedom. One harmful product, bought at the wrong time and in the wrong way, such as the highly leveraged mortgage derivative products (toxic assets) that

---

v. In 19th century England, a guinea was a gold coin.

precipitated the banking crisis of 2007-2008, can undermine decades of freedom. Financial products are dangerous without proper advice. Misleading advertising aside, they do not lead to freedom.

Most unfortunately, at present almost all financial companies are product companies, including banks, insurance companies, brokerages, mutual fund companies, private equity, hedge funds, venture capital companies, finance companies, and others. To buttress their control of financial services and enhance their profits, these companies make enormous political contributions (just as do energy companies and drug companies, where analogous concerns exist). Not only do these companies and their efforts at political control frustrate our life plans, they are also, with their political power, prime suspects for causing rising inequality, the collapse of democracy, species extinction, and war.

Often products, such as couches, cars, paper clips, and tomatoes, are easy to test and evaluate. But financial products are not so easy given their sophistication, the uncertainty of future economic conditions, our reliance on the products over a lifetime, and their purpose to maximize our capacity to live all aspects of our life plans. Like ticking time bombs, they can hide faults for decades. Moreover, financial product companies have long systematically traded on people's dreams of freedom to sell counter-productive or defective products. This is enabled when there is no coherent life plan, nor fiduciary obligation on the part of the company. Financial companies must model integrity if they are to deliver freedom, and financial products must be designed and sold with an integrity that supports architectures of freedom. The idea, fostered by both corporations and government, that maximizing corporate profits is a right measure of economic efficiencies, is fraudulent if the profits are at the expense of consumer freedom.

Companies must not make their profits from selling products embedded in their advice. That's sales, and a conflict of interest, not trustworthy advice.

As we see in the following map,

> *Delivered without unbiased advice, financial products only provoke and exploit our acquisitive nature.*

They depend on and feed our addictions to materialism. We are left measuring ourselves by how much we can consume. I have called it refrigerator economics—how much can we stuff into our refrigerator? Who has the largest refrigerator? Without being grounded in the self-knowledge of our life plan and our meaningful purpose, we forget who we are. We become reactive, fearful, and grasping. The present moment is lost in the mirror of forgetfulness.

Products
Each Cell a Product

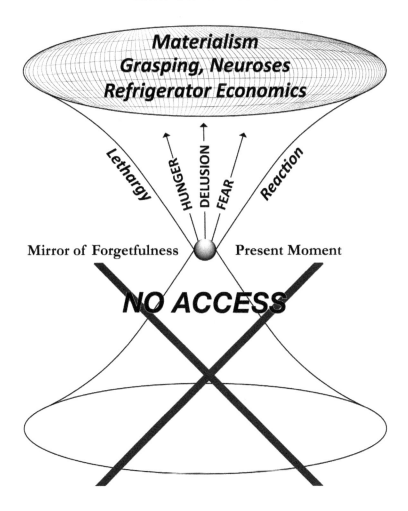

Institutions

It is absurd that financial product companies that have no interest in our freedom should wield such outsized political influence in our great democracy, a democracy that is dedicated to freedom.

Language conveys culture. It conveys civilization. From person to person, it conveys meaning and the heart. But with the institutional language of product companies, we can't easily discern the truth. The advertising-speak, on websites and in brochures, is self-serving and often deceptive. It is permeated with implications intended to sell products more than to tell the truth and consumers are baffled.

> *Consumers mistakenly think of the following as services rather than products: mortgages, mutual funds, savings accounts, stocks, bonds, certificates of deposit, money market accounts, tax shelters, insurance, derivatives, and more. They are products, with carefully embedded profit margins, engineered without consideration for their impact on your personal life plan.*

Profits derived from these products, rather than freedom for consumers, have long been the dominant focus and motivating power in the financial "services" industry. And even in academia—the Nobel prize-winning economist Milton Friedman considered profits the only social responsibility of business.[31]

For over 100 years, financial products have been central to nearly every financial scandal and the worst economic crises, including the Great Depression, the recent Banking Crisis and the Great Recession.

Sales processes mislead consumers into confusing safety or a high rate of return with freedom. A narrow focus on products is merely a distraction from that proper focus for consumers—the freedom to be accomplished by following their life plans. Marketing and political power enable corporations to mislead consumers and shift societal focus from freedom to products.[w]

The resulting low trust levels for financial advisers and financial services undermine public confidence in our economic and political systems and help create a massively inefficient allocation of human resources. Financial products must be vetted, their risks fully identified and analyzed, hopefully by advisers who are fiduciaries to their clients, before they can be recommended with advice as we define it. Regulators and politicians should have no ties or political debts to product companies or surrogates, no conflicts of interest.

When you seek financial advice, you want someone who is your fiduciary, who places your interests first, who honors your life plan, charges fees only (not commissions), and has a holistic approach to finance. They would not be affiliated with any product company but be trained to choose from amongst all available products for your benefit.[x]

---

w. The costs in human freedom of the institutional dominance of product companies are immense. They go unreported in our economic system because we focus on transactions rather than individual freedom. But excess profits to the product industry have been calculated in: Gerald Epstein, Juan Antonio Montecino, "Overcharged: The High Cost of High Finance," Roosevelt Institute, July 12, 2016.
Although huge ($23 trillion estimated over 33 years) these costs are but a fraction of the costs to society of the loss of human freedom when product companies' profits dominate standards of financial advice.

x. See Appendix Two on finding a financial adviser.

Moments: A Paradigm Shift

> *As we move toward a Golden Civilization, we find ourselves in an economics of moments of freedom, rather than moments of transactions.*

What happens to economics and economic theory as moments of freedom replace product transactions? The question reframes how we understand economics.

Life Planning delivers moments of freedom. Shouldn't all financial advice? Should not economics and democracy at large deliver freedom as well?

> *If you maximize the opportunity of freedom for people, their dreams, and their experience of freedom, you increase their clarity, stimulate their passionate purposes, and maximize their productivity.*

When we produce freedom more than products, people will deliver into the world the best that they can be. But moments of freedom require truth as their chalice rather than deceptions and innuendo, integrity rather than the artifice of sales and statistics. Moments of freedom are filled with peace and authenticity as much as exhilaration. Financial services must deliver these things rather than the distrust and the cynicism that now pervades our contemporary culture dominated by profits and products.

The new maps we've created point us toward freedom, rather than products. At their center is the one real thing, the present moment, within which freedom resides. As a consequence of maps that haven't included freedom or wisdom, humanity has focused on the accumulation of products, stealing from Mother Earth (space) and from future generations (time).

> *What a difference it will make as it becomes clear that freedom and wisdom are both the pinnacles and the basis of human experience, and that the greatest products in life are moments of time, present moments, that are awake and filled with freedom.*

Action Steps and Basic Principles for Products

1. The greatest products that we own are our life, time, freedom, and health. Focus on them. Protect them. Nurture them.

2. Be vigilant in your choices of products: Will the product increase (or diminish) your moments of freedom? Will it enhance or weaken your ability to act with integrity and authenticity? Ask these same questions for financial products you already own.

3. Insist that product providers not use words like advice, specialist, education, or consulting when their primary function is sales. They are not the fiduciaries of your freedom. Their profits come first.

4. Insist on stricter standards for truth in advertising. Be wary of implications of freedom in advertising. Freedom is something you, not product companies, control through faithful implementation of the life plan devised by you and a fiduciary adviser.

5. Insist on product information that is simple and accurate. Ask for product comparisons. Vet this information through a holistic, fiduciary, fee-only, Life Planning adviser.

6. Perform a risk analysis for any new or "contemporary" products and consider that risk in terms of your life plan.

7. Insist on warnings on financial products, advising consumers to seek out fiduciary advice before purchase. Shun products lacking such a warning.

> *You should be able to trust your adviser as you trust your doctor—with your life. Life, and freedom, are what your life plan delivers.*

8. Support elimination of product company influences in politics and democracy. Banks, insurance companies, hedge funds, mutual fund companies, and brokerage firms should not be allowed to contribute to political campaigns, and lobbying should be severely curtailed.

Markets

*What will markets look like if they are to sustainably,
and with integrity, deliver freedom to all
for a thousand generations?*

> *In a Golden Civilization, markets are flourishing, wildly cre-
> ative, and free. It is this free nature that brings ever-increasing
> freedoms to us. Money and markets have a dynamic nature—
> they give us instant rewards for good work and instant choices
> for purchase.*

But traditional markets have limitations in regard to freedom:

- Freedom is poorly measured by dollars.

- The self-interest that has traditionally been supposed to motivate
markets provides at best limited access to true freedom.

- Hierarchies of power make a mockery of market freedoms for
the rest of us.

> *In a Golden Civilization, in addition to minimizing the mar-
> ket-dominating influences of hierarchies of power, two economic
> principles flourish. As we incorporate them, they revolutionize,
> stabilize, clarify, and free individuals, markets, and society:*

> *First, markets that maximize human freedom are driven more by self-knowledge than self-interest.*
>
> *Second, moments of freedom replace moments of transaction as the dominant focus of economics. This focus on freedom maximizes the efficient allocation of human capital which flourishes in freedom. Moments of freedom turbocharge innovation, solving societal problems and protecting human society with the authenticity that is at their core.*

In a Golden Civilization, the whole focus of society is on freedom. Freedom is its breath. It is the purpose of democracy to name, establish, and sustain freedoms for each of us. And it is the dynamic function of markets to deliver these freedoms in exchanges.

As their focus shifts from moments of transaction to delivering moments of freedom, markets change in three ways:

1. Services aim to deliver freedoms, both practical and profound. They give us more access to both time and space (through travel, greater ease, and knowledge, for example). New services save us time, giving us more moments. Additionally, they transform the nature of time bringing us experiential freedoms through media, culture, trainings, and wisdom practices, creating more awake moments for everyone.

2. Products are delivered by institutions dedicated not only to profits but also to experiences of freedom for their customers and employees, valuing and developing self-knowledge amongst their stakeholders and transforming the momentary experiences of exchange into moments of greater freedom and authenticity in the relationship.

3. Advice replaces sales. It comes from adviser-mentors who recognize freedom inside themselves and are determined to deliver it for consumers. Their relationship skills and the quality of their listening bring moments of freedom. When an economy becomes advice-driven, individuals explore the whole range of freedom: present moments, interior spaces, Great Spirit, virtues, and transparency, as well as the products, markets, and services that support that freedom.

The Flourishing of Markets

Markets encourage human society and culture to flourish by establishing the space for us to efficiently communicate and trade with each other. Civilization becomes more creative and dynamic, developing freedoms as well as authenticity, character, and wisdom. There are no limits to growth in these latter areas, even as limits to economic growth (driven by self-interest and measured by money) remain an academic and policy concern. If, instead of maximizing freedom throughout society, markets of self-interest deliver deceit, cynicism, distrust, inequality, autocracy, species extinction, and war, then clearly something is seriously wrong with our markets and our systems of society (the integrities) that underlie it.

Charts Tell a Story

Free markets involve buyers and sellers of relatively equal weight, easy access for new sellers, buyers, and products, and competitive alternatives. Free markets are driven by the individual actions of each party acting in self-interest (or self-knowledge), facilitating competition and new alternative products where consumers determine which products are best.

Markets start with the purchase of, or an exchange of money for, something we need or value, perhaps a product. Often the exchange involves some aspect of our dream of freedom, an image of the person we wish to become. Ideally, each partner in the transaction comes closer to their dream of freedom as a result, but an institution, often the seller in contemporary society, has no dream of freedom. It is a factory that aims at profits by manufacturing products. If our markets are dominated by institutions with more power than we have and, as a consequence, we sacrifice too much of our dream in uneven ex-changes, the world becomes darkened for us. In contrast, in a Golden Civilization, institutions are our servants.

In an ideal exchange in an ideal market, the power of the purchaser is roughly equal to the power of the seller. Thus, they can negotiate the price or the terms of the exchange to something fair to both.

Idealized Classical Economics

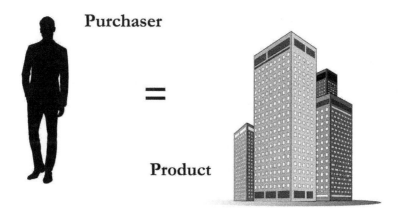

Purchaser

=

Product

In reality, our marketplace for most items is dominated by large institutions. The consumer has little or no say in the purchase price or terms of exchange. Indeed, most terms of exchange in today's litigious world make a mockery of free markets. Whether renting a car, buying an app, or even visiting a website, often the "terms" are pages of small print protecting the large institution. They are onerous to read, much less to understand, and so often updated or changed as to be impossible to keep up with. The inequity of the market exchange in these conditions is testimony to the power of the "house" in our institutionally dominated society. Yet, these largely unread agreements stand up in courts of law.

In addition, by and large, the only competition is between large institutions.

The Reality of the Economic Marketplace

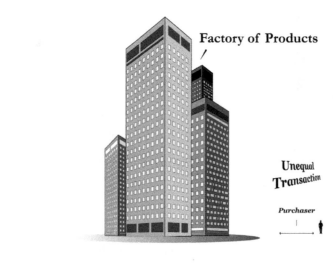

Factory of Products

Unequal Transaction

Purchaser

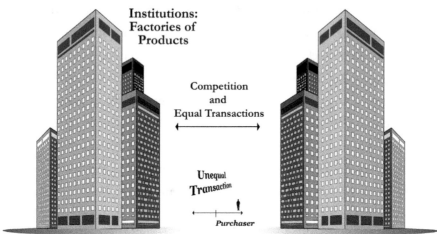

Institutions: Factories of Products

Competition and Equal Transactions

Unequal Transaction

Purchaser

Factory of Products in Time & Space

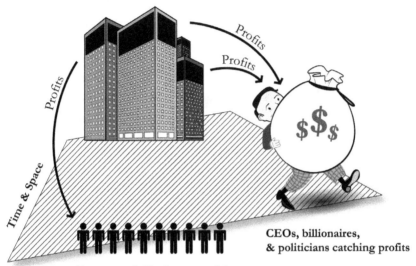

**Investors & Retirees catching
their profits only after CEOs
take theirs**

**CEOs, billionaires,
& politicians catching profits**

Successful companies (modern factories) with their market power produce such reliable and systematic profits that CEOs, billionaires, and the political elite profit in explicit and innumerable ways. As a consequence, they find it in their 'self-interest' to ignore unsustainable, negative externalities (e.g., pollution, inequality, oligarchy, autocracy, and war) for civilization and the unrealized dreams of freedom of its people.

Market domination has the advantage for its profiteers of reliable and predictable streams of profits, whereas open markets mean a more chaotic but flourishing stream of innovation.

In economic theory, demand for a product increases in quantity as its price falls. Prices often fall due to economies of scale as greater quantities are produced. The chart of this economic function is the most famous in all of economics. Here, where the supply and demand curves cross in a moment of time determines the most efficient quantity of product to be produced as well as its price. This is very useful, very elegant, classical economics. It is used to produce the reliable profits the economic and political elite along with ordinary investors and retirees demand from their institutions.

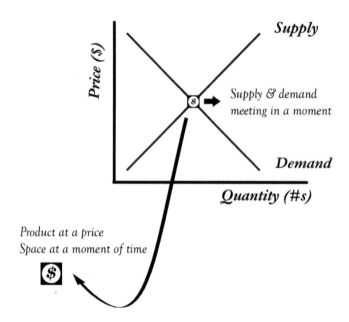

You can put this whole diagram on one of our grids of time and space (see below), as a moment of economic reality. Of course, for us human beings, moments are extraordinary things. Can economic reality match or capture or deliver our experience of what a moment is? How efficient can markets be in the delivery of human freedom if the market's understanding of moments doesn't match our own, but is instead confined merely to the grids of time and space where products and profits are created?

Contrasting the Value of Moments of Space-Time Economics with the Value of Moments of Freedom

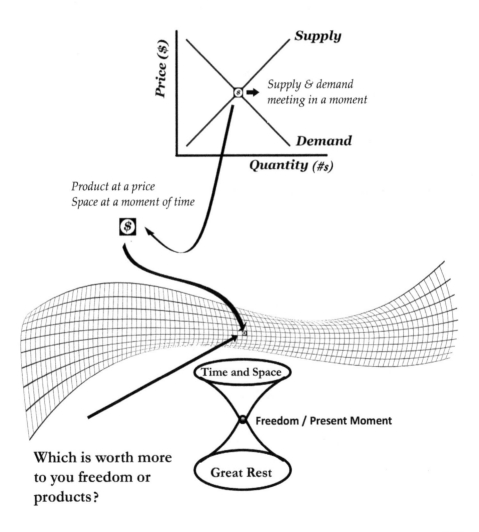

Which is worth more to you freedom or products?

The truth is, if the focus of our markets is just performance on the grid, they will not work efficiently for human freedom.

> *Present moments are singularities of extraordinary depth, explosive in their vitality, profoundly human, and articulating the widest ranges of human experience.*
>
> *Present moments are where freedom resides. They are to be fiercely distinguished from market moments on the grid of time and space that identify quantity and price points for purchases and sales. In economics, it is moments of freedom that have the greatest value.*

Whether about transactions or freedom, markets are initiated by an act of listening and followed by an act of engagement. For institutions, where listening takes the form of data gathering, it's lethargic in our chart because it's mechanical. There is no authentic relationship with the present moment or with another person. The engagement then is marketing and manufacturing, creating products or selling them.

For individuals, in contrast, listening, whether to supply or demand, is all about authenticity. Listening for each of us can touch freedom at the present moment and can reach all the way to the depths of Great Spirit. We listen in order to engage. In a Golden Civilization, these relationships are trustworthy, if not sacred.

Much of this is lost in institutionally dominated markets:

The World of Markets, Products, and Institutions

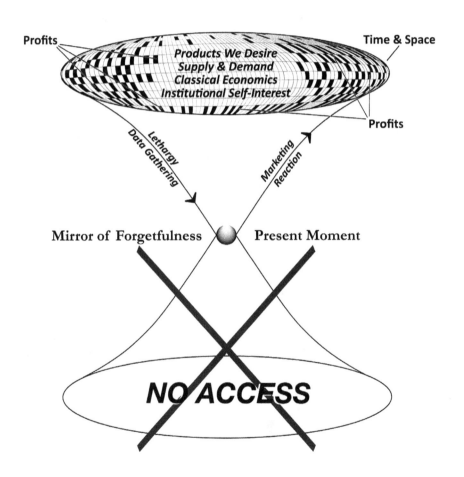

In this map of Markets, Products, and Institutions, we see markets of products arising from unconscious factory forces with no access to the depth and awakening possible in present moments. For individuals, institutionally dominated markets stimulate worlds that are incomplete, worlds of illusion, driven by desire and aversion. The stronger the institutional hold on our freedom, the more materialistic, less organic, and less real, our civilization becomes. There is less heart.

In contrast, in a Golden Civilization markets maximize awakened experiences for all. Freedom itself is the focus of free markets, facilitated by the efficient pricing and quantity of products, rather than the hierarchical purposes of corporations or governments toward profits, power, and control.

In a free market of individuals, motivated by self-knowledge and awakening, the focus on freedom brings ongoing access to virtues such as kindness, compassion, creativity, and generosity, as opposed to an institutional world motivated by self-interest and profits.

When individuals are more free, they engage in society more productively, solving problems that we have sometimes relied on government to do.

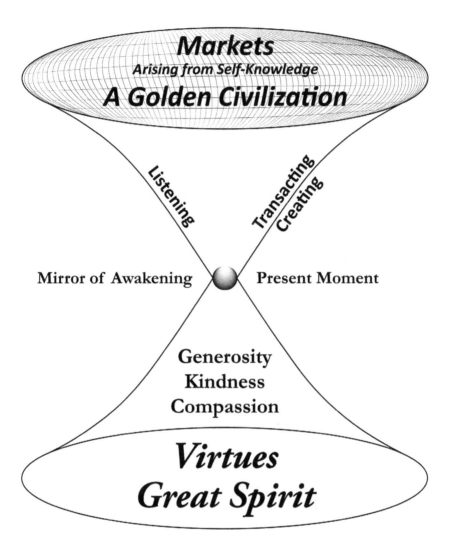

What happens to market efficiency if market dominating institutions can sell products that don't deliver what they promise? What if we buy those products but don't find the freedom that was implied?

I think the following chart accurately describes financial markets where product sales masquerade as financial advice. (The chart can be applied to other products and services as well.) Here, we see how the consumer is deluded or intentionally deceived with false dreams of freedom, and instead materialism is embedded and eats away at civilization.

The Trap of Materialism and How Markets Facilitate It

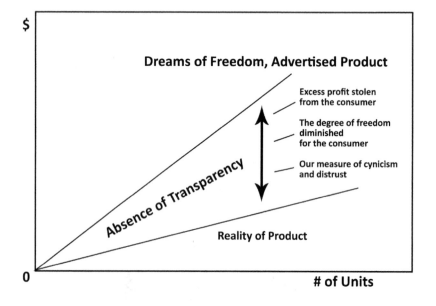

In markets dominated by institutions and confined to the grid of space-time, freedom is illusory. What is promised (and purchased) as freedom instead steals our dreams of freedom from us and gives them as profits to the factories and institutions who value money over freedom.

> *There is more freedom in a moment of self-knowledge than in all market transactions. As we have discovered, self-knowledge arises from listening to the present moment in a way that either takes us into the depths of our being or awakens us to engagement with the world in a way that matches who we are, that is filled with authenticity and actualizes our life plan.*

A Golden Civilization sustainable for thousands of years requires much higher standards of integrity toward the delivery of freedom than we have required or experienced to now. When freedom is wrapped around a product in a sales pitch, it often wins the sale because freedom is what we want. But there is no real freedom there. Our freedom requires great care in a world of limited financial resources, where over-purchasing products diminishes our freedom and gives excess profits to corporations.

> *The delivery of freedom by for-profit institutions has been as inefficient as it has been inauthentic. Advertising aside, it is not their purpose to deliver freedom to us, and freedom itself is not in the nature of these institutions.*

It is inappropriate that advertisements are alluring rather than truthful and completely transparent, that they play on our desires rather than respect our individual passions for freedom. Institutions are ignorant of our freedom, as are the billionaires that direct them. They certainly have no more understanding of freedom than those among us who are wise, spiritually free, and free of material trappings. The wealthy and their institutions have no advantage over any of us when it comes to understanding and enjoying freedom, but they can, unfortunately, wield power and money to bend our paths away from freedom. If we allow them.

Free Markets and Public Policy

Markets work best when they are 'free.' They maximize the efficient allocation of products delivering the best price to each of us and the best quantity to society. As consumers, efficient markets mean we have more resources for what we care about most. The freer the markets in general, the freer we are. The freedom of markets has had a great deal to do with the explosions of growth in the world over the last 250 years. Freedom of markets has given to many greater leisure and longer lives.

The benefits of free markets are often described as arising from a balancing of individual self-interests. But our markets are not markets of individuals. Too often, the self-interest of large institutions overwhelms and undermines the freedom of markets, belittling the self-interest of individual consumers. The recent Banking Crisis and Great Recession are examples of this. See the resulting massive corporate settlements listed in Appendices Eight and Nine. The recent fraudulent misrepresentations of Wells Fargo and Volkswagen to millions of consumers are also examples. Rather than delivering freedom, these corporations, with all their wealth and power, stole it.

Market dominance not only diminishes our freedom, but also inhibits growth and increases unease and distrust in society. We feel quite appropriately that we are being "taken" by forces much larger than us and that markets are rigged against us. Rather than modeling integrity, markets become playgrounds of power, riddled with conflicts of interest.

Of course, we don't always want markets to be free when issues of public policy require urgent or alternative action or when dominant institutions deliver the best service. But there is a cost to us as a society, as well as to each of us individually, even for these allowed exceptions. Efficient allocations of resources are thrown off. Products can become more expensive or more scarce. Corruption increases whenever power replaces market forces, and whenever profit holds sway over freedom. Innovation is stifled. For markets to maximize the delivery of human freedom, they require an ethos of integrity in their operations (ensuring ease of access and entry) and authenticity in their relationships with each of us. Institutional dominance in for-profit markets does not permit either. This is a political issue, not an economic issue, as you might first think.

In a Golden Civilization, politicians would, as figures of wisdom, deliberate what market structures are best for society. In particular, they would be watchful where competitive forces fail to materialize or fail to deliver freedom. But in our day, money determines political agenda, debate, and outcomes. Money puts the politicians in office and defines what they will vote for. Thus, the politics of markets is controlled by narrow and powerful forces rather than by heralds of wisdom or by personal freedom. Given the media power of large institutions, markets are marred with fake proclamations of virtue that proceed to dominate our politics. What politicians of the right mean when they praise free markets are merely markets that are free of government regulation. They don't mind large corporations inhibiting markets as long as their political contributions are sizeable.

Politicians on the left, on the other hand, are not as appreciative of the benefits of free markets at all. They know that market dominance delivered under the banner of free markets has been harmful. So, they disparage free markets, without distinguishing the difference between true free markets and institution-dominated markets.

Politicians on both the right and left seek government action that will siphon more money into the coffers of their donors. Thus, our democracy is bought, the rich get richer, and democracy gets poorer.

It is clear that democratically determined adjustments to market behavior are essential to diminish the corruption and inequities that can accompany institutional dominance of markets. Wise adjustments can inspire innovation and ethical behavior. For example, democratic responses to the growing encroachment of civilization on other species and vital ecosystems have resulted in many individuals becoming global citizens, bringing their Entrepreneurial Spirit to serve the welfare of the planet and its species. Markets shift from old economies to new. Although democratic action must always be sensitive to the inefficient allocation of resources, "for profit" efficiencies are not always for the benefit of civilization and indeed can end it by exacerbating planetary crises, inequality, and warfare.

The financial services industry is not alone. There are problems in many industries of society that cry out for both democratic wisdom and the efficiencies of markets for solutions. For example, the cost and availability of pharmaceuticals is an area where society has yet to determine the most beneficial balance between incentives for market innovation (and profits) and the human imperative to diminish suffering, disease, and death. The field of medicine, with its advisers (doctors), products (drugs, devices, services, etc.), and its product companies (Big Pharma manufacturers, pharmacies, diagnostic machine companies, insurance providers, etc.) has noteworthy overlaps with financial services and presents similar threats to our well-being.

> *There are three conclusions to our discussion of Markets*
> *so far:*
> *1. Protect the freedom of markets as much as possible.*
> *2. Limit the power of institutional self-interest to*
> *dominate markets. Dominated markets aren't free.*
> *3. Strengthen the wisdom factor in democratic*
> *decision-making, diminishing the influence of institu-*
> *tional self-interest as a significant factor in political*
> *debate.*

Markets of Self-Interest and their Externalities

Markets driven by self-interest can contain remarkable efficiencies but also disastrous, often unanticipated and unseen inefficiencies that cry out for invigorated democracy and wisdom. Economists call these inefficiencies negative externalities. They can include war, pollution, species extinction, famine, grotesque inequalities, and autocracy.

Markets of Self-Interest, their Efficiencies and Negative Externalities

Efficiencies
Optimal Pricing of Goods and Services
Profits
Competition Motivating Creativity
Matching of Innovations and Rewards

Inefficiencies and Negative Externalities
Pollution and Species Extinction
Famine
War
Painful and Unwanted Inequalities
Oligarchy Rather Than Democracy
Clever leaders rather than wise
Massive regulations required to balance the self-interest of the rich and institutions against society's interests
Societal Polarizations
Cynicism and Distrust

These externalities contain implications not only in regard to the freedom of markets but also for the possibility of democracy, freedom of the press, and the quality of leadership required for a Golden Civilization. We must recognize the negative roles that markets of self-interest, money, and power can play in the crises that ravage our world—at the expense of planetary resources and human freedom.

When we truly consider the possible and real externalities of a self-interest-based economics, with wisdom we must consider their costs.

We must ask ourselves how much economic growth, how much of the wealth of nations, how much of our potential lifestyles is being taken from us, now and from our future? How much is the debt being levied on future generations? How much life, resource, and resilience is being stolen from Mother Earth that cannot be replenished?

Many questions follow:

Adding the cost of negative externalities to the benefits we accrue, is the combination worth the debts we have to repay?

How will we repay these debts and can we?

Can these debts be funded by future growth, or is this notion merely the argument of those who accrue short-term profits without having to account for negative externalities?

How much damage from these externalities is due to the self-interests of institutions using their power and wealth to trump the wisdom and self-knowledge of humanity?

And perhaps the most fearful question of them all: If the billionaires, governments, corporations, and other institutions that made the decisions to take from our common heritage now control the media, the research institutes, and our democracy, how will we ever find out the truth? Are we too late?

In the largest decisions of civilization, we need wisdom and self-knowledge rather than self-interest. In a Golden Civilization, we openly gather information so that elected figures of wisdom make these difficult decisions, always under our direction. We cannot allow vital information to be monopolized by power brokers or figures of avarice to serve their narrow self-interests at our expense.

Some Native American peoples have looked forward seven generations in their planned care of the earth.[y] With the complexities of technology, where Mother Earth is involved, we should be looking forward a thousand generations or more.

Institutions

A third of financial executives who said they made more than $500,000 annually have witnessed or have firsthand knowledge of wrongdoing in the workplace.

From a survey of 1,200 traders, portfolio managers, investment bankers and hedge fund professionals on both sides of the Atlantic.[32]

Institutions and Integrity

As we suggested at the beginning of the book, integrity in all institutions, systems, and infrastructure is as essential in a technological society as it is in missions to Mars, Jupiter, and the Moon. Indeed, humanity and Earth are on far more complex journeys than the Apollo or Galileo spacecraft, much more complex than NASA could hope to design. A Golden Civilization requires far greater care in building and guarding its integrities than our technologies do. Without impeccable integrity in our social and political systems and in our markets and exchanges, there will be no Golden Civilization for us to arrive at or any of us left to thrive within it.

---

y.   The Seventh Generation Principle dates to The Great Law of Iroquois Confederacy and refers to the concept that the decisions made today should benefit the children seven generations (about 140 years) hence.

> *Integrity requires institutions to value living systems and the freedom of creatures in those systems more than they value profits and power.*
>
> *The grid of time and space is a perfect model for a factory and machine civilization. It works well for technology and for countable things, like money. The grid can be broken down to ever smaller sizes. Its pieces can be analyzed, manipulated, bought, and sold. The grid is perfect for a command and control society, a society of hierarchy and inequality, or a society facing war or disaster. But the grid does not serve the humanity within us. It is a terrible model for freedom, wholly inadequate for a living system like Mother Earth. Freedom must include the whole of us, our whole map. The present moment, creative action, and Great Spirit are all elements of freedom and of free beings.*

Fiduciary Responsibility of Institutions

A strong corporation generally prefers to dominate a market rather than compete in one that is open and free, where new products might supplant their own. This puts institutions in direct conflict with the ideals of free markets and human freedom.

Lao Tse of ancient China wisely warned us: "More laws mean more outlaws." The fewer regulations we have, the healthier and more free the society. However, the very artifice of incorporation, while perhaps desirable, creates the need in society to counter the single-minded focus of the corporation on profits and self-interest within its envelope of limited liability. Failures of integrity and actions of institutions that diminish consumer freedom or harm the planet, stifle entrepreneurial endeavor and foster a climate of deceit and hypocrisy.

Not just corporations, but billionaires, with their power, act like institutions. We must keep in mind that in addition to whatever benefits they may have bestowed upon civilization, and regardless of the great efficiencies they might have added, they have also lucked into, like a lottery, (or pushed their way into) enormous access to capital—and the ownership of factories whose main and most reliable product is profit and power. As a democracy, we've given them that power. And what we have given if it is not for the benefit of civilization, we can also take away. As we lay the foundation of a Golden Civilization we must keep in mind that the more harm one can do (as in shouting fire in a crowded theater) the less free society can allow one to be. This goes for institutional power as well as individual.

> *The larger the institution, government, billionaire or corporation, the greater its responsibility in civilization to model integrity and deliver freedom.*

Markets are precious venues of trust and exchange. They are where consumers can access and build their dreams of freedom. Market dominance, if it is countenanced at all, must carry with it immense and solemn responsibility.

For markets to model integrity and deliver freedom, institutions must be human—or humane. They must assume a fiduciary responsibility not only to their shareholders but to all they come in contact with and to all whom they influence.

> *The largest corporations have a fiduciary obligation to the planet, to our democracy and to the freedom of all human beings. Their drive for personal profit must be held within and subject to this fiduciary obligation.*

The following chart describes the cycles that civilization goes through without the ethical norms, systems, and structures that are the foundation of a Golden Civilization.

Model Integrity, Deliver Freedom

Economic Cycles of Idealism, Efficiency, Tyranny, and Revolt

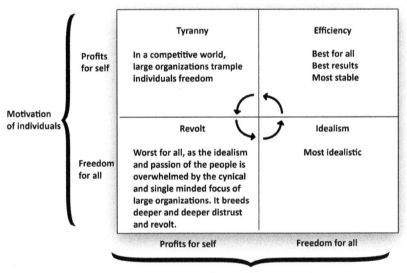

For a healthy society, and as individuals, we want to reside in the right two quadrants: Idealism and Efficiency. But for large organizations to do so requires them to shift from a "profits for self" mentality to being the fiduciary of human freedom. Markets operate in different

ways in each quadrant. Markets in the left quadrants, when dominated, are inefficient and trample over individual freedoms. A Golden
Civilization resides in the right quadrants, where institutions align
with individual freedom, self-knowledge is fostered, and democracy
reigns.[z] Good government sits entirely on the right-hand side of the
design. For these changes to occur requires a change of ethos in our
culture and clear definitions of fiduciary obligations in our laws.

Institutions: Non-Profits and Freedom of Speech

We briefly discussed corporate-front groups in the Media chapter.

> *One of the great flaws of modern democracy, and civilization
> at large, is the notion that a corporation has as much right
> to freedom and free speech as citizens do—or possibly more,
> since they provide jobs. This belief undermines civilization
> by surrendering individual freedoms to institutions far more
> powerful than we are.*
>
> *Institutions are not citizens in democracy and are not meant
> to be free. Their freedom to operate and influence is a parody
> of individual freedom. They are meant to be our servants.
> Their speech is not from one human being to another, but from
> an impersonal, powerful, single-minded force to individual
> human beings.*

Although composed of people, the institutions themselves are artificial
constructs of power, not people. In a Golden Civilization, institutions
are humane. Their speech is limited to truth-telling except in the case

---

z.   See Appendix Four: Corruption, for the widespread global distrust of
countries and their institutions, and for how far away from fiduciary responsibility our governments and corporations are perceived to be.

of obvious fictions like moviemaking. Even there, it is not right for large institutions to dominate the field. In all fields of culture, we must strive for free markets rather than dominated ones. Even nuance, let alone blunt force, used by large organizations in marketing or advertising represents a theft from transparency and honesty, robbing us of freedom by implying deliverables—freedom—that will never be realized.

Both for-profits and non-profits are single-minded in the pursuit of their agendas. For that reason, they should be limited by law in their power and influence. If they lack integrity or fail in their fiduciary duty to consider the larger societal purpose of freedom for all, there must be fierce consequences.

Large for-profit corporations have long funded non-profit organizations with misleading names and obscured missions to feign support for consumers, public health, or the environment, when actually they support or pursue objectives that are just the opposite. This subterfuge is an abuse of power and, where consequences to our health and safety are concerned, can be deadly. Some well-documented tactics of corporate-front groups include:

- Promoting "scientific" conclusions far from the mainstream to deceive citizens or consumers, further corporate interests, and maximize profits rather than reveal and inform.

- Using watered-down referendums to divert votes from bona fide reforms and concerned citizens.

- Commanding media space as if they were the "balanced" or mainstream "alternative" viewpoint, when really their "freedom of speech" is just bought by money and their paper-thin scientific studies.

- Hiring scientists (by the corporation, and therefore not independent) often without revealing to the public the corporate source.

- Using mockery, negative branding, and name calling in lieu of genuine debate to block or pass legislation.

These are all acts of fraud and should be adjudicated as such.

Often these non-profits distribute their tainted messaging via national media, without being identified as corporate-funded front groups.

Major market dominators have long and extensively employed these tactics, including companies in the food, energy, financial, automobile, tobacco, pharmaceutical, and retail industries. A great source for authoritative information on these corporate-front groups is sourcewatch.org.

As a consequence, the public loses faith in the non-profit sector, which also pursues noble and charitable purposes. The cynicism and hypocrisy of large organizations is infectious.

Our ancestors once struggled with how to tell a prophet from a false prophet. In today's corporate culture, our task is to distinguish a noble non-profit from the funded information factories pretending to be one.

For markets to function effectively as places of exchange, they must be honest. In a Golden Civilization, corporate-front groups are banned. There are three ways markets, and thus society, are corrupted:

- Corporate-front groups become another tool for large corporations to manipulate markets to keep them from being free.

- Corporations interfere with democratic decision-making—markets are, and should be, a useful tool for democracy, not the other way around.

- Deceit of the public by large institutions results in cynicism, distrust, and polarization.

> *Distrust undermines all of our institutions. Cynicism is not appropriate, right, or healthy in a Golden Civilization. It is a societal disease that robs us of our innocence, and thus of ourselves, and of the truth of things. It robs us of what is profound and of what connects us to all other beings. It diminishes the possibility of authenticity in our relationships. It indicates something is wrong and that hypocrisy rules the roost.*

The solutions to these deceits? Nonprofit fronts pursuing corporate agendas must declare in all communications, including letterhead and websites, who their corporate and billionaire sponsors are. But this is a mere stopgap measure. We should immediately move to end these fronts by legislation or, alternatively, revise the rights that the voting public has granted corporations and end their ability to fund non-profits. The corporate contract, along with its limited liability, must come with clear responsibilities.

Ultimately, in a Golden Civilization, these fronts do not exist at all. Corporations express their views plainly, with full transparency, and if they stray from messaging or actions beneficial to the public, then the consumers in the free and open market, and the voters and their wise representatives in democracy, react swiftly and appropriately in response.

It would be a shame to curtail corporate funding for charitable causes. But the less than honorable intentions and actions of many corporations and their front groups demand a re-examination of tax laws and corporate charters to clean up abuse. The cleanest approach would be for corporations to stick to their "for-profit" pursuits. Let society find other less sullied ways to fund good causes than to give large profit-focused corporations the opportunity to look better than they are.

There are many opportunities for "for-profit" corporations to do good as they make and sell products and services for profit. To benefit the greater good, let them make better products with only the healthiest of environmental footprints. Let them give better service. Reduce CEO salaries and pay workers more. Support the life plans of employees and grant flexible hours to allow quality time for family and to pursue passions. Make the workplace joyful and healthy. Model equality. Encourage employees to organize around their own interests, not the corporation's. Integrate mindfulness, listening, inspiring, and problem-solving skills into the workplace. Model respectful communications and group process. Make kindness and humility part of everyone's experience. Seek to create great experiences for corporate vendors, customers, and shareholders. These actions demonstrate to all the fiduciary nature of institutions and their dedication to the values of a Golden Civilization. They are worth spending money on.

Institutions Don't Breathe

Let's revisit a fundamental fact and its implications for the structures of civilization and of our freedom. Institutions don't breathe. They have no heart. They can't be mindful the way we can. They can't do inner listening. There is no "inner" there. They cannot access the present moment, nor the Great Spirit. They can't experience or know freedom. They are corporate leviathans. They have their single purposes. Given that, how can we expect them to respect or foster our freedom? In a Golden Civilization, it would be wonderful to trust them so much. To earn that trust, their integrity must be impeccable—and their humanity.

We're Barely at the Beginning of Civilization, of Complexity, and of Systems of Accountability

We think of ourselves as a greatly advanced civilization with freedoms adorning our society like jewels. Yet we've recently experienced the most scandal-ridden of economic times with multi-billion-dollar settlements resulting from bank and other financial malfeasance. A few minor figures have been sanctioned or jailed, but no major players. Corrective laws were passed but then revised or withdrawn before they could even engender real reform. The financial institutions at the heart of the scandals are more politically powerful than ever. Predictably, considering these facts, there has been no change in ethos in the broader culture. See Appendices Eight and Nine for a Financial Times spreadsheet summarizing the crisis from 2007 to 2015. While the spread doesn't include the earlier Enron or KPMG scandals or the more recent scandals involving Wells Fargo, it nevertheless captures the extensive criminal activity in the financial services industry in the subject timeframe. Most of the cited companies remain among the most powerful in the world.

We have also recently seen major auto manufacturers deceive the public, fraudulently selling "clean" cars that pollute the earth. We've seen oil companies and their surrogates deny climate change to preserve their markets for oil. We've seen drug companies gouge individual consumers and their health insurance for thousands of dollars. We've seen new financial frauds since the banking crisis engineered by large financial corporations stealing money, time, and freedom from millions of consumers for corporate profit.

In a Golden Civilization, none of this would happen. There would be a clearer sense of and pride in corporate fiduciary responsibility.

We're barely 250 years into the industrial revolution, barely at the beginning of complex civilization, a mere fraction of the 20-million-year lifespan of our nearest primates. With continuing rapid increases in knowledge and technology, unless we change our path, civilization cannot survive the negative externalities of another 250 years: the wars, pollution, surveillance, inequalities, autocracies, cynicism, and distrust. But, as a civilization and as a species, we are young and we are powerful.

We can create and become anything we want. Easily, we can change the rules to guarantee a thriving civilization and a fertile planet for a thousand generations. Given the complexities of knowledge we face, we must not wait. It must be our highest priority.

To end corruption and inspire our civilization with its own integrity and dedication to freedom, we must ensure that corporate penalties for fraud and malfeasance are much greater than occurred following the Great Recession of 2008. The financial settlements in that case were a trivial cost of doing business for corporations, hardly penalties at all. In such severe cases in the future, charters to practice and rights to advertise should be revoked; CEOs and boards should be held personally accountable. Some argue that if the US raises its corporate standards it will lose business to less forthright countries. That is why such standards must become global. We must understand this as we, the global community, move from being warring states to being members of a planetary culture. We should consider doing business only with countries that recognize and adhere to these standards. We will need stronger whistle-blower protections and rewards, vigorous investigative journalism, and commitment from watchful citizens to make this work.

The community of nations must recognize that we are not each other's enemies—our common enemies are corruption, ignorance, greed, lust for power, envy, fear, narcissism, and false (and real) entitlement. These are the enemies that all of us must be willing to face and tame inside ourselves as we deny them fertile soil in our institutions.

The growing threats to civilization mean that delay is not an option. Lobbyists, lawyers, and purchased politicians will balk and say, "Oh no, that can never be done quickly." But it's not so difficult. Every election counts. It's time to identify what would be ideal for a Golden Civilization to thrive, with integrity and freedom, for a thousand generations. Make it law. Make penalties so severe that institutions will never again fail the standards of integrity.

And if they nonetheless do fail our rising standards, we must provide dislocated employees who were not in the direct line of fraudulent activity much greater protection in terms of basic income, unemployment benefits, and Life Planning. The innocent should not suffer. Instead, we can help them find their passion and their freedom.

Our objectives could not be more clear: free markets of institutional dominance; create a fiduciary institutional culture; free society of deceit, cynicism, and distrust; and bring into being a Golden Civilization, where individual freedom is supported by all institutional structures. As the ethos of our culture becomes inherently humane, there will be little need to further legislate or regulate activities within that culture. But in the short-term, if we need laws to bound the damaging actions of reckless institutions and wealth, then so be it.

The Balance of Markets and Democracy in a Golden Civilization

Balancing the freedom of markets with market regulations is one of the most pressing policy and hot-button political issues of our times. But we cannot even determine society's best systems for freedom and integrity as long as democracy and markets are dominated by large money forces. We must first clear away market dominance, conflicts of interest, and corruption.

> *A paradox: Both free markets and regulatory actions threaten large corporations. Either can reduce the organization's power or viability. That is the hallmark of creative capitalism and egalitarian democracy—both are levelers and innovators. Both rely on, inspire, and stand for freedom. To truly embrace capitalism and democracy, we must also be mindful of, and be willing to bear their costs by providing support for those who may be harmed. Up to now, many of our policies have aimed at propping up corporations when they fail or act fraudulently. This practice has diminished freedom, encouraged corruption, and spread cynicism and distrust. It would be far less costly to society to let the poorly managed companies fail and to double or even triple support for displaced workers and to provide Life Planning to inspire their own Entrepreneurial Spirit. In a Golden Civilization, individuals and their freedoms matter most. If institutions fail us rather than serve us, they must go.*

As we have indicated, freedom as well as entrepreneurial endeavor will arise more from increasing levels of virtue and authenticity in society, from greater access to present moments, and from life plans pursued, than it will from policy decisions that maximize corporate profits.

To maximize freedom for us all, the rules of markets and their structures must become the province of figures of wisdom, freely elected by an awake constituency.

Where society has basic requirements, like it has for clean air and water, health care, and education, there will tend to be dominant institutions with free markets clustered around, percolating with innovation. Market competition and wise democracy ensure an open path for those innovations. Too often it is otherwise. In my own field of financial services, during my 40-year professional life as a financial adviser and teacher, I have witnessed instead the market dominance of financial product companies and the commanding purchasing power they were allowed with politicians and the media. Great innovations arose amongst independent financial advisers, but there was little access to markets. Such access would have greatly altered centers of power in financial services and government, brought greater trust throughout society, and delivered greater freedom to all but those who held the reins of power.

In a Golden Civilization, institutions in the marketplace inspire trust, deliver freedom, and delight us with their beneficence and transparency.

The Future: Markets of Freedom

In the future, economic growth will be measured in moments of freedom rather than in currency. Growth will be understood as driven by self-knowledge rather than by self-interest.

Our most important policy question is how do we achieve the greatest efficiency of markets in the delivery of moments of freedom to all.

With a societal shift to valuing self-knowledge, there will be markets we can now hardly imagine, markets that transcend even our notions of market behavior. These will be markets of freedom; markets of awakening; markets of the present moment and the flourishing of life itself; markets of the qualities of mind and energy that deliver freedom; markets of virtues, attention, focus, patience, understanding, dedication, courage, kindness, compassion, curiosity, flexibility, rapture, tranquility, and equanimity.

These markets will enrich individuals (and civilization) far more than the markets of exchange and self-interest that our governments, economists, and the wealthy have to now favored. They will not be organized as efficiencies in grids of space-time but rather as efficiencies of access to the present moment, virtues, Great Spirit, and efficiencies of transparency. The economics will be more of relationships and interior spaces of personal freedom than an economics of money. Rather than mechanical and widespread, they will be deep. Rather than efficiencies of transaction, they will be markets of experiences of transformation, their efficiencies measured by access to freedom, wisdom, and compassion. Mediated at first through purchased settings of time and space, they will morph into democratic freedoms and rights.

All markets (whether conscious or unconscious, freedom or transaction-based) are centered around the present moment and the nuances of listening, selfless gathering, and engagement, but especially markets of freedom. Within those nuances are markets of cultural exchange. But we hardly notice them, because the present moment is so brief, selflessness so profound, and we ourselves so inexperienced. More than the refrigerator economics of boxes of space-time, in our quests for freedom and self-knowledge, we want explosions of consciousness, clarity, exhilaration, and peace. As our understanding of freedom grows, we want the whole map to be our realm of economics, not individual pieces of the grid, however jewel-like they appear to be.

In the current grid of the marketplace, deception, false surfaces, hypocrisy, half-truths, and lies imprison both seller and buyer. The economics is unsustainable. There is no access to the interior spaces of self-knowledge, wisdom, and freedom. Each lie blocks a pathway, throws a cloud of deception over a pathway to freedom.

The Balance of Self-Knowledge and Self-Interest

There is a word for the deep interior markets of freedom. They are the gathering places of self-knowledge. Self-knowledge incorporates both the quiet listening we call mindfulness and the passionate self-knowing that arises in Life Planning and that moves us forward into engagement with the world. In markets of self-knowledge rather than self-interest, the boxes and cells of space-time are permeated with awareness, wisdom, and freedom.

Self-interest is a natural and necessary subset of self-knowledge, but without self-knowledge, the negative externalities of self-interest kill us. The problem for markets as we have created them, is that institutions do not have self-knowledge.

> *The only way to achieve a self-knowledge economy is to reduce the power of institutions and increase the self-knowledge of the individuals within them.*

In a Golden Civilization, self-knowledge flourishes. It is the primary goal for leaders and in education, the media, and culture. Even within institutions, self-knowledge becomes more dominant than self-interest, as institutions demonstrate their fiduciary duty to society.

In the map that follows, self-knowledge occupies the bottom half, but through the singularity of the present moment and the mirror of awakening, self-knowledge enters into the world of time and space. Self-interest remains confined to the grid in the top portion of the map.

How Self-Knowledge Permeates Self-Interest

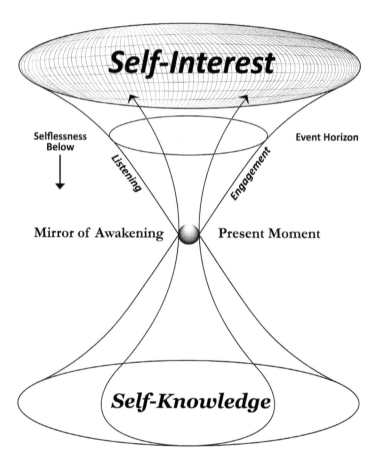

We cannot map properly the enormous territory of self-knowledge. In a conscious universe, awake with human creativity and freedom, it is infinitely larger than the territory of self-interest. Self-knowledge permeates the universe. Self-interest, a subset, is a mere parody of self-knowledge.

The Circle of Self-Interest Held Within the Infinity of Self-Knowledge

Self-Knowledge

These next two charts illustrate relationships and differences between economies based on self-interest and self-knowledge. First, a summary of some core elements of the economics of self-knowledge and self-interest.

Core Elements of a Self-Knowledge Economics	Core Elements of a Self-Interest Economics
Moments of Freedom	Transactions of Buyers and Sellers
Mentors, Advisers, Financial Life Planners	Markets
Innovation/Entrepreneurial Spirit Flourishing in Everyone	Competition for Scarce Resources
Internal/External, Self/Global, Conscious/Unconscious Configurations	Space-Time Configurations
Freedom & Authenticity Orientation	Transaction Orientation

A self-knowledge economy is more efficient for civilization than a self-interest economy. It is naturally grounded in who we are, in our authenticity, freedom, and virtues. Here are some of the benefits and externalities of each.

Self-Knowledge Benefits and Externalities	Self-Interest Benefits and Externalities
Pricing and Profits, Innovation and Rewards	Pricing and Profits, Innovation and Rewards
Planetary Culture	Warring States Culture
Integrity/Freedom	Massive Inequality
Wisdom	Cleverness
Authenticity	Pollution, Famine, Banking Crises, War
Virtue/Happiness	Envy, Greed
Universal Entrepreneurial Spirit Flourishing for Everyone	Entrepreneurial Spirit Available Only to Venture Capital and Private Equity Machines
Democracy	Oligarchy/Autocracy
Acceptance of Oneself and Others	Opposition of Oneself to Others
Sufficiency	Scarcity
Free Markets/Global Markets	Markets Dominated by Product Companies, by Power, and by Political Cronyism
Minimal Regulation Required in Ethos of Authenticity	Massive Regulation Required where Self-Interest Dominates Self-Knowledge
Compassion and Cooperation	Societal Polarization
Creativity from Wisdom	Creativity from Competition

A society ruled by self-interest lurches from crisis to crisis. It fosters excess, creates war, and poisons the planet. Yes, it can innovate, but only at the cost of economic extremes and instability. A society ruled by self-knowledge, within which self-interest plays an important role, is more stable. Rather than arising from a spectrum of avarice, innovation is driven by the passions of people to bring freedom and compassion into the world. It is driven by wisdom.

We aspire for our world to be bountiful and humane, not manufactured or digitized, not controlled by hierarchies of power. Such hierarchies are merely tools, meant to serve us all. The sustainable foundation of a Golden Civilization are great hearts, free and flourishing, shaping the hierarchies of power as we wish and need them to be, not the other way around.

As our economics shift from self-interest to self-knowledge, we shift from a universe that is dominated by unconscious forces to one that is vital with conscious forces, where we recognize ourselves as the beating heart of the universe we occupy. In an unconscious universe, sentient beings are separate from each other. They are vulnerable to being ruled by forces larger than themselves, driven by institutions, religions, dictators, or deceits, or by fate or instinct or karma, or by biology or DNA. An unconscious world is often polarized, its fragile architecture patched together by clinging to beliefs. It is a world incapable of peace, completeness, or presence, a world where brute force and death itself constantly overwhelm freedom and life. Alternatively, in a conscious universe, our experience is authentic, organic, and alive. We consciously co-create the universe with all other awakened beings. Awakening itself flourishes in every moment. Even death is an awakening.

Consider again our maps of an unconscious civilization contrasted with a civilization that is awake.

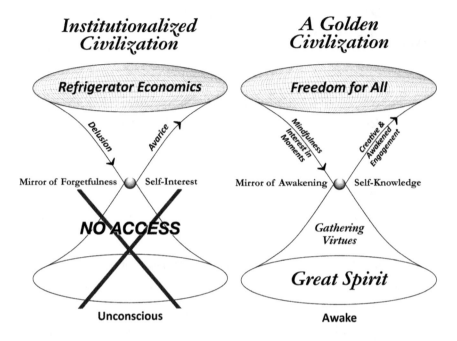

It is our task to bring increasing levels of freedom to markets where they are dominated and to explore greater qualities within markets, as we ourselves become free. When resources are limited, markets are necessary to allocate them most efficiently throughout society. Where the resources of wisdom and self-knowledge are available to all, markets are more about articulating the most efficient pathways to freedom for each of us. Their ultimate purpose is less about making money than about maximizing freedom for all. For that task they require great integrity. In a Golden Civilization, it must be clear to all that markets have great integrity and are trustworthy. In a Golden Civilization, integrity blossoms into authenticity and the resource of freedom is unlimited. Markets themselves become free, organic, and alive.

Action Steps and Basic Principles for Markets

> *Markets are most efficient and transformational when they are designed to model integrity and deliver freedom. In a Golden Civilization, this is what they do.*

Here are some action steps to take us there.

1. Support free markets, democratized, competitive, with access to all.

2. Dramatically reduce institutional dominance and influence in markets (including corporate, governmental, and non-profit).

3. Cultivate zero tolerance throughout society for institutional corruption and lack of integrity. There should be dramatic penalties for failures of institutional integrity.

> **a.** Institutional crimes should be punished far more severely than individual crimes if we are to have institutions of integrity as the norm and freedom for all as the expectation. A million small thefts by a corporation should be punished as if it were one million thefts, not just one, and punished explicitly, in addition, for abuse of power. Harm to society includes the spread of cynicism and distrust which, of course, is immeasurable in all senses of the word. We must impose and enforce much stricter standards on the false implications of language and image in advertising. There should be nothing but truth in advertising. No nuance or implication beyond what is true. And establish consumer fiduciaries to watch over the standard.

b. The loss of freedom to advertise in all forms of media should be just one consequence of failures of integrity.

c. Eliminate corporate "personhood" where its power has been abused, in particular its ability to influence elections and the proper function of democracy.

4. Hold corporations and governments accountable for negative externalities going forward a thousand generations. Globalize tax systems so that there is no escape from these responsibilities.

5. Eliminate all corporate political (and non-profit if necessary) contributions. Under the guise of goodness, they deceive populations, dominate markets, and destroy human freedom.

6. Outlaw corporate-front groups.

7. Redesign the corporate charter governing limited liability of corporations to fiercely discourage failures of integrity; make such failures as intolerable to owners, Boards of Directors, senior managers, and employees as they are to all consumers and citizens.

8. Provide Life Planning and significant temporary financial support for those who lose jobs due to corporate failure resulting from market forces or regulatory action. Rather than allow the despair of loss, provide the vision and means for employees to again feel the passion for freedom.

9. Bring a humane, mindful, and fiduciary culture into all aspects of institutional life.

10. Encourage training and availability of financial advisers and advice that models integrity and delivers freedom to all. Our greatest resource is our human capital. The market's primary purpose is to maximize the efficient allocation of human capital, by aligning it with the individual pursuit of freedom.

11. Strengthen democracy everywhere. Where there is a failure of markets to model integrity or to deliver freedom, the real failure is in our democracy which has the responsibility and—we must always remember—the power to determine the structure of markets and the rules and regulations by which they can most efficiently function.

12. The efficiency of markets must be measured in degrees of human freedom, not by profits or other financial measurements. Spread self-knowledge everywhere through education, experiences of freedom, mindfulness, and Life Planning.

13. Deliver and encourage the study and experience of moments of freedom, so that markets most efficiently deliver them.

   a. Study the nature of the present moment, both through scientific studies and experientially.

   b. Seek to understand, experience, and then deliver individual dreams of freedom, and thus Entrepreneurial Spirit and self-knowledge into the world.

   c. Institute democratic reforms to maximize individual freedom.

   d. Encourage the practice of mindfulness and its study.

   e. Encourage the study and experience of awakening in all its traditions.

   f. Encourage and study virtue, kindness, and compassion in all their guises. Seek to understand their benefits and how best to teach and deliver them. Be fierce where markets deny them.

14. Equal to human capital, the greatest resource we have is our Earth systems and the complex species that have evolved to maximize efficiencies within their environment. Markets must work to preserve and continue to maximize these efficiencies, which means their own experiences of freedom, and to maximize communications across species.

Leaders

We should live in such a way that if others followed our example,
this very earth would be heaven.

~Iswar Chandra Vidyasagar,
as quoted in The Gospel of Sri Ramakrishna

Great leaders inspire us to be better people than we are.

In difficult situations, leaders make the difference, regardless of the machineries of power. They are not the machinery, but are the light in its midst, the heart at its center. Without them, machinery saps our souls.

Great leaders bear suffering gladly, deeply, and willingly for their people. They experience their anger or shame or fear or guilt, without acting them out on others, without taking them out on themselves. They inspire us in the midst of such feelings. A great leader moves through darkness into light. Against all odds, they find vigor, strength, and vision and take us there. They inspire others long after they are gone. Great leaders open up heaven for us. They show us a personal path that will make us a better person and the earth a better place.

Leaders are dedicated to our individual freedom as much as they are to our communities. That's how they touch us, and then inspire us.

In a Golden Civilization, leaders of corporations, of governments, and of non-profits inspire us to go beyond what we thought was possible. They are not separated from us by multi-million dollar salaries and gated residences. They lead us by their humanity and humility, by their presence within their companies and communities, by donating their personal time to worthy causes, by connecting with their consumers, by their listening, by their example, by their belief in our freedom and by their understanding of the values of a Golden Civilization. They are one of us.

If a leader is not virtuous, we copy their lack of virtue and are no more true to them than they are to us. If a leader is not virtuous, even to ourselves there is a taint. People trust great leaders, they gather around them, they follow them. Masters of the present moment, they have great insight, live simply, and know freedom.

True leaders, where institutional power has grown corrupt, do not fear or block whistle-blowers—indeed, they lead among them. They speak the truth, and from the vantage point of their leadership positions, they expose the truth to ward off damage to society.

Shareholders are important, but not as important as nor as great a responsibility as democracy, the public, and Mother Earth.

> *If you seek success, look within. Perfect yourself and external success will follow. Develop authenticity and act with integrity and people will look to you for your wisdom and walk with you.*

Obstacles to Great Leadership

Even a little greed and selfishness turn strength into weakness, knowledge into ignorance, care into cruelty, and purity into defilement, thus ruining one's character.[33]

~Huanchu Daoren

Learn from the mistakes of others. You can't live long enough to make them all yourself.

~Eleanor Roosevelt

Great leadership depends on the natural unfolding of our character into wisdom and self-knowledge. The obstacle? The knot of self-centeredness and hypocrisy that blocks each of our completeness.

It is astonishing to find the following quote, more than two thousand years old, from the Huainan civilization in the Han Dynasty of China. It should cause us to reflect on leaders we choose today in our democracy, and on the consequences of the great inequalities we have created in society.

"There are three dangers in the world:
- *To have many privileges but few virtues is the first danger.*
- *To be high in rank but low on ability is the second danger.*
- *To receive a large salary without personally accomplishing much is the third danger."* [34]

> **The greatest danger both for the world and for ourselves is to hold a leadership position, responsible for many people, and to lack the virtue and the nobility of character to truly lead.**

Leadership suffers greatly when self-interest rules over wisdom, and the power of money corrupts decision-making. The problem is magnified by the way we internally map our world as a grid of time and space filled with experiences that can be bought and things that can be possessed. These are but fools' gold. To a great leader, a great heart and the unobstructed flow of freedom it delivers are all in all. Conflicts with these values that arise from money or power interests undermine relationships and make leadership impossible.

> **Where personal profits or the profits of businesses come before the delivery of freedom to others or of modeling integrity within ourselves, we are no longer leaders. Business and profit have had a very low correlation to nobility of character. Very few great leaders emerge in a culture dominated by self-interest.**

In fact, we've cultivated a tawdriness of leadership in our institutional structures. Two specimens of evidence: financial rewards tantamount to bribery and confidentiality (or non-disclosure) contracts. Here are results excerpted from a recent poll conducted in the financial services industry: "28% of respondents earning $500,000 or more a year said their company's confidentiality policies and procedures barred the reporting of potential illegal or unethical activities directly to law enforcement or regulatory authorities. A quarter of respondents earning $500,000 or more have signed or been asked to sign a confidentiality agreement that would prohibit reporting illegal or unethical activities to the authorities."[35]

And "27% of those surveyed disagree that the financial services industry puts the best interests of clients first. This figure rises to 38% for those earning $500,000 or more per year...Nearly one-third of respondents (32%) believe compensation structures or bonus plans in place at their company could incentivize employees to compromise ethics or violate the law."[36] Surely those earning over $500,000 should be leaders in society, not servile to institutional unethical behavior. In a Golden Civilization, such practices would be unthinkable.

Rich bosses do not easily, or normally, make great leaders. Extremes of salary and wealth without ethics at their base, undermine the integrity, dignity, and generosity of honest labor. They undermine the development of virtue by fixing our eyes on a false prize. They undermine entrepreneurial endeavor by diminishing the relative freedom of the less entitled. Does the extreme inequality in society inspire us to live entrepreneurial lives, vital lives, communal lives? Or does it inspire discontent, buying lottery tickets and other forms of gambling, gaming the system and, among the wealthy, utilizing tax havens? How can there be great leadership under such conditions? Extreme inequality is a breeding ground for the polarizations in society that lead to racism, fascism, dictatorships, violence, and war.

It is the darkness of our age and the failure of democracy, of economics, and of leadership itself that leaders have not grounded us in something deeper than self-interest. How profoundly disconcerting it has been to experience leaders as arrogant, self-centered, corrupt, and foolish rather than wise, inspiring us to be better people. In the future, we will see this as a disease that festered in society. When our leaders are grabbers and takers, we likewise are tempted to grab and take.

All of Us as Leaders

Strong people don't need strong leaders.
~ Ella Baker

In a Golden Civilization, great leaders are everywhere. The structures of civilization foster them. Their emergence into society is natural and organic. They walk among us, not separately. They are us. Each of us is born to become a leader. Leadership fulfills the Entrepreneurial Spirit into which we are born, and which we cultivate like a guiding star throughout our lives.

Recently I was asked to reflect back and consider what advice I would give my younger self. I responded that if there was just one thing it would be this:

 • Be true to yourself; don't compromise who you are. Be authentic in everything you do.

But then I thought further, and added:

• Attain within yourself perfect simplicity;[aa] that is the surest path to authenticity.

• Look deeply at the human nature of everyone you meet.

• Be humble in light of, well...everything.

• Observe those who are wise, learn from them, model what you do after them, especially in small moments and minute particulars, as William Blake calls them.

• Learn also from those who are not wise; ironically, they have much to teach.

> *When someone does you wrong, they harm themselves more than you. Instead of letting it trouble you, observe your response to them. There is something there—in your response—that can make you wise.*

Leaders call forth many strengths. Depending on circumstances, they discover and model the virtues needed to tackle the dilemmas we find ourselves facing. When necessary, leaders are on fire with Entrepreneurial Spirit, inspiring us with their energy to do great deeds. At other times, they model patience, equanimity, or acceptance because that is what is needed. We all know of such leaders; we've seen them. We follow them, because they model integrity and virtue. In the democracy of a Golden Civilization, our education system will foster these qualities in everyone; every occupation becomes a field of leadership and virtue.

---

aa T.S. Eliot, Little Gidding: "A condition of complete simplicity (costing not less than everything)."

> *There are people who say there can be only a few leaders. I don't agree. There can be only a few bosses and only in crises. We must all be leaders in doing what is right, in modeling integrity and delivering freedom in our fields of expertise, our specialties, our spheres of influence, our daily interactions, and of course in the passionate pursuits that arise out of our life plans. Otherwise, how can we trust each other?*

Personally, I want each person I meet in their own domain to be a leader, to lead me safely, gently out of uncertainty, out of self-judgment, out of suffering, into the open space and lovely fields and gardens of freedom.

The Spectrum of Leadership

Everyone as a leader ⟷ Leaders of the most powerful organizations, hierarchical leaders. A world weighted on this end of the spectrum is a world that diminishes freedom; a world instead focused on money and power.

> *The real leaders are among the people, they are in the marketplace, in the cities, on the factory floors. They live on farms, on mountain tops, on the edge of waters, in small towns and suburbs, and deep within the forest's wall. In their own way, each of them practices mindfulness and pursues virtue. They are awake and kind.*

It is critical, for a Golden Civilization, that we institutionalize great leadership throughout society, and become a democracy that is filled with great leaders in every walk of life, from childhood through adulthood.

> *Like birds in a flock changing direction in the sky above us, a new leader emerges, as capable of leading the flock as the previous leader. All of us must be ready to claim the mantle of leadership.*

Paths of Leadership

Human life is made freer by minimization. For example, if you party less, you avoid that much more frenzy, and if you speak less, you avoid that much more resentment. If you think less, your vital spirit doesn't get worn out, and if you are less clever, your wholeness can be preserved. Those who seek not to lessen daily but to increase daily are really fettering their lives.[37]

~Huanchu Daoren

The best thing to do with the best things in life is to give them up.

~Dorothy Day

When our view is locked to the grid of time and space, to refrigerator economics, we can neither see nor breathe. We lose our humanity. But the grid is only a tiny corner of what is real. We know how transparency in economics and politics is crucial to understanding the true state of mundane things. This is the transparency of space-time. But there is a greater transparency to achieve in each of us—the transparency that is awake. It takes in the whole universe. It transcends cells on the grid, by leveraging the power of the present moment to serve as a portal to the deepest experiences of truth and freedom. Its markers are the absence of greed, envy, and aversion as drivers of our grasping nature. For our civilization to thrive, we need both aspects of transparency: the first for our civilization to function with fairness; and the second to develop our great hearts, our Entrepreneurial Spirits, and our wise leaders.

Often, we seek solitude to achieve transparency within ourselves and to develop wisdom. It is in solitude that we can observe ourselves most clearly and, when stressed, we seek it. Some walk the beach, others visit the park, go to mountains or forests, or sit along rivers or streams. We reduce the "noise" and clear our minds. But, the most direct route to solitude is to find it inside ourselves. In the power of the present moment, we can access solitude and find great rest whenever we are in need. Solitude opens us up, deepens self-knowledge, builds authenticity, and strengthens sincerity. It provides space for present moments and freedom.

On our maps of mindfulness, we find great rest at the base of the map, but it is the transparency of the present moment that brings us there. The present moment is everything; nothing ever happens outside of it. If you want to be at peace, master the present moment and how it changes. Master through mindfulness how selflessness arises. This is the most powerful skill a leader can learn, regardless of field, profession, or domain.

> *If you master the present moment, you have mastered everything.*

> *The present moment is the hidden jewel—hidden in plain sight. In the rush of life, we forget about it. But it is where everything happens; it is where freedom happens. It is the hidden jewel of civilization, of great leadership and life itself. When we are awake in the present moment, a Golden Civilization arises all on its own.*

Leaders at ease in the present moment model how the universe becomes aware of itself and creates itself, gathering virtue at the base of our maps, and distributing it into civilization.

Here are some Maps of Leadership that display how this is done, how virtues arise through the authenticity and freshness of the moment into the grid of time and space. By so doing, leaders inspire us to do likewise. I've started with a map of how Tai Chi works, because it is analogous to how, through the transparency of the present moment, we gather virtues reflected at the base of our map. And then we distribute them through time and space. In Tai Chi, practitioners often focus on the tan t'ien, an energy center in the body just below the navel. As they do so they gather chi (energy) from their base (Mother Earth), packing it into the tan t'ien, from which they then distribute the chi, directing it to good purpose in the world around them. In a similar way, self-knowledge can enter into a world of self-interest and spread virtue, authenticity, compassion, and forgiveness into the world.

Through the power and the transparency of the present moment, we gather what is profound, shown at the base of the map, and deliver it into civilization.

Transformations of Leadership

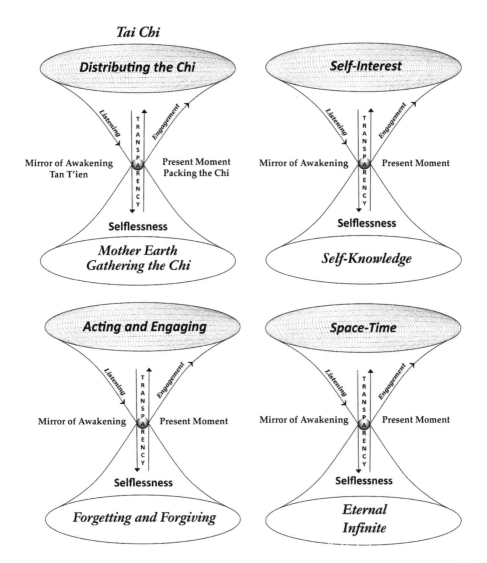

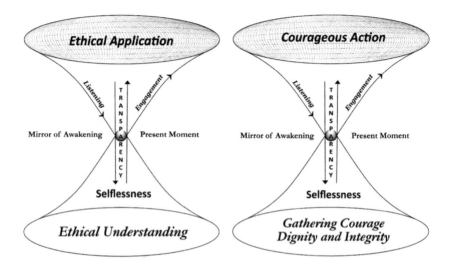

Training

> When sages are in high positions, the people are pleased with their
> government; when sages are in low positions, the people look up
> to their ideas. When petty people are in high positions, it is not
> possible to rest easy even for a moment.

~The Book of Leadership and Strategy:
Lessons of the Chinese Masters Translated by Thomas Cleary

> Yesterday, I was clever, and I wanted to change the world,
> today I am wise, and I want to change myself.

~Rumi

We need standards for our leaders—standards for ourselves as leaders—that are learned and practiced from childhood.

If we continue to train more for self-interest, profit, and advantage than for integrity and freedom, our systems will require endless repair, until they reach a point where they will not hold. Only wise leadership can guide us to reshape our systems as we must.

Wisdom can be accumulated by study or by experience, both of which can take a lifetime. It can also be learned experientially with wise teachers. And it can be learned through meditative or contemplative practice that constantly returns the practitioner to a place of integrity and authenticity inside themselves. All virtues can be learned in these ways: courage, patience, kindness, compassion, equanimity, generosity, vigor, respect, honesty, understanding, emotional sensitivity, and many others. However we learn wisdom so that it becomes organic within us; it must be learned and by all of us.

If leaders are to inspire us to be better people than we are, they must understand and have empathy for the full range of human experience. They must understand the nature of freedom inside themselves. And in the world, they must understand what it is to be poor. They must develop an acceptance and an intelligence regarding the wide range of human culture, the history of Mother Earth and other species, and the revelations of science and experiential and contemplative practices.

Training for leaders includes:

Basic Requirements

   1. A multi-day program that

> • Clarifies and delivers participants into their dreams of freedom, their life plans, so that their authenticity becomes alive and transparent.

> • Teaches inner listening.

> • Strengthens all listening skills.

> • Develops empathy.

> • Inspires participants to believe in the goodness and dreams of freedom of everyone they meet.

> • Develops the skills needed to support other people pursuing their dreams of freedom and the skills to deliver them into those dreams.

> • Provides the foundation for leadership that is empathic and inspired, kind and entrepreneurial, supportive and engaged.

You might think all of this is a big ask, but as a trainer I assure you it can all be trained in a matter of days.

   2. For leaders in the highest offices, a one to three-month mindfulness retreat that focuses on mastery of the present moment. This training would establish leaders in a practice that delivers greater patience, clarity, kindness, and self-knowledge, while diminishing the distractions of self-interest.

Ongoing Requirements

1. Reside one week each year in an impoverished community, living just as they live, so leaders have a deep sense of what freedom for all and what economic reality for all means.[ab]

2. Participate for one week each year in a contemplative/mindfulness/meditation retreat to cultivate the present moment and to better understand the highest reaches of human freedom possible within oneself and the challenges of achieving them.

• Practice a different tradition and learn from a new teacher each year to expand one's empathy and understanding of other people.

• Explore the relationship between freedom and wisdom.

• Learn how to end wars inside oneself.

• Learn how to transform suffering into wisdom inside oneself and in others.

Contemplative practice is our greatest strength because it goes deep inside us, where our virtue and wisdom reside.

3. Ongoing weekly leadership coaching in either group or individual settings, dedicated to ethical issues and the values of a Golden Civilization, to keep integrity central.

• One hour a week with an executive coach specializing in values, integrity, and wisdom to bring an ethical lens to challenging or problematic situations or decisions while minimizing conflicts of interest.

---

ab. It's time to create and participate in programs across all of civilization that facilitate this, whether through religious or civic or secular non-profit organizations.

- Coaching would include, where necessary, leaders learning to live in the communities their workers live in, to go amongst them, to not build walls between them.

- Coaching would include how to retrain or replace leaders who exhibit arrogance and high regard for self-interest.

4. Allow at least one week per year for liberal arts/multi-cultural education, to develop awareness, respect, and appreciation for all cultures and species, all history, all of science, and for the many varieties of systems of thought.

We need councils of wise elders, leadership and wisdom councils, chosen for their hearts and their wisdom, not dominated by financiers or lawyers. People with simplicity and humility rather than MBAs, PhDs, and JDs.

Such standards for leadership will help ensure wise leaders emerge. I imagine a society of wise elders, or an Organization of Wise Leaders (OWL, if you will), that would gather leaders from across the world within it.

OWL membership would require, in addition to the basic and annual requirements, that the member's salary not exceed the lowest paid employee by more than 20 times. It would also require two years of work experience, preferably in entrepreneurial endeavor.

To further foster its ideals, OWL could award annual prizes for ethical leadership at the global, national, regional, and local levels, including awards for specific disciplines.

In training, leaders would be evaluated against benchmarks for positive qualities like humility, sincerity, reliability, and empathy, and also judged for negative qualities such as arrogance and self-centeredness. Over years of training, they would witness and experience character development in themselves and others and learn how that development delivers freedom into the world. Self-knowledge builds authenticity from which right actions arise naturally. A great teacher once said that first there is realization, then there is manifestation.

Action Steps and Basic Principles for Leaders

Knowing what must be done does away with fear.

~Rosa Parks

The most difficult thing is the decision to act.
The rest is merely tenacity.

~Amelia Earhart

Of the Seven Integrities, leadership is the most powerful—the integrity most capable of inspiring both rapid and comprehensive change. Achieving a Golden Civilization in the midst of and in spite of the countless flaws in society that keep us from it is a leadership issue.

For example, one such leadership-related barrier in society is cheating. A study[38] of leaders and advisers in the financial services industry revealed that "more than half of respondents–52%–felt it was likely that their competitors have engaged in unethical or illegal activity to gain an edge in the market." Such corruption and cheating are to be expected. If leaders in government and corporations model and are rewarded for avarice or self-interest, avarice is what the culture will respond with. If they model integrity and virtue, integrity and virtue is what will emerge. In addition, if leaders in financial services (not to mention business and government) established zero tolerance for cheating in their firms, overnight we would see the difference, and within a few years, the institutions would be clean. Within ten years, the whole culture would begin to realize that something different was happening, and within twenty, within a single generation, globally there would be a completely different ethos around money.

Such change requires our leaders in government to themselves model virtue. This would engender trust, and if we can trust our leaders, each other, and the products and services we buy, the impact on economic efficiency and economic growth would be enormous.

Cleverness is not a virtue, although many think it is.

> *Replace cunning with the passion to deliver freedom to all and our economic model will be the basis of culture and government for millennia to come. A great leader lives simply, establishes democracy, ends war, and inspires each of us to become a better person. You are that leader and your time is now.*

Basic Principles and Actions for Leadership

1. Dedicate yourself to the delivery of freedom for all sentient beings.

2. Be prepared to be a leader in any and all endeavors.

3. Join or create the communities where your passion and skills can make the most difference in the creation of a Golden Civilization. Make the commitment to make it happen inside yourself.

4. Always inspire others to be their best selves, to be better than they are.

5. In all things, challenge yourself to act with authenticity and integrity.

6. Act to end the extremes of inequality that separate communities and build walls of exclusion.

7. Stand up to abuses of institutional power, whether by government, corporations, the media, non-profits, or billionaires. Make yourself heard. Neither their power nor their right to speech is larger than yours.

8. Insist that our leaders have no conflicts of interest. Our elected politicians serve us and must be a fiduciary to us in all things. Hold them accountable.

9. Become a body of wisdom; build wisdom inside yourself; include all of Earth in your embrace.

10. Take leadership in your communities by hosting or participating in conversations about creating and maintaining a Golden Civilization. Make it happen. Conversations lead to actions, and actions bring results.[ac]

---

ac. See Appendix Ten: Community Conversations for a Golden Civilization.

11. In every moment live as if the Golden Civilization were already here. Live into the dream of it. Live the vision you wish it to be. Act with the kindness, listen with the care. Lead where there is a vacuum. And take note at every place where the Golden Civilization has clearly not arrived, both inside yourself and without. Bring those moments to your Golden Civilization Conversations, creating a participative democracy that addresses every change we need to make to bring the Golden Civilization into being and to constantly and sustainably renew it.

Daily: Live your life plan.
- Practice mindfulness.
- Deepen your self-knowledge.
- Model listening deeply and empathically.
- Free yourself both from institutions without, and from desire and aversion within.
- Seek to master virtue and the present moment.
- Cultivate selflessness.
- Deliver freedom.

Annually:
- Spend a week every year in poverty.
- Spend a week every year in contemplation.

CODA

The Foundation
of
A Golden Civilization

The core unit of economics, the building block of democracy and even of time and space, is the same, a moment of freedom. Moments of freedom are how the universe breathes. They are both its breath and its beating heart. They take place only at the present moment. For a Golden Civilization to thrive, we must learn how to access the wisdom that flourishes in these moments, waking up within them constantly, and delivering them into all realms.

> *Mindfulness is not a trivial exercise that we do merely to allay stress, or to maintain health, or achieve longevity of our bodies and brains. Being mindful in the present moment links us with all other creatures and grounds us in the subtle nature of all that we share. It takes us to the heart of creation, of civilization, and to the heart of freedom.*

Universe of Beings
A Celebration of Moments

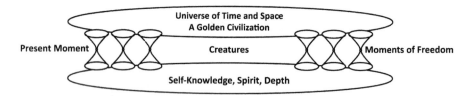

As we see in our maps, all creatures have access to the present moment. All have access to great depth. They are our siblings. Many of their ancestors were our ancestors. And in the interweaving ecologies of planet Earth, we all need each other in the widest and most profound sense.

In a Golden Civilization, all creatures have rights, and we aspire to always increase our skills of communication among species.

Our map of the universe, of being, includes all beings coexisting in time and space. Our map to a Golden Civilization is centered on life itself, breathing in the present moment. As citizens of the world, the world is our democratic responsibility. It is up to us to ensure that all species have a voice in a Golden Civilization; all have freedom and life.

In mindfulness, the closer that we come to the present moment, the more awake and alive we become. The more present we are, the more freedom we have, the healthier the planet is, and the closer we come to each other as we arise together from the same place–the only place any of us have ever known, or will ever know—just this moment, the birthplace of our Golden Civilizations.[ad]

---

ad. Speculatively, one can imagine, something even more profound about the present moment. As shown in the next two charts, it is conceivable that whole universes and all Golden Civilizations arise from the combination of great depth and the twirling, transcendent mirror of the present moment.

The Map of all Universes, Infinite Possibilities

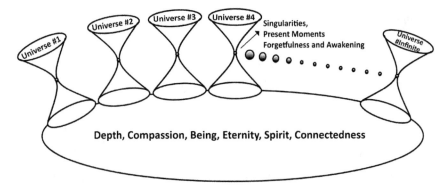

Out of One Present Moment, One Singularity
Infinite Beings, Infinite Worlds

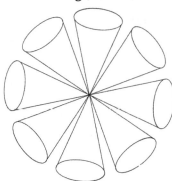

Honor the Ancestors

I have dedicated this book to Mother Earth and her Golden Civilizations. In particular, I dedicate it to the three places where I wrote the book. First, to that wild, global, energized city of London that over thousands of years crafted economics and democracy— and to the particular (and ominous) location in the city where I wrote, just yards from where Edward Gibbon at the beginning of the Industrial Revolution composed *The Decline and Fall of the Roman Empire*.

Second, to Serenity Point, a spit of land reaching out into a lake, ice age created, named by the Native Americans who lived here for thousands of years before myself. Just for the last several years, as I've been writing, Serenity Point has been surrounded by swans, inspirational for their beauty and fidelity. It has also been surrounded just for this time, by turtles, resting on logs, symbols of longevity as I hope the Golden Civilization will be.

Third, to the youngest place on Earth and its most creative, to the Hawaiian Islands and my spiritual home. And in particular to the landscape between Ka`uiki and Ka iwi o Pele in Hana, Maui, where Pele, goddess of the volcano, Kamapua`a, god of the hunt, Ai`ai and Ku`ulakai, god of the fish, the recent queen of Hawai`i, Ka`ahumanu, and Maui himself resided and performed wonders. And to my personal guide, the spirit of Le`houla, an ancient beach and the maiden who gave it her name.

Final Action Steps

I hope you will consider taking these action steps within the context of doing what you do best, what brings you most alive, and what makes you happy. In other words, as each of us lives fully our life plans, a Golden Civilization naturally comes into being.

I think there are three levels of action for each of us.

1. Cultivate meditative depth within.

2. Take action—politically, socially, culturally, in all of our communities.

3. Live with authenticity—live your life plan.

In regard to the political actions we might take to establish a Golden Civilization, the most urgent is removing money permanently from both politics and media, and simultaneously beginning the conversations within every community and with every human being envisioning a Golden Civilization. Then the great tasks of our time, like a mighty river, establishing the global movement for democracy and its freedoms and ending war in this generation.

Insist that all institutions model integrity and deliver freedom. In each endeavor of your own, in each facet of your society, in each institution where you participate, insist on behavior that will bring a Golden Civilization. Raise the standards of integrity across all fields of endeavor. A Golden Civilization will arise naturally by each of us hoisting it in our own lives, each of us focusing on our own domain and being willing to challenge within that domain, the institutions that cross it. A thousand generations will remember our efforts, and in their own present moments of freedom, they will thank us.

APPENDICES

Appendix One:
The Practice of Mindfulness

Find a spot where you can sit quietly and without interruption. Find a posture that is relatively erect and yet at ease. Commit to sitting completely still for 20 minutes—completely still, without moving, even for an itch or painful sensation (unless you feel the pain will harm you). Close your eyes and feel for a minute or two the many random sensations over the whole of your body. Gradually bring your focus to the sensations of breathing, either at the belly or in the nostrils. Quiet the mind by resting in the rhythm of the breath. Whenever a thought arises, let it go, and gently but directly bring your awareness back to the sensations of breathing. It doesn't matter how many times the mind wanders, nor how alluring or annoying your thoughts may be. As soon as you notice that you are thinking, let go of the thoughts and return directly and without judgment to the breath. As the mind relaxes, sharpen your awareness by noticing the qualities of each sensation that you feel at the nostrils or the belly, whichever location you have chosen as your primary focus for the meditation. Notice the movement, texture, temperature, and feel the shapes and dimensionality of each sensation as you touch them with your awareness, continuing to let your thoughts go. It doesn't matter how many times the mind wanders, or how still the mind becomes, if you notice you are not present to moments of sensation, return to them directly.

A practice as simple as this one cultivates the present moment, where freedom resides. Practicing twenty minutes a day will change your life, bringing more moments of freedom to you every day; done longer, its impact will grow greater and greater.

There are many mindfulness courses of instruction and applications available online and in communities. If you would like a book to guide you, I have written a simple yet comprehensive introduction to mindfulness practice that you can use throughout your life: *Transforming Suffering into Wisdom: Mindfulness and the Art of Inner Listening. Applying Meditation to Everyday Life*, Serenity Point Press, 2015. It is available from Amazon and on Kindle.

Appendix Two: Life Planning, EVOKE, and Finding a Financial Adviser

Many years ago, I devised an economic system that, through Life Planning, democratizes Entrepreneurial Spirit. For years I have taught this system to financial advisers all over the world. It is a process of listening that delivers freedom into the lives of clients. I call the process by the acronym EVOKE®. The five-phase process moves from Exploration (listening) to Vision, to resolving Obstacles, to Knowledge (financial plan), to Execution. Those who practice EVOKE tend to call themselves Life Planners, or financial Life Planners, to distinguish themselves from the more traditional product-oriented financial advisers.

I have written widely about the EVOKE process, including a book for advisers (*Lighting the Torch: The Kinder Method of Life Planning*) and one for consumers (*Life Planning for You: How to Design & Deliver the Life of Your Dreams*). The consumer book is accompanied by a free website (**www.lifeplanningforyou.com**) where thousands of people from all over the world have created their own life plans.

My view is this: for one to be a great financial adviser, one must first be a great life planner, dedicated to client dreams of freedom. And to be a great life planner, one must first have been life planned—must first know the freedom that is possible within oneself before advising others. Then, as the adviser listens to a client, they rest firmly in the roots of freedom as they listen, completely dedicated to achieving that same freedom in their clients.

In addition to listening, there are a variety of exercises life planners use to help clients design their dreams of freedom in the Vision phase of EVOKE. The signature exercise I teach is called The Three Questions. Here they are, meant to be responded to sequentially. If you wish to try them, please pause with each of them. Let each question sink in and then address it with authenticity, self-knowing, and compassion.

Question #1

Imagine that you are financially secure, and you have enough money to take care of your needs, now and in the future.

How would you live your life? Would you change anything?

In answering this question, let yourself go. Don't hold back on your dreams.

Describe a life that is complete, that is richly yours.

Question #2

Imagine that you visit your doctor, who tells you that you have only five to ten years to live. However, you won't ever feel sick, but you will have no prior notice of the moment of your death.

What will you do in the time you have remaining to live?

Will you change your life and how will you do it?

Question #3

Imagine this time that your doctor shocks you with the news that you have only one day left to live. Reflecting on your life, on your accomplishments, and on all the things you had anticipated doing, the things you looked forward to, ask yourself:

What did I miss? Who did I not get to be?

What did I not get to do?

For most, The Three Questions clarify their priorities with a jolt. They are on fire to accomplish those dreams they have neglected, particularly following Question #3. It is that fire that drives the formation of their life plan. Occasionally, some are discouraged at realizing the goals they have forgotten, taken for granted, or abandoned. But a practiced life planner is adept at turning that discouragement into inspiration to resolve issues and accomplish goals of passion and freedom. In fact, there is a moment in a Life Planning engagement that we advisers call Lighting the Torch, when clients come alive with an abiding energy and confidence. Financial advice thus brings their Entrepreneurial Spirit into the world.

How to find an adviser who is dedicated to advice rather than product sales?

A) How do you find a holistic adviser? Globally, Certified Financial Planner (CFP®) designees (and also Chartered in the UK, and others) have a breadth of knowledge about money matters. Their education, which can take several years to accomplish, covers investments, risk and insurance, taxes, estate planning, retirement, and general financial planning including budgets and cash flow.

B) How do you find a fiduciary adviser? Most simply hire a CFP® designee. A CFP® is required to act as a fiduciary and put client interests first. In the United States, a Registered Investment Advisor is an additional designation required to act as a fiduciary.

C) How do you find a fee-only adviser? A fee-only adviser receives fees directly and only from the consumer for advisory services rendered, never from a product company. The most common forms of fee-only structures are hourly, project-based, retainer, or a percentage charge for the total amount of assets under management (AUM) if the adviser is working as an investment adviser. If they invest your assets, they don't take custody of them. (Make sure that is the case.) Your assets are held in your own personal account by an independent third-party custodian. If you wish, and your adviser is authorized, you can grant your adviser a limited trading authority. With fiduciary responsibility, your adviser should seek out the most appropriate products or services for you, your life plan, and your pursuit of your dreams of freedom.

Some leading associations of fee-only planners in America:

1. NAPFA (www.napfa.org): The National Association of Personal Financial Advisors is the oldest and most established of the fee-only associations. Formed in 1983 in reaction to the predominance of commission-based charging, NAPFA revolutionized compensation structures for financial advice. NAPFA's members are required to be compensated strictly by fees, never by commissions.

2. Fee-only organizations that support the middle market. Too often, fee-only advisers have million-dollar minimums for client investments. These three organizations generally do not; their advisers will often work virtually with clients from all over the country:

   a. Garrett Planning Network (www.garrettplanningnetwork. com): Started by Sheryl Garrett in 2000. Its member advisers are encouraged to use an hourly fee-only model.

   b. Alliance for Comprehensive Planners (ACP) (www.acplanners.org): Formerly known as Cambridge Advisors, founded by Bert Whitehead. ACP is a community of tax-focused financial planners operating under a retainer model. They are strictly fee-only and follow a holistic approach.

   c. XY Planning Network (www.xyplanningnetwork.com): Founded by Michael Kitces with a focus on Generation X and Generation Y clients.

D) How do you find a life planner? If you want a Registered Life Planner® (RLP®), trained in the EVOKE process, start with the list of over 400 RLPs on www.kinderinstitute.com.

If there is no RLP® in your immediate area, many will work virtually over the Internet. The Kinder Institute has also trained over 2,500 planners across 30 countries and six continents in at least two-days-worth of Life Planning training, with special emphasis on listening and goal-setting skills. Most of these advisers, too, are listed on www.kinderinstitute.com. Most CFPs and fee-only planners have had at least some Life Planning training. You can also search other Life Planning organizations with non-EVOKE methodologies such as Money Quotient and Sudden Money.

E) How can you discern from an adviser's investment philosophy whether they are more dedicated to delivering advice than to selling products?

One possible clue (though not a guarantee): Many fiduciary advisers in recent decades have shifted from active investing to passive investing, in index funds or ETFs, which reduces costs and taxes for the consumer. Before you choose active investing, listen closely to arguments for passive investing. Since active investing has an element of gambling to it, and no one can know the future, the odds are you will do better with passive, though in any period of time there will always be active strategies that beat passive. How do you find a winning active strategy for the longer term? How do you know when to switch strategies? Studies say you can't do either very well and trying to do so will generally lower your rate of return.

Appendix Three: Income Inequality

Here is a list of 2017 compensation packages of the top five CEOs of American companies as reported by The New York Times in May 2018.[39]

Company	CEO	Compensation
Broadcom (AVGO)	Hock E. Tan	$103,211,163
First Data (FDC)	Frank J. Bisignano	$102,210,396
Live Nation Entertainment (LYV)	Michael Rapino	$70,615,760
CBS (CBS)	Leslie Moonves	$68,375,015
Liberty Media/Qurate Retail Group	Gregory B. Maffei	$67,220,132

Contrast these salaries with the following chart:

	Annual Realized Pay
Annual salary of our most trusted profession–Nurses [40]	$70,000 [41]
Average salary of a K-12 teacher	$58,353 [42]
Salary of a person earning the federal minimum wage ($7.25/hour)	$15,080
More than a billion people in the world live on less than $1.25/day	$456 [43]

Appendix Four: Corruption

The corruption we see and the distrust we feel toward our institutions is experienced all over the world and across all industries, and particularly toward government institutions. Transparency International produces an annual Global Corruption Barometer. Among the key findings of its 2013 survey of more than 114,000 people in 107 countries were the following:[44]

- **"Bribery is widespread.**
Overall, more than one in four people (27 percent) report having had to pay a bribe in the last 12 months when interacting with key public institutions and services.

- **Public institutions entrusted to protect people suffer the worst levels of bribery.**
...the police and the judiciary...31 percent of people who came into contact with the police report having had to pay a bribe...
judiciary...24 percent...

- **The democratic pillars of societies are viewed as the most corrupt.**
Around the world, political parties, the driving force of democracies, are perceived to be the most corrupt institution."

The report goes on: "On a scale of one to five, where one means 'corruption is not a problem at all' and five means 'corruption is a very serious problem', the average score across the countries surveyed was 4.1."

Political parties scored 3.8 out of a scale of five. The survey concluded, "it is the actors that are supposed to be running countries and upholding the rule of law that are seen as the most corrupt..."

Among the consequences: "When people are not in a position to afford a bribe, they might be prevented from buying a home, starting a business or accessing basic services. Corruption can, and often does, infringe on fundamental rights. For those surviving on less than US$2 a day, and for women who are the primary caretakers of children around the globe, corruption and bribery are particularly devastating."

"When powerful groups buy influence over government decisions or when public funds are diverted into the coffers of the political elite, ordinary people suffer."

The Corruption Perceptions Index 2014, also from Transparency International, broadens our understanding of corruption to countries worldwide as you can see in the following map and chart. Over two-thirds of countries measure below 50, where 100 would represent integrity and lack of corruption.

Even in America where we pride ourselves on our free markets and our democracy, measured against other developed countries we fare quite poorly. With a score of 74 the US is far below the leading countries of Denmark at 92 and New Zealand at 91. Among the worst of global powers, India comes in at 38, China at 36 and Russia at 27. [45]

SCORE

Highly corrupt — Very clean

0-9 10-19 20-29 30-39 40-49 50-59 60-69 70-79 80-89 90-100   No data

RANK	COUNTRY/TERRITORY	SCORE
1	Denmark	92
2	New Zealand	91
3	Finland	89
4	Sweden	87
5	Norway	86
5	Switzerland	86
7	Singapore	84
8	Netherlands	83
9	Luxembourg	82
10	Canada	81
11	Australia	80
12	Germany	79
12	Iceland	79
14	United Kingdom	78
15	Belgium	76
15	Japan	76
17	Barbados	74
17	Hong Kong	74
17	Ireland	74
17	United States	74
21	Chile	73
21	Uruguay	73
23	Austria	72
24	Bahamas	71
25	United Arab Emirates	70
26	Estonia	69
26	France	69
26	Qatar	69
29	Saint Vincent and the Grenadines	67
30	Bhutan	65
31	Botswana	63
31	Cyprus	63
31	Portugal	63
31	Puerto Rico	63
35	Poland	61
35	Taiwan	61
37	Israel	60
37	Spain	60
39	Dominica	58
39	Lithuania	58
39	Slovenia	58
42	Cape Verde	57
43	Korea (South)	55
43	Latvia	55
43	Malta	55
43	Seychelles	55
47	Costa Rica	54
47	Hungary	54
47	Mauritius	54
50	Georgia	52
50	Malaysia	52
50	Samoa	52
53	Czech Republic	51
54	Slovakia	50
55	Bahrain	49
55	Jordan	49
55	Lesotho	49
55	Namibia	49
55	Rwanda	49
55	Saudi Arabia	49
61	Croatia	48
61	Ghana	48
63	Cuba	46
64	Oman	45
64	The FYR of Macedonia	45
64	Turkey	45
67	Kuwait	44
67	South Africa	44
69	Brazil	43
69	Bulgaria	43
69	Greece	43
69	Italy	43
69	Romania	43
69	Senegal	43
69	Swaziland	43
76	Montenegro	42
76	Sao Tome and Principe	42
78	Serbia	41
79	Tunisia	40
80	Benin	39
80	Bosnia and Herzegovina	39
80	El Salvador	39
80	Mongolia	39
80	Morocco	39
85	Burkina Faso	38
85	India	38
85	Jamaica	38
85	Peru	38
85	Philippines	38
85	Sri Lanka	38
85	Thailand	38

287

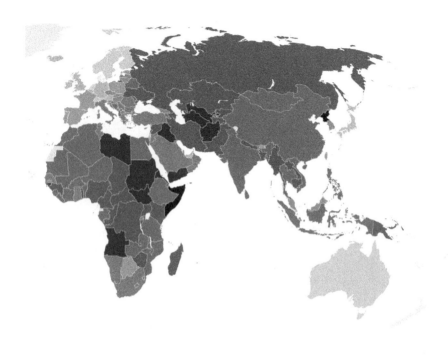

RANK	COUNTRY/TERRITORY	SCORE	RANK	COUNTRY/TERRITORY	SCORE	RANK	COUNTRY/TERRITORY	SCORE	RANK	COUNTRY/TERRITORY	SCORE
85	Trinidad and Tobago	38	110	Kosovo	33	136	Cameroon	27	156	Cambodia	21
85	Zambia	38	110	Malawi	33	136	Iran	27	156	Myanmar	21
94	Armenia	37	115	Côte d'Ivoire	32	136	Kyrgyzstan	27	156	Zimbabwe	21
94	Colombia	37	115	Dominican Republic	32	136	Lebanon	27	159	Burundi	20
94	Egypt	37	115	Guatemala	32	136	Nigeria	27	159	Syria	20
94	Gabon	37	115	Mali	32	136	Russia	27	161	Angola	19
94	Liberia	37	119	Belarus	31	142	Comoros	26	161	Guinea-Bissau	19
94	Panama	37	119	Mozambique	31	142	Uganda	26	161	Haiti	19
100	Algeria	36	119	Sierra Leone	31	142	Ukraine	26	161	Venezuela	19
100	China	36	119	Tanzania	31	145	Bangladesh	25	161	Yemen	19
100	Suriname	36	119	Vietnam	31	145	Guinea	25	166	Eritrea	18
103	Bolivia	35	124	Guyana	30	145	Kenya	25	166	Libya	18
103	Mexico	35	124	Mauritania	30	145	Laos	25	166	Uzbekistan	18
103	Moldova	35	126	Azerbaijan	29	145	Papua New Guinea	25	169	Turkmenistan	17
103	Niger	35	126	Gambia	29	150	Central African Republic	24	170	Iraq	16
107	Argentina	34	126	Honduras	29	150	Paraguay	24	171	South Sudan	15
107	Djibouti	34	126	Kazakhstan	29	152	Congo Republic	23	172	Afghanistan	12
107	Indonesia	34	126	Nepal	29	152	Tajikistan	23	173	Sudan	11
110	Albania	33	126	Pakistan	29	154	Chad	22	174	Korea (North)	8
110	Ecuador	33	126	Togo	29	154	Democratic Republic of the Congo	22	174	Somalia	8
110	Ethiopia	33	133	Madagascar	28						
			133	Nicaragua	28						
			133	Timor-Leste	28						

Corruption Perceptions Index 2014 by Transparency International is licensed under CC.BY-ND 4.0

What are the costs of corruption? According to a report by the anti-poverty organization One, as reported by the BBC: [46]

"Corruption inhibits private investment, reduces economic growth, increases the cost of doing business and can lead to political instability.

But in developing countries, corruption is a killer. When governments are deprived of their own resources to invest in health care, food security or essential infrastructure, it costs lives and the biggest toll is on children."

The report goes on to say that "if corruption was eradicated in sub-Saharan Africa:

• Education would be provided to an additional 10 million children per year

• Money would be available to pay for an additional 500,000 primary school teachers

• Antiretroviral drugs for more than 11 million people with HIV/Aids would be provided"

Appendix Five:
Freedom of the Press Worldwide

Reporters Without Borders compiles the World Press Freedom Index through a qualitative survey combined with quantitative records of abuses to journalists. The survey includes questions regarding "pluralism, media independence, media environment and self-censorship, legislative framework, transparency, and the quality of the infrastructure that supports the production of news and information.

Here is the ranking of press freedom by country in 2017:[47]

Ranking 2017

2017 World Press Freedom Index

1	Norway	7.60
2	Sweden	8.27
3	Finland	8.92
4	Denmark	10.36
5	Netherlands	11.28
6	Costa Rica	11.93
7	Switzerland	12.13
8	Jamaica	12.73
9	Belgium	12.75
10	Iceland	13.03
11	Austria	13.47
12	Estonia	13.55
13	New Zealand	13.98
14	Ireland	14.08
15	Luxembourg	14.72
16	Germany	14.97
17	Slovakia	15.51
18	Portugal	15.77
19	Australia	16.02
20	Surinam	16.07
21	Samoa	16.41
22	Canada	16.53
23	Czech Republic	16.91
24	Namibia	17.08
25	Uruguay	17.43
26	Ghana	17.95
27	Cabo Verde	18.02
28	Latvia	18.62
29	Spain	18.69
30	Cyprus	19.79
31	South Africa	20.12
32	Liechtenstein	20.31
33	Chile	20.53
34	Trin. & Tob.	20.62
35	Andorra	21.03
36	Lithuania	21.37
37	Slovenia	21.70
38	OECS	22.10
39	France	22.24
40	U.K	22.26
41	Belize	23.43
42	Burkina Faso	23.85
43	United States	23.88
44	Comoros	24.33
45	Taiwan	24.37
46	Romania	24.46
47	Malta	24.76
48	Botswana	24.93
49	Tonga	24.97
50	Argentina	25.07
51	P. N. Guinea	25.07
52	Italy	26.26
53	Haïti	26.36
54	Poland	26.47
55	Mauritania	26.49
56	Mauritius	26.67

57	Madagascar	26.71	86	Togo	30.75
58	Senegal	26.72	87	Seychelles	30.86
59	Dominican R.	26.76	88	Greece	30.89
60	Guyana	26.80	89	Kyrgyzstan	30.92
61	Niger	27.21	90	Peru	30.98
62	El Salvador	27.24	91	Israel	31.01
63	South Korea	27.61	92	Nicaragua	31.01
64	Georgia	27.76	93	Mozambique	31.05
65	Bosnia-Herz.	27.83	94	Liberia	31.12
66	Serbia	28.05	95	Kenya	31.20
67	Fiji	28.64	96	Panama	32.12
68	Lesotho	28.78	97	Tunisia	32.22
69	Mongolia	28.95	98	East Timor	32.82
70	Malawi	28.97	99	Lebanon	33.01
71	Hungary	29.01	100	Nepal	33.02
72	Japan	29.44	101	Guinea	33.15
73	Hong Kong	29.46	102	Ukraine	33.19
74	Croatia	29.59	103	Brazil	33.58
75	N. Cyprus	29.88	104	Kuwait	33.61
76	Albania	29.92	105	Ecuador	33.64
77	Guinea Bissau	30.09	106	Montenegro	33.65
78	Benin	30.32	107	Bolivia	33.88
79	Armenia	30.38	108	Gabon	34.83
80	Moldova	30.41	109	Bulgaria	35.01
81	Côte d'Ivoire	30.42	110	Paraguay	35.64
82	Kosovo	30.45	111	Macedonia	35.74
83	Tanzania	30.65	112	Uganda	35.94
84	Bhutan	30.73	113	C. African Rep.	36.12
85	Sierra Leone	30.73	114	Zambia	36.48

115	Congo-Brazzaville	36.73		145	South Sudan	48.16
116	Mali	38.27		146	Bangladesh	48.36
117	Maldives	39.30		147	Mexico	48.97
118	Guatemala	39.33		148	Russia	49.45
119	United Arab Emirates	39.39		149	Tajikistan	50.27
120	Afghanistan	39.46		150	Ethiopia	50.34
121	Chad	39.66		151	Singapore	51.10
122	Nigeria	39.69		152	Swaziland	51.27
123	Qatar	39.83		153	Belarus	52.43
124	Indonesia	39.93		154	D.R. of Congo	52.67
125	Angola	40.42		155	Turkey	52.98
126	Oman	40.46		156	Brunei	53.72
127	Philippines	41.08		157	Kazakhstan	54.01
128	Zimbabwe	41.44		158	Iraq	54.03
129	Colombia	41.47		159	Rwanda	54.11
130	Cameroon	41.59		160	Burundi	55.78
131	Burma	41.82		161	Egypt	55.78
132	Cambodia	42.07		162	Azerbaijan	56.40
133	Morocco / W. Sahara	42.42		163	Libya	56.81
134	Algeria	42.83		164	Bahrain	58.88
135	Palestine	42.90		165	Iran	65.12
136	India	42.94		166	Yemen	65.80
137	Venezuela	42.94		167	Somalia	65.95
138	Jordan	43.24		168	Saudi Arabia	66.02
139	Pakistan	43.55		169	Uzbekistan	66.11
140	Honduras	43.75		170	Laos	66.41
141	Sri Lanka	44.34		171	E. Guinea	66.47
142	Thailand	44.69		172	Djibouti	70.54
143	Gambia	46.70		173	Cuba	71.75
144	Malaysia	46.89		174	Sudan	73.56

175	Vietnam	73.96
176	China	77.66
177	Syria	81.49
178	Turkmenistan	84.19
179	Eritrea	84.24
180	North Korea	84.98

Appendix Six:
Declining Democracy

The V-Dem Institute from the University of Gothenburg presents in its Annual Democracy Report 2018 "Democracy for All?"[48] a comparison of the states of democracy of 178 countries between 2007 and 2017. It is a remarkable study from which we have included its signature chart with score and confidence intervals based on the following indicators: suffrage, elected officials, clean elections, freedom of association, freedom of expression and alternative sources of information, rule of law, judicial constraints on the executive, legislative constraints on the executive, an egalitarian component, a participatory component, and a deliberative component. The chart included here demonstrates the advances and backslides of countries from 2007 (lighter markings), just prior to the US banking crisis, to the first year of Donald Trump's presidency (darker markings). Note how dramatically the U.S. has fallen as a democracy in just a brief ten year period.

FIGURE 1.6: COUNTRIES BY SCORE ON V-DEM'S LIBERAL DEMOCRACY INDEX (LDI) 2017 AND 2007.

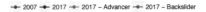

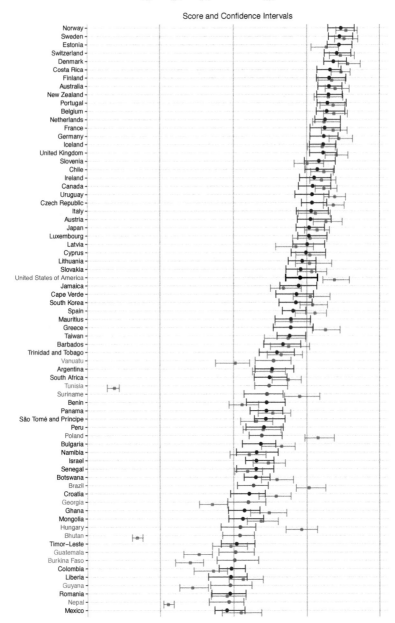

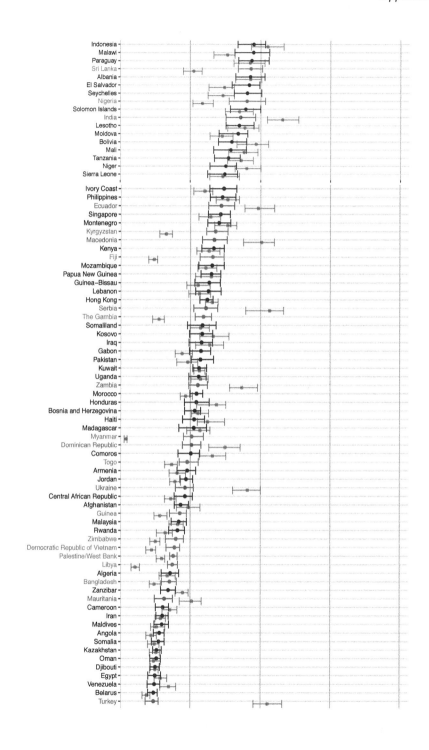

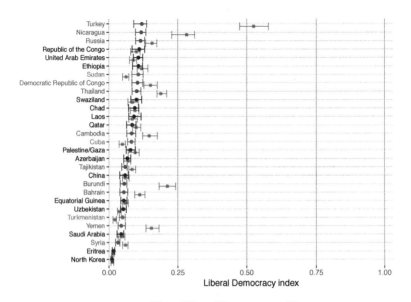

Liberal Democracy index

•— 2007   •— 2017   •— 2017 – Advancer   •— 2017 – Backslider

Appendix Seven:
Distrust of Professions

Distrust pervades much of civilization. Surveys from Edelman, Harris, Gallup, Ipsos, Roy Morgan, Price Waterhouse, and others all proclaim it. Of particular concern is the distrust of government, media, and financial services, three of the institutions essential for a healthy democracy and civilization. Notice how nursing is the benchmark for a trustworthy profession, and how far these other professions are from that standard. Here are samples of surveys of professions in the English-speaking world. Note: Outside the English-speaking world, distrust is often higher.

In the US from Gallup surveys, here are the percentage of respondents rating the "honesty and ethical standards" of the following professions either high or very high: [49]

"Very High" or "High" ratings for Ethics and Honesty	U.S Adults
Occupations	%
Nurses	80%
Bankers	23%
Lawyers	21%
Business Executives	17%
Insurance Sales People*	15%
Advertising Practitioners	10%
Car Sales People	8%
Members of Congress	7%
Lobbyists**	6%

* From a 2012 Gallup survey, not available thereafter
** From a 2013 Gallup survey, not available thereafter
All other results from 2014

In Canada, from an Ipsos Reid and Reader's Digest survey, here are the percentage of respondents rating the following professions "extremely trustworthy."[50]

Professions	Extremely Trustworthy
Firefighters	77%
Ambulance Drivers / Paramedics	74%
Pharmacists	70%
Nurses	69%
Airline Pilots	65%
Doctors	65%
Farmers	58%
Canadian Soldiers	58%
Teachers	52%
Veterinarians	51%
Dentists	50%
Police Officers	46%
Judges	42%
Daycare Workers	39%
Food Safety Inspectors	37%
Electricians	37%
Psychologists/Councelors	35%
Accountants	34%

Chiropractors	**30%**
Airport Security Guard	**29%**
Plumbers	**28%**
Church Leaders	**24%**
Financial Advisors	**22%**
Journalists	**18%**
Television & Radio Personalities	**17%**
Lawyers	**16%**
Auto Mechanics	**16%**
Airport Baggage Handlers	**12%**
CEO's	**11%**
Local Politicians	**6%**
Bloggers	**6%**
National Politicians	**6%**
Car Sales People	**5%**
Telemarketers	**4%**

In Australia, from a Roy Morgan survey, here are the percentage of respondents rating the following professions high or very high for "ethics and honesty."[51]

Ratings for Ethics and Honesty Survey for Australia

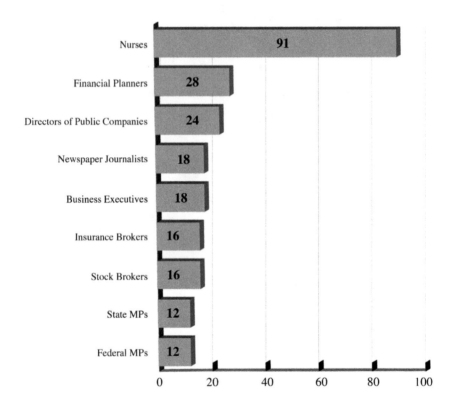

In the UK, from an Ipsos MORI poll, here are the percentage of respondents who do NOT trust the following professions to tell the truth.[52]

Do not trust to tell the truth %	
Doctors	9%
Teachers	11%
Scientists	11%
Judges	13%
Television news readers	24%
The ordinary man/woman in the street	26%
Clergymen/priests	27%
Police	28%
Pollsters	34%
Civil Servants	38%
Trade union officials	47%
Business leaders	57%
Estate Agents	70%
MPs in general	70%
Journalists	72%
Bankers	75%
Politicians generally	77%

In the UK, from a Price Waterhouse Cooper's survey, here are the percentage of respondents who trust the following professions.[53]

Percentage of Customers Who Trust

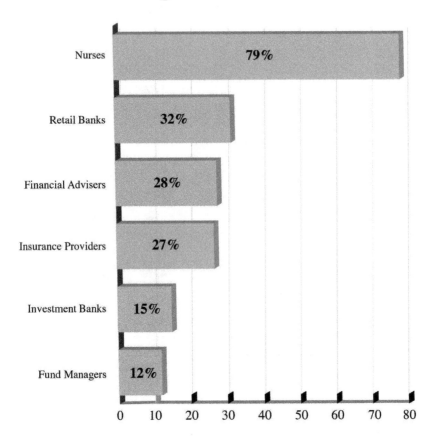

Appendix Eight:
Summary of the Banking Crisis

The Financial Times reported the total settlements and fines by financial institutions from 5/30/2007 to 7/21/2015.[54] Here is a summary of the following spreadsheet (Appendix Nine).

Bank	Grand Total
Bank of America / Merrill Lynch	$ 57,961,300,000
JPMorgan Chase	$ 32,220,200,000
Citigroup	$ 14,847,800,000
Wells Fargo	$ 9,673,230,000
BNP Paribas	$ 8,900,000,000
Deutsche Bank	$ 4,503,500,000
Credit Suisse	$ 4,352,000,000
UBS	$ 4,015,800,000
Barclays	$ 3,648,000,000
HSBC	$ 3,473,500,000
SunTrust	$ 2,878,000,000
Royal Bank of Scotland	$ 2,186,000,000
Goldman Sachs	$ 2,176,500,000
Morgan Stanley	$ 1,910,850,000
Commerzbank	$ 1,450,000,000
Standard Chartered	$ 967,000,000

Ally Financial	$ 840,300,000
Rabobank	$ 800,000,000
ING Bank	$ 619,000,000
Bank of Tokyo-Mitsubishi	$ 573,600,000
Lloyds TSB Bank	$ 567,000,000
US Bank	$ 465,200,000
PNC	$ 416,100,000
Flagstar Bank	$ 265,050,000
GMAC Mortgage	$ 230,000,000
Lloyds Banking Group	$ 191,000,000
Bank Leumi	$ 130,000,000
Societe Generale	$ 122,000,000
Aurora Bank	$ 93,000,000
Wegelin	$ 74,000,000
State Street	$ 70,000,000
TD Bank	$ 52,500,000
RBC	$ 50,910,000
MetLife	$ 49,200,000
Everbank	$ 44,000,000
Capital One Bank	$ 38,500,000
Fifth Third Bancorp	$ 26,000,000
Liechtenstein Bank	$ 23,800,000
Sovereign Bank	$ 16,000,000
United Bank for Africa	$ 15,000,000
Ocean Bank (Miami)	$ 10,900,000
TCF	$ 10,000,000
Union Bank of California	$ 10,000,000

Wachovia	$ 10,000,000
American Express	$ 9,000,000
Zions First National Bank	$ 8,000,000
Bank of New York Mellon	$ 7,300,000
Pacific National Bank	$ 7,000,000
AIG	$ 6,100,000
Australia and New Zealand Bank Group	$ 5,700,000
Citizens Bank (Royal Bank of Scotland)	$ 5,000,000
Doha Bank	$ 5,000,000
Pamrapo Savings Bank	$ 5,000,000
Saddle River Valley Bank	$ 4,100,000
Citizens Republic Bancorp	$ 3,600,000
Intesa Sanpaolo	$ 2,900,000
Chevy Chase Bank	$ 2,850,000
Saehan Bank	$ 2,200,000
Luther Burbank	$ 2,000,000
Midwest BankCentre	$ 1,450,000
Woodforest National Bank	$ 1,000,000
Grand Total	**$ 161,054,940,000**

Appendix Nine:
Spreadsheet of Banking Crisis

The Financial Times reported the following settlements and fines arising from the banking crisis 2007-2015.[55]

Bank	Settlement or Fine	Million	Date	Reason	Description	Regulator
Barclays	10.9	Million	5/30/2007	Market Manipulation	Settled charges of insider trading.	Securities and Exchange Commission
Union Bank of California	10	Million	9/14/2007	Sanctions/Money Laundering/Tax Evasion	Settled Bank Secrecy Act compliance charges.	Office of the Comptroller of the Currency
HSBC	10.5	Million	10/12/2007	Market Manipulation	Settled claims of facilitating pension fund fraud.	Securities and Exchange Commission
United Bank for Africa	15	Million	4/22/2008	Sanctions/Money Laundering/Tax Evasion	Settled Bank Secrecy Act compliance charges.	Office of the Comptroller of the Currency
Wachovia	10	Million	4/24/2008	Market Manipulation	Penalty for oversight failures regarding relationships with payment processors.	Office of the Comptroller of the Currency
JPMorgan Chase	25	Million	8/15/2008	Market Manipulation	Settlement over auction rate securities manipulation, in conjunction with the Florida Office of Financial Regulation and the North American Securities Administrators Association.	New York Attorney General
Morgan Stanley	35	Million	8/25/2008	Market Manipulation	Settlement over auction rate securities manipulation, in conjunction with the Florida Office of Financial Regulation and the North American Securities Administrators Association.	New York Attorney General
Bank of America	50	Million	10/8/2008	Market Manipulation	Auction rate securities settlement.	Securities and Exchange Commission
RBC	9.8	Million	10/8/2008	Market Manipulation	Auction rate securities settlement.	Securities and Exchange Commission
RBC	10.71	Million	11/25/2008	Lending/Consumer Practices	Settled charges of improper mortgage underwriting .	Department of Justice
Lloyds TSB Bank	175	Million	1/9/2009	Sanctions/Money Laundering/Tax Evasion	Settlement violations of International Emergency Economic Powers Act (Iran, Sudan sanctions).	Department of Justice
Lloyds TSB Bank	175	Million	1/9/2009	Sanctions/Money Laundering/Tax Evasion	Settlement violations of International Emergency Economic Powers Act (Iran, Sudan sanctions).	New York County District Attorney

Bank	Amount		Date	Category	Description	Agency
Lloyds TSB Bank	175	Million	1/9/2009	Sanctions/Money Laundering/Tax Evasion	Settlement violations of International Emergency Economic Powers Act (Iran, Sudan sanctions).	New York County District Attorney
UBS	780	Million	2/19/2009	Sanctions/Money Laundering/Tax Evasion	Settled tax evasion allegations.	Securities and Exchange Commission
Doha Bank	5	Million	4/20/2009	Sanctions/Money Laundering/Tax Evasion	Fine for Bank Secrecy Act compliance violations.	Office of the Comptroller of the Currency
Goldman Sachs	60	Million	5/11/2009	Mortgage Backed Securities	A settlement over subprime mortgage backed securities.	Massachusetts Attorney General
Australia and New Zealand Bank Group	5.7	Million	8/24/2009	Sanctions/Money Laundering/Tax Evasion	Settled sanctions violations charges (Sudan, Cuba).	Department of Treasury
Credit Suisse	268	Million	12/16/2009	Sanctions/Money Laundering/Tax Evasion	Settled sanctions violations charges (Iran, Burma, Sudan, Cuba, Libya).	Department of Treasury
Credit Suisse	268	Million	12/16/2009	Sanctions/Money Laundering/Tax Evasion	Settled sanctions violations charges (Iran, Burma, Sudan, Cuba, Libya).	New York County District Attorney
Lloyds TSB Bank	217	Million	12/22/2009	Sanctions/Money Laundering/Tax Evasion	Settled sanctions violations charges (Iran, Sudan, Libya).	Department of Treasury
Bank of America	150	Million	2/4/2010	Mergers/Acquisitions	Settlement for failure to disclose Merrill Lynch bonuses and financial losses before 2008 merger.	Securities and Exchange Commission
State Street	50	Million	2/4/2010	Mortgage Backed Securities	Settlement for misleading investors about mortgage backed securities.	Securities and Exchange Commission
State Street	10	Million	2/4/2010	Mortgage Backed Securities	Settlement over misleading investors about mortgage backed securities.	Massachusetts Attorney General
State Street	10	Million	2/4/2010	Mortgage Backed Securities	Settlement over misleading investors about mortgage backed securities.	Massachusetts Secretary of State
AIG	6.1	Million	3/4/2010	Lending/Consumer Practices	Settled charges of discrimination against minority borrowers.	Department of Justice
Wells Fargo	50	Million	3/12/2010	Sanctions/Money Laundering/Tax Evasion	Settled Bank Secrecy Act compliance violations against Wachovia.	Office of the Comptroller of the Currency
Pamrapo Savings Bank	5	Million	3/29/2010	Sanctions/Money Laundering/Tax Evasion	Settled Bank Secrecy Act compliance violations.	Department of Justice
Morgan Stanley	14	Million	4/29/2010	Market Manipulation	Settled claims of block crude oil trade manipulation.	Commodity Futures Trading Commission
Royal Bank of Scotland	500	Million	5/10/2010	Sanctions/Money Laundering/Tax Evasion	Settled charges of Bank Secrecy Act, Trading with the Enemy Act and International Emergency Economic Powers Act violations against ABN Amro Bank.	Department of Justice
Morgan Stanley	102.7	Million	6/25/2010	Mortgage Backed Securities	A settlement over bank's handling of subprime mortgages.	Massachusetts Attorney General

Goldman Sachs	550	Million	7/15/2010	Mortgage Backed Securities	Settled charges of misleading investors over mortgage backed securities (Abacus CDO).	Securities and Exchange Commission
Citigroup	75	Million	7/29/2010	Mortgage Backed Securities	Settled charges of misleading investors about mortgage backed securities.	Securities and Exchange Commission
Barclays	298	Million	8/18/2010	Sanctions/Money Laundering/Tax Evasion	Settled sanctions violations charges (Cuba, Iran, Sudan) .	Department of Justice
Saehan Bank	2.2	Million	10/4/2010	Market Manipulation	Resolved False Claims Allegations with the Small Business Administration.	Department of Justice
Woodforest National Bank	1	Million	10/7/2010	Lending/Consumer Practices	Settlement for consumer law compliance violations.	Office of the Comptroller of the Currency
Bank of America	137.3	Million	12/7/2010	Market Manipulation	Settled charges of bid rigging in municipal bond derivatives market, in conjunction with the Securities and Exchange Commission, IRS, Office for the Controller of the Currency and 20 other State attorneys general.	Department of Justice
Bank of America	1350	Million	12/31/2010	Mortgage Repurchases	Settlement resolving repurchase requests of faulty Countrywide mortgage sales. Bank agreed to repurchase liabilities.	Freddie Mac
Bank of America	1520	Million	1/3/2011	Mortgage Repurchases	Settlement resolving repurchase requests of faulty Countrywide mortgage sales. Bank agreed to repurchase liabilities.	Fannie Mae
Zions First National Bank	8	Million	2/10/2011	Sanctions/Money Laundering/Tax Evasion	Settled Bank Secrecy Act compliance violations.	Office of the Comptroller of the Currency
Pacific National Bank	7	Million	3/23/2011	Sanctions/Money Laundering/Tax Evasion	Settled Bank Secrecy Act compliance violations.	Office of the Comptroller of the Currency
Wells Fargo	11	Million	4/5/2011	Mortgage Backed Securities	Settled charges of Wachovia misconduct in sale of credit default obligations tied to mortgage backed securities .	Securities and Exchange Commission
UBS	160	Million	5/4/2011	Market Manipulation	Settled municipal bond rigging allegations (paid to federal and state agencies).	Department of Justice
UBS	90.8	Million	5/4/2011	Market Manipulation	Settled municipal bond rigging allegations .	New York Attorney General
Citizens Republic Bancorp	3.6	Million	5/5/2011	Lending/Consumer Practices	Settled discrimination claims against minority borrowers.	Department of Justice
US Bank	1.2	Million	5/20/2011	Lending/Consumer Practices	Penalty for failure to meet FHA mortgage underwriting standards.	Department of Housing and Urban Development
Bank of America	20	Million	5/26/2011	Lending/Consumer Practices	Paid as foreclosure relief to military borrowers (BAC	Department of Justice

					HomeLoans - formerly Countrywide).	
Morgan Stanley	2.35	Million	5/26/2011	Lending/Consumer Practices	paid as foreclosure relief to military borrowers (Saxon Mortgage Services, MS subsidiary).	Department of Justice
JPMorgan Chase	2	Million	6/14/2011	Lending/Consumer Practices	Fine for marketing and sale of faulty credit protection product.	Office of the Comptroller of the Currency
Midwest BankCentre	1.45	Million	6/15/2011	Lending/Consumer Practices	Settled discrimination claims against minority borrowers.	Department of Justice
JPMorgan Chase	153.6	Million	6/21/2011	Mortgage Backed Securities	Settled charges of misleading investors over CDOs .	Securities and Exchange Commission
JPMorgan Chase	211	Million	7/1/2011	Market Manipulation	Settling municipal bond rigging allegations, in conjunction with the Department of Justice, the IRS and the Office for the Controller of the Currency.	Securities and Exchange Commission
JPMorgan Chase	35	Million	7/7/2011	Market Manipulation	Settled claims of municipal bond rigging.	Office of the Comptroller of the Currency
JPMorgan Chase	92	Million	7/11/2011	Market Manipulation	Settled claims of municipal bond rigging.	State Attorneys General
JPMorgan Chase	51.2	Million	7/11/2011	Market Manipulation	Settled claims of municipal bond rigging.	Securities and Exchange Commission
JPMorgan Chase	50	Million	7/11/2011	Market Manipulation	Settled claims of municipal bond rigging.	Internal Revenue Service
Wells Fargo	85	Million	7/20/2011	Lending/Consumer Practices	Settles claims of steering borrowers into subprime loans.	Federal Reserve
JPMorgan Chase	88.3	Million	8/1/2011	Sanctions/Money Laundering/Tax Evasion	Settled sanctions violations allegations (Cuba, Iran, Sudan).	Department of Treasury
Ocean Bank (Miami)	10.9	Million	8/9/2011	Sanctions/Money Laundering/Tax Evasion	Penalty for Bank Secrecy Act compliance violations, in conjunction with the Treasury and the Florida Office of Financial Regulation.	Federal Deposit Insurance Corporation
Goldman Sachs	13	Million	9/1/2011	Lending/Consumer Practices	A settlement over robosigning allegations; applied to borrowers as principal writedowns.	New York Department of Financial Services
RBC	30.4	Million	9/27/2011	Market Manipulation	Settles claims of selling unsuitable investments to school districts.	Securities and Exchange Commission
Morgan Stanley	4.8	Million	9/30/2011	Market Manipulation	Settles charges of restraining competition in the New York City electricity market. .	Department of Justice
Citigroup	285	Million	10/19/2011	Mortgage Backed Securities	Settles claims of misleading investors on CDO purchases tied to mortgage securities.	Securities and Exchange Commission
Wells Fargo	37	Million	10/21/2011	Market Manipulation	Settling bid rigging and other municipal bond market practices against Wachovia .	US Southern District Court of New York

Bank of America	20	Million	11/10/2011	Lending/Consumer Practices	Paid as foreclosure relief to military borrowers.	Department of Justice
Citigroup	20.5	Million	11/15/2011	Mortgage Backed Securities	A settlement over allegations of misleading credit unions on MBS purchases.	National Credit Union Administration
Deutsche Bank	145	Million	11/15/2011	Mortgage Backed Securities	A settlement over allegations of misleading credit unions on MBS purchases.	National Credit Union Administration
Royal Bank of Scotland	52	Million	11/28/2011	Mortgage Backed Securities	Settled charges of unlawful mortgage securitization.	Massachusetts Attorney General
Wells Fargo	58.1	Million	12/8/2011	Market Manipulation	Settling bid rigging and other municipal bond market practices against Wachovia; paid to 26 state AGs.	State Attorneys General
Wells Fargo	46	Million	12/8/2011	Market Manipulation	Settling bid rigging and other municipal bond market practices against Wachovia.	Securities and Exchange Commission
Wells Fargo	34.5	Million	12/8/2011	Market Manipulation	Settling bid rigging and other municipal bond market practices against Wachovia.	Office of the Comptroller of the Currency
Wells Fargo	20	Million	12/8/2011	Market Manipulation	Settled claims of municipal bond rigging.	Office of the Comptroller of the Currency
Wells Fargo	8.9	Million	12/8/2011	Market Manipulation	Settling bid rigging and other municipal bond market practices against Wachovia .	Internal Revenue Service
Bank of America	335	Million	12/21/2011	Lending/Consumer Practices	A settlement to resolve Countrywide discrimination claims against minority borrowers.	Department of Justice
Bank of New York Mellon	1.3	Million	12/22/2011	Market Manipulation	Settlement of auction rate securities manipulation case (paid to TX, NY, FL).	New York Department of Financial Services
Bank of America	200	Million	2/1/2012	Market Manipulation	Settles charges over Libor rate-rigging scandal.	Federal Deposit Insurance Corporation
Ally Financial	310	Million	2/9/2012	Foreclosures	Part of the National Mortgage Settlement; $200m paid as relief to borrowers, $110m paid to federal and state regulators; in conjunction with the Department of Justice and State attorneys general.	Department of Housing and Urban Development
Bank of America	11820	Million	2/9/2012	Foreclosures	Part of the National Mortgage Settlement; $8.6bn paid as relief to borrowers, $3.2bn paid to federal and state regulators; in conjunction with the Department of Justice and State attorneys general.	Department of Housing and Urban Development
Citigroup	2205	Million	2/9/2012	Foreclosures	Part of the National Mortgage Settlement; $1.8bn paid as relief to borrowers, $415m paid to federal and state regulators; in conjunction	Department of Housing and Urban Development

					with the Department of Justice and State attorneys general.	
JPMorgan Chase	5290	Million	2/9/2012	Foreclosures	Part of the National Mortgage Settlement; $4.2bn paid as relief to borrowers and in principal writedowns, $1.1bn paid to federal and state regulators; in conjunction with the Department of Justice and State attorneys general.	Department of Housing and Urban Development
Wells Fargo	5350	Million	2/9/2012	Foreclosures	Part of the National Mortgage Settlement; $4.3bn paid as relief to borrowers, $1bn paid to federal and state regulators; in conjunction with the Department of Justice and State attorneys general.	Department of Housing and Urban Development
Citigroup	158.3	Million	2/15/2012	Lending/Consumer Practices	Settlement over False Claims Act violations; false certifications of residential mortgages.	Department of Housing and Urban Development
Flagstar Bank	132.8	Million	2/24/2012	Lending/Consumer Practices	Settlement over False Claims Act violations; false certifications of residential mortgages.	Department of Housing and Urban Development
JPMorgan Chase	20	Million	4/4/2012	Lending/Consumer Practices	Settlement over unlawful handling of Lehman Brothers' customer funds.	Commodity Futures Trading Commission
Goldman Sachs	22	Million	4/12/2012	Lending/Consumer Practices	Settlement for improper information disclosure measures.	Securities and Exchange Commission
Bank of New York Mellon	6	Million	4/16/2012	Lending/Consumer Practices	Penalty for breaches regarding mutual fund investment vehicle.	Federal Reserve
Deutsche Bank	202	Million	5/10/2012	Lending/Consumer Practices	Settled False Claims Act violations, false certifications of residential mortgages.	Department of Housing and Urban Development
SunTrust	21	Million	5/31/2012	Lending/Consumer Practices	Settlement resolving lending discrimination allegations.	Department of Justice
ING Bank	619	Million	6/12/2012	Sanctions/Money Laundering/Tax Evasion	Settles sanctions violations claims (Cuba, Burma, Sudan, Libya, Iran, in conjunction with the Department of Justice and the New York County District Attorney.	Department of Treasury
Barclays	200	Million	6/27/2012	Market Manipulation	Penalty for LIBOR rate manipulation.	Commodity Futures Trading Commission
Barclays	160	Million	6/27/2012	Market Manipulation	Penalty for LIBOR rate manipulation.	Department of Justice
Wells Fargo	175	Million	7/12/2012	Lending/Consumer Practices	A settlement resolving discrimination allegations against minority borrowers.	Department of Justice

Capital One Bank	35	Million	7/17/2012	Lending/Consumer Practices	Debt collection, credit/identity monitoring compliance.	Office of the Comptroller of the Currency
MetLife	3.2	Million	8/7/2012	Lending/Consumer Practices	Settlement over loan servicing and foreclosure processing deficiencies.	Federal Reserve
Wells Fargo	6.5	Million	8/14/2012	Mortgage Backed Securities	Settles charges of misleading investors about mortgage backed securities.	Securities and Exchange Commission
Barclays	176	Million	8/18/2012	Sanctions/Money Laundering/Tax Evasion	Settled sanctions violations charges (Sudan, Iran, Burma, Cuba).	Department of Treasury
Luther Burbank	2	Million	9/12/2012	Lending/Consumer Practices	Settlement resolving allegations of lending discrimination.	Department of Justice
Bank of America	370	Million	9/13/2012	Lending/Consumer Practices	Settlement resolving discrimination allegations against recipients of disability income.	Department of Justice
Standard Chartered	340	Million	9/14/2012	Sanctions/Money Laundering/Tax Evasion	Settles Iran sanctions violations charges.	New York Department of Financial Services
American Express	9	Million	10/1/2012	Lending/Consumer Practices	Settled claims over marketing and debt collection practices and compliance deficiencies.	Federal Reserve
JPMorgan Chase	296.9	Million	11/1/2012	Mortgage Backed Securities	Settles claims of misleading investors over mortgage backed securities.	Securities and Exchange Commission
Credit Suisse	120	Million	11/16/2012	Mortgage Backed Securities	Settles claims of misleading investors over residential mortgage backed securities.	Securities and Exchange Commission
Goldman Sachs	1.5	Million	12/7/2012	Market Manipulation	Penalty for trading supervision failures.	Commodity Futures Trading Commission
Standard Chartered	132	Million	12/10/2012	Sanctions/Money Laundering/Tax Evasion	Settlement over sanctions violations (Cuba, Burma, Iran, Sudan).	Department of Treasury
Standard Chartered	100	Million	12/10/2012	Sanctions/Money Laundering/Tax Evasion	Settlement over sanctions violations (Cuba, Burma, Iran, Sudan).	Federal Reserve
Standard Chartered	95	Million	12/10/2012	Sanctions/Money Laundering/Tax Evasion	Settlement over sanctions violations (Cuba, Burma, Iran, Sudan), in conjunction with the New York County District Attorney.	Department of Justice
HSBC	1256	Million	12/11/2012	Sanctions/Money Laundering/Tax Evasion	Settlement over sanctions violations (Cuba, Burma, Iran, Libya).	Department of Justice
HSBC	500	Million	12/11/2012	Sanctions/Money Laundering/Tax Evasion	Settlement over sanctions violations (Cuba, Burma, Iran, Libya).	Office of the Comptroller of the Currency
HSBC	375	Million	12/11/2012	Sanctions/Money Laundering/Tax Evasion	Settlement over sanctions violations (Cuba, Burma, Iran, Libya).	Department of Treasury
HSBC	165	Million	12/11/2012	Sanctions/Money Laundering/Tax Evasion	Violations of sanctions (Cuba, Burma, Iran, Libya).	Federal Reserve

Bank of Tokyo-Mitsubishi	8.6	Million	12/12/2012	Sanctions/Money Laundering/Tax Evasion	Settlement over sanctions violations (Burma, Iran, Cuba).	Department of Treasury
UBS	700	Million	12/19/2012	Market Manipulation	Penalty for Libor rate rigging allegations.	Commodity Futures Trading Commission
UBS	500	Million	12/19/2012	Market Manipulation	Penalty for Libor rate rigging allegations.	Department of Justice
Wegelin	74	Million	1/3/2013	Sanctions/Money Laundering/Tax Evasion	Penalty for assisting US citizens in tax evasion.	Department of Justice
Aurora Bank	93	Million	1/7/2013	Foreclosures	Independent Foreclosure Review settlement resolving improper foreclosure processing allegations; $93m paid into borrower relief fund, $149 paid to foreclosure prevention efforts	Office of the Comptroller of the Currency
Bank of America	11600	Million	1/7/2013	Mortgage Repurchases	Settlement resolving repurchase requests of faulty mortgage sales. Bank agreed to repurchase liabilities; includes $1.3bn fee for servicing obligations	Fannie Mae
Bank of America	2886	Million	1/7/2013	Foreclosures	Independent Foreclosure Review settlement resolving improper foreclosure processing allegations; $1.1bn paid into borrower relief fund, $1.8bn paid to foreclosure prevention efforts.	Office of the Comptroller of the Currency
Citigroup	794	Million	1/7/2013	Foreclosures	Independent Foreclosure Review settlement resolving improper foreclosure processing allegations; $307m paid into borrower relief fund, $487m paid to foreclosure prevention efforts.	Office of the Comptroller of the Currency
JPMorgan Chase	1958	Million	1/7/2013	Foreclosures	Independent Foreclosure Review settlement resolving improper foreclosure processing allegations; $753m paid into borrower relief fund, $1.2bn paid to foreclosure prevention efforts.	Office of the Comptroller of the Currency
MetLife	46	Million	1/7/2013	Foreclosures	Independent Foreclosure Review settlement resolving improper foreclosure processing allegations.	Office of the Controller of the Currency
PNC	180	Million	1/7/2013	Foreclosures	Independent Foreclosure Review settlement resolving improper foreclosure processing allegations; $69m paid into borrower relief fund, $111m paid to foreclosure prevention actions	Office of the Comptroller of the Currency
Sovereign Bank	16	Million	1/7/2013	Foreclosures	Independent Foreclosure Review settlement resolving improper foreclosure	Office of the Comptroller of the Currency

					processing allegations; $6m paid into borrower relief fund, $10m paid to foreclosure prevention efforts.	
SunTrust	163	Million	1/7/2013	Foreclosures	Independent Foreclosure Review settlement resolving improper foreclosure processing allegations; $63m paid into borrower relief fund, $100m paid to foreclosure prevention actions.	Federal Reserve
US Bank	208	Million	1/7/2013	Foreclosures	Independent Foreclosure Review settlement resolving improper foreclosure processing allegations; $80m paid into borrower relief fund, $128m paid to foreclosure prevention efforts.	Office of the Comptroller of the Currency
Wells Fargo	1991	Million	1/7/2013	Foreclosures	Independent Foreclosure Review settlement resolving improper foreclosure processing allegations; $766m paid into borrower relief fund, $1.2bn paid to foreclosure prevention efforts.	Office of the Comptroller of the Currency
Goldman Sachs	330	Million	1/16/2013	Foreclosures	Independent Foreclosure Review settlement resolving improper foreclosure processing allegations; paid into borrower relief fund and foreclosure prevention actions.	Federal Reserve
Morgan Stanley	227	Million	1/16/2013	Foreclosures	Independent Foreclosure Review settlement resolving improper foreclosure processing allegations; paid into borrower relief fund and foreclosure prevention actions.	Federal Reserve
HSBC	249	Million	1/18/2013	Foreclosures	Independent Foreclosure Review Settlement - $96m paid into borrower relief fund, $153m paid to foreclosure prevention efforts.	Office of the Comptroller of the Currency
Deutsche Bank	1.5	Million	1/22/2013	Market Manipulation	Settlement over energy market manipulation.	Federal Energy Regulatory Commission
PNC	7.1	Million	1/25/2013	Lending/Consumer Practices	Fine for failure to comply with Small Business Administration loan underwriting standards.	Department of Justice
TCF	10	Million	1/25/2013	Sanctions/Money Laundering/Tax Evasion	Fine for Bank Secrecy Act violations.	Office of the Comptroller of the Currency
Royal Bank of Scotland	325	Million	2/6/2013	Market Manipulation	Fine for Libor rate rigging practices.	Commodity Futures Trading Commission
Royal Bank of Scotland	150	Million	2/6/2013	Market Manipulation	Fine for Libor rate rigging practices.	Department of Justice

Bank	Amount		Date	Category	Description	Agency
Bank of America	165	Million	3/29/2013	Mortgage Backed Securities	A settlement over sales of poor MBS securities to corporate credit unions.	National Credit Union Administration
Capital One Bank	3.5	Million	4/24/2013	Lending/Consumer Practices	Fine for failure to properly account for auto finance losses.	Securities and Exchange Commission
Citizens Bank (Royal Bank of Scotland)	5	Million	4/29/2013	Lending/Consumer Practices	Fine for consumer banking deficiencies.	Office of the Comptroller of the Currency
Citigroup	250	Million	5/28/2013	Mortgage Backed Securities	Settled charges of securities laws violations in connection mortgage-backed securities sales to Fannie Mae and Freddie Mac; settlement amount disclosed January 2014	Federal Housing Finance Agency
Bank of Tokyo-Mitsubishi	250	Million	6/20/2013	Sanctions/Money Laundering/Tax Evasion	Fine for sanctions violations (Iran, Sudan, Myanmar).	New York Department of Financial Services
Intesa Sanpaolo	2.9	Million	6/28/2013	Sanctions/Money Laundering/Tax Evasion	Fine for sanctions violations (Iran, Cuba, Sudan).	Department of Treasury
Citigroup	968	Million	7/1/2013	Mortgage Repurchases	Settlement resolving repurchase requests of faulty mortgage sales. Bank agreed to repurchase liabilities.	Fannie Mae
Barclays	435	Million	7/16/2013	Market Manipulation	Settlement over energy market manipulation claims.	Federal Energy Regulatory Commission
UBS	885	Million	7/25/2013	Mortgage Backed Securities	Settled charges of securities laws violations in connection mortgage-backed securities sales to Fannie Mae and Freddie Mac; $470m paid to Freddie Mac, $415m paid to Fannie Mae.	Federal Housing Finance Agency
GMAC Mortgage	230	Million	7/26/2013	Foreclosures	Independent Foreclosure Review settlement resolving improper foreclosure processing allegations	Federal Reserve
JPMorgan Chase	410	Million	7/30/2013	Market Manipulation	Settlement for energy market manipulation charges.	Federal Energy Regulatory Commission
Liechtenstein Bank	23.8	Million	7/30/2013	Sanctions/Money Laundering/Tax Evasion	Settlement resolving charges of aiding US tax evasion.	Department of Justice
UBS	50	Million	8/6/2013	Mortgage Backed Securities	Settled charges of misleading investors about CDOs tied to mortgage securities.	Securities and Exchange Commission
Everbank	44	Million	8/23/2013	Foreclosures	Independent Foreclosure Review settlement resolving improper foreclosure processing allegations; $37m paid as borrower relief, $6m to foreclosure prevention programs	Office of the Comptroller of the Currency

Barclays	36.1	Million	9/10/2013	Mortgage Backed Securities	A settlement resolving mortgage backed security violations.	Massachusetts Attorney General
JPMorgan Chase	300	Million	9/18/2013	Market Manipulation	Penalty for unsafe derivatives trading activity (London Whale).	Office of the Comptroller of the Currency
JPMorgan Chase	60	Million	9/18/2013	Lending/Consumer Practices	Settlement over faulty consumer product billing practices .	Office of the Comptroller of the Currency
JPMorgan Chase	329	Million	9/19/2013	Lending/Consumer Practices	Fine for illegal credit card practices; $309m paid in refunds to consumers, $20m paid as cash penalty.	Consumer Financial Protection Bureau
JPMorgan Chase	200	Million	9/19/2013	Market Manipulation	Penalty for unsound investment oversight and controls (London Whale).	Federal Reserve
JPMorgan Chase	200	Million	9/19/2013	Market Manipulation	Penalty for unsound investment oversight and controls (London Whale).	Securities and Exchange Commission
TD Bank	37.5	Million	9/20/2013	Sanctions/Money Laundering/Tax Evasion	Penalty for anti-money laundering violations.	Office of the Comptroller of the Currency
Saddle River Valley Bank	4.1	Million	9/23/2013	Sanctions/Money Laundering/Tax Evasion	Penalty for Bank Secrecy Act compliance violations.	Office of the Comptroller of the Currency
TD Bank	15	Million	9/23/2013	Market Manipulation	Penalty for facilitating Scott Rothstein Ponzi scheme.	Securities and Exchange Commission
Citigroup	395	Million	9/25/2013	Mortgage Repurchases	Settlement resolving repurchase requests of faulty mortgage sales. Bank agreed to repurchase liabilities.	Freddie Mac
Wells Fargo	869	Million	9/27/2013	Mortgage Repurchases	Settlement resolving repurchase requests of faulty mortgage sales. Bank agreed to repurchase liabilities.	Freddie Mac
Chevy Chase Bank	2.85	Million	9/30/2013	Lending/Consumer Practices	Settled charges of discrimination against minority borrowers.	Department of Justice
SunTrust	65	Million	9/30/2013	Mortgage Repurchases	Settlement resolving repurchase requests of faulty mortgage sales. Bank agreed to repurchase liabilities.	Freddie Mac
JPMorgan Chase	6000	Million	10/1/2013	Mortgage Backed Securities	Part of $13bn settlement; $4bn paid as relief to consumers, $2bn paid as civil penalty	Department of Justice
JPMorgan Chase	4000	Million	10/1/2013	Mortgage Backed Securities	Part of $13bn settlement; settles federal and state claims by FHFA.	Federal Housing Finance Agency
JPMorgan Chase	1400	Million	10/1/2013	Mortgage Backed Securities	Part of $13bn settlement; settles securities claims brought by NCUA.	National Credit Union Administration
JPMorgan Chase	613.8	Million	10/1/2013	Mortgage Backed Securities	Part of $13bn settlement; settles claims by state New York.	New York

JPMorgan Chase	515.4	Million	10/1/2013	Mortgage Backed Securities	Part of $13bn settlement; settles federal and state securities claims brought by FDIC.	Federal Deposit Insurance Corporation
JPMorgan Chase	298.9	Million	10/1/2013	Mortgage Backed Securities	Part of $13bn settlement; settles federal and state claims by state of California.	California
JPMorgan Chase	100	Million	10/1/2013	Mortgage Backed Securities	Part of $13bn settlement; settles claims by state of Illinois.	Illinois
JPMorgan Chase	34.4	Million	10/1/2013	Mortgage Backed Securities	Part of $13bn settlement; settles claims by state of Massachusetts.	Massachusetts
JPMorgan Chase	19.7	Million	10/1/2013	Mortgage Backed Securities	Part of $13bn settlement; settles claims by state of Delaware.	Delaware
SunTrust	968	Million	10/10/2013	Foreclosures	Part of the National Mortgage Settlement; $500m paid as borrower relief, $468m paid as fine to federal and state regulators; in conjunction with the Department of Justice .	Department of Housing and Urban Development
SunTrust	373	Million	10/10/2013	Mortgage Repurchases	Settlement resolving repurchase requests of faulty mortgage sales. Bank agreed to repurchase liabilities.	Fannie Mae
JPMorgan Chase	100	Million	10/16/2013	Market Manipulation	Settlement over unsound investment oversight and controls (London Whale).	Commodity Futures Trading Commission
JPMorgan Chase	4000	Million	10/25/2013	Mortgage Backed Securities	Settlement over securities laws violations in connection with mortgage-backed securities sales. $2.7bn paid to Freddie Mac, $1.3bn paid to Fannie Mae.	Federal Housing Finance Agency
JPMorgan Chase	670	Million	10/25/2013	Mortgage Repurchases	Settlement resolving repurchase requests of faulty mortgage sales. Bank agreed to repurchase liabilities.	Fannie Mae
JPMorgan Chase	480	Million	10/25/2013	Mortgage Repurchases	Settlement resolving repurchase requests of faulty mortgage sales. Bank agreed to repurchase liabilities.	Freddie Mac
Ally Financial	475	Million	10/29/2013	Mortgage Backed Securities	Settlement over securities laws violations in connection with mortgage-backed securities sales	Federal Housing Finance Agency
Ally Financial	55.3	Million	10/29/2013	Mortgage Backed Securities	Settled charges of misleading investors over mortgage backed securities.	Federal Deposit Insurance Corporation
Rabobank	475	Million	10/29/2013	Market Manipulation	Settled false reporting charges regarding Libor and Euribor.	Commodity Futures Trading Commission
Rabobank	325	Million	10/29/2013	Market Manipulation	Settled false reporting charges regarding Libor and Euribor.	Department of Justice
Flagstar Bank	121.5	Million	11/6/2013	Mortgage Repurchases	Settlement resolving repurchase requests of faulty	Fannie Mae

					mortgage sales. Bank agreed to repurchase liabilities.	
Wells Fargo	335.23	Million	11/6/2013	Mortgage Backed Securities	Settled charges of misleading investors over mortgage backed securities.	Federal Housing Finance Agency
Fifth Third Bancorp	26	Million	11/22/2013	Mortgage Repurchases	Settlement resolving repurchase requests of faulty mortgage sales. Bank agreed to repurchase liabilities.	Freddie Mac
US Bank	56	Million	12/10/2013	Mortgage Repurchases	Settlement resolving repurchase requests of faulty mortgage sales. Bank agreed to repurchase liabilities.	Freddie Mac
Bank of America	131	Million	12/12/2013	Mortgage Backed Securities	Settled with SEC over allegation Merrill Lynch failed to tell investors in a CDO named Norma that a hedge fund had helped select, then bet against, the portfolio underlying the CDO.	Securities and Exchange Commission
PNC	89	Million	12/12/2013	Mortgage Repurchases	Settlement resolving repurchase requests of faulty mortgage sales. Bank agreed to repurchase liabilities.	Freddie Mac
Royal Bank of Scotland	50	Million	12/13/2013	Sanctions/Money Laundering/Tax Evasion	Settled allegations it allowed 3,500 transactions involving Iranian and Sudanese entities.	NYS Department Financial Services
Royal Bank of Scotland	50	Million	12/13/2013	Sanctions/Money Laundering/Tax Evasion	Settled allegations it allowed 3,500 transactions involving Iranian and Sudanese entities.	Treasury and the Federal Reserve
Deutsche Bank	1925	Million	12/20/2013	Mortgage Backed Securities	Settlement over alleged violations of securities laws in connection with mortgage-backed securities; $1.63bn paid to Freddie Mac and $300m to Fannie Mae	Federal Housing Finance Agency
Flagstar Bank	10.75	Million	12/27/2013	Mortgage Repurchases	Settlement resolving repurchase requests of faulty mortgage sales. Bank agreed to repurchase liabilities.	Freddie Mac
HSBC	83	Million	12/30/2013	Mortgage Repurchases	Settlement resolving repurchase requests of faulty mortgage sales. Bank agreed to repurchase liabilities.	Fannie Mae
PNC	140	Million	12/30/2013	Mortgage Repurchases	Settlement resolving repurchase requests of faulty mortgage sales. Bank agreed to repurchase liabilities.	Fannie Mae
Wells Fargo	591	Million	12/30/2013	Mortgage Repurchases	Settlement resolving repurchase requests of faulty mortgage sales. Bank agreed to repurchase liabilities.	Fannie Mae
JPMorgan Chase	1700	Million	1/7/2014	Sanctions/Money Laundering/Tax Evasion	Signed a deferred prosecution agreement with the US attorney's office in Manhattan for failing to alert regulators	Department of Justice

				about suspicions bankers had over Madoff.	
JPMorgan Chase	350	Million	1/7/2014	Sanctions/Money Laundering/Tax Evasion	Settled findings of widespread deficiencies in the bank's AML program including failing to report suspicions about Madoff and other cases of suspicious activity.	Office of the Comptroller of the Currency
JPMorgan Chase	614	Million	2/4/2014	Lending/Consumer Practices	Settled charges of defrauding federal agencies by underwriting poor quality mortage loans	Department of Justice
Morgan Stanley	1250	Million	2/4/2014	Mortgage Backed Securities	Settled charges of misleading investors over mortgage backed securities.	Federal Housing Finance Agency
Credit Suisse	196	Million	2/21/2014	Sanctions/Money Laundering/Tax Evasion	Settled charges of providing brokerage and advisory services to foreign clients without regulator approval	Securities and Exchange Commission
Societe Generale	122	Million	2/27/2014	Mortgage Backed Securities	Settled charges of misleading investors over mortgage backed securities.	Federal Housing Finance Agency
Credit Suisse	885	Million	3/21/2014	Mortgage Backed Securities	Settled charges of misleading investors over mortgage backed securities.	Federal Housing Finance Agency
Bank of America	9330	Million	3/26/2014	Mortgage Backed Securities	Settled charges of misleading investors over mortgage backed securities.	Federal Housing Finance Agency
Bank of America	772	Million	4/9/2014	Lending/Consumer Practices	Settlement over charges of misleading customers on credit card protection products. $727m refunded to consumers, $20m paid to CFPB and $25m paid to Office of the Comptroller of the Currency	Consumer Financial Protection Bureau
Barclays	280	Million	4/24/2014	Mortgage Backed Securities	Settled charges of misleading investors over mortgage backed securities.	Federal Housing Finance Agency
Credit Suisse	1800	Million	5/19/2014	Sanctions/Money Laundering/Tax Evasion	Penalty after pleading guilty to charges of helping Americans evade taxes overseas	Department of Justice
Credit Suisse	715	Million	5/19/2014	Sanctions/Money Laundering/Tax Evasion	Penalty after pleading guilty to charges of helping Americans evade taxes overseas	New York Department of Financial Services
Credit Suisse	100	Million	5/19/2014	Sanctions/Money Laundering/Tax Evasion	Penalty after pleading guilty to charges of helping Americans evade taxes overseas	Federal Reserve
SunTrust	968	Million	6/17/2014	Lending/Consumer Practices	Settlement in conjunction with HUD, CFPB and 49 state attorneys general addressing mortgage origination, servicing and foreclosure abuses	Department of Justice

Royal Bank of Scotland	100	Million	6/19/2014	Mortgage Backed Securities	Settled charges of misleading investors over mortgage backed securities.	Federal Housing Finance Agency
BNP Paribas	8900	Million	6/30/2014	Sanctions/Money Laundering/Tax Evasion	Pleaded guilty to illegally processing transactions in countries subject to US sanctions (Sudan, Cuba, Iran)	Department of Justice
HSBC	10	Million	6/30/2014	Foreclosures	Settled charges of improper foreclosure-related charges submitted to Department of Housing and Urban Development	Department of Justice
US Bank	200	Million	6/30/2014	Lending/Consumer Practices	Settled charges of defrauding the Federal Housing Administration by underwriting poor quality mortages	Department of Justice
SunTrust	320	Million	7/3/2014	Lending/Consumer Practices	Resolved criminal charges of misleading customers seeking mortgage relief through the Home Affordable Modification Program	Department of Justice
Citigroup	7000	Million	7/14/2014	Mortgage Backed Securities	Settled charges of misleading investors over mortgage backed securities. $4bn paid to Department of Justice, $500m to Federal Deposit Insurance Corporation and $2.5bn paid as borrower relief.	Department of Justice
Morgan Stanley	275	Million	7/24/2014	Mortgage Backed Securities	Settled charges of misleading investors on the sale of residential mortgage backed securities. Funds returned to affected investors.	Securities and Exchange Commission
Lloyds Banking Group	191	Million	7/28/2014	Market Manipulation	Settles charges over Libor rate-rigging scandal. Includes $86m penalty paid to Department of Justice.	Commodity Futures Trading Commission
Bank of America	16650	Million	8/6/2014	Mortgage Backed Securities	Settlement to resolve allegations of misselling mortgage-backed securities. The pact involves several US agencies, including the Federal Deposit Insurance Corp, and state attorneys-general.	Department of Justice
Standard Chartered	300	Million	8/19/2014	Sanctions/Money Laundering/Tax Evasion	Settlement for failing to improve procedures for identifying suspicions transactions following a 2012 settlement over sanctions violations	New York Department of Financial Services
Goldman Sachs	1200	Million	8/21/2014	Mortgage Backed Securities	Settled charges of misleading investors over mortgage backed securities.	Federal Housing Finance Agency

HSBC	550	Million	9/12/2014	Mortgage Backed Securities	Settled charges of misleading investors over mortgage backed securities.	Federal Housing Finance Agency
Wells Fargo	5	Million	10/9/2014	Lending/Consumer Practices	Settlement resolving charges of discriminating against consumers who were pregnant or on maternity leave	Department of Housing and Urban Development
Bank of America	250	Million	11/12/2014	Market Manipulation	Fine assessed for unsafe and unsound practices related to the bank's foreign exchange trading business	Office of the Comptroller of the Currency
Citigroup	350	Million	11/12/2014	Market Manipulation	Fine assessed for unsafe and unsound practices related to the bank's foreign exchange trading business	Office of the Comptroller of the Currency
Citigroup	310	Million	11/12/2014	Market Manipulation	Resolved charges of facilitating the manipulation of global foreign exchange benchmark rates; settlement in conjunction with UK and Swiss regulators	Commodity Futures Trading Commission
HSBC	275	Million	11/12/2014	Market Manipulation	Resolved charges of facilitating the manipulation of global foreign exchange benchmark rates; settlement in conjunction with UK and Swiss regulators	Commodity Futures Trading Commission
JPMorgan Chase	350	Million	11/12/2014	Market Manipulation	Fine assessed for unsafe and unsound practices related to the bank's foreign exchange trading business	Office of the Comptroller of the Currency
JPMorgan Chase	310	Million	11/12/2014	Market Manipulation	Resolved charges of facilitating the manipulation of global foreign exchange benchmark rates; settlement in conjunction with UK and Swiss regulators	Commodity Futures Trading Commission
Royal Bank of Scotland	290	Million	11/12/2014	Market Manipulation	Resolved charges of facilitating the manipulation of global foreign exchange benchmark rates; settlement in conjunction with UK and Swiss regulators	Commodity Futures Trading Commission
UBS	290	Million	11/12/2014	Market Manipulation	Resolved charges of facilitating the manipulation of global foreign exchange benchmark rates; settlement in conjunction with UK and Swiss regulators	Commodity Futures Trading Commission
Bank of Tokyo-Mitsubishi	315	Million	11/18/2014	Sanctions/Money Laundering/Tax Evasion	Penalty for misleading reglators about transactions in countries subject to sanctions; a follow up to the $250m fine paid in 2013	New York Department of Financial Services
Bank Leumi	130	Million	12/22/2014	Sanctions/Money Laundering/Tax Evasion	Fine for facilitating tax evasion by US clients	New York Department of Financial Services

Bank	Amount	Unit	Date	Type	Description	Agency
UBS	15	Million	1/15/2015	Market Manipulation	Settled accusations of violating federal securities laws in its dark pool operation	Securities and Exchange Commission
Commerzbank	1450	Million	3/12/2015	Sanctions/Money Laundering/Tax Evasion	Settlement for alleged business dealings in countries subject to US sanctions (Sudan, Iran)	New York Department of Financial Services
Deutsche Bank	800	Million	4/23/2015	Market Manipulation	Settled charges of manipulation, false reporting of Libor and Euribor	Commodity Futures Trading Commission
Deutsche Bank	775	Million	4/23/2015	Market Manipulation	Settled charges of manipulation, false reporting of Libor and Euribor	Department of Justice
Deutsche Bank	600	Million	4/23/2015	Market Manipulation	Settled charges of manipulation, false reporting of Libor and Euribor	New York Department of Financial Services
Bank of America	205	Million	5/20/2015	Market Manipulation	Settled allegations of rigging foreign exchange markets and Libor benchmark	Federal Reserve
Barclays	650	Million	5/20/2015	Market Manipulation	Guilty plea and fine for price manipulation in foreign exchange markets	Department of Justice
Barclays	485	Million	5/20/2015	Market Manipulation	Settled charges of attempted manipulation and false reporting of foreign exchange benchmark rates	New York Department of Financial Services
Barclays	400	Million	5/20/2015	Market Manipulation	Settled charges of attempted manipulation and false reporting of foreign exchange benchmark rates	Commodity Futures Trading Commission
Barclays	342	Million	5/20/2015	Market Manipulation	Settled allegations of rigging foreign exchange markets and Libor benchmark	Federal Reserve
Barclays	115	Million	5/20/2015	Market Manipulation	Penalty for attempted manipulation of and false reporting of ISDAFIX benchmark rates	Commodity Futures Trading Commission
Barclays	60	Million	5/20/2015	Market Manipulation	Extra fine for Libor	Department of Justice
Citigroup	925	Million	5/20/2015	Market Manipulation	Guilty plea and fine for price manipulation in foreign exchange markets	Department of Justice
Citigroup	342	Million	5/20/2015	Market Manipulation	Settled allegations of rigging foreign exchange markets and Libor benchmark	Federal Reserve
JPMorgan Chase	550	Million	5/20/2015	Market Manipulation	Guilty plea and fine for price manipulation in foreign exchange markets	Department of Justice
JPMorgan Chase	342	Million	5/20/2015	Market Manipulation	Settled allegations of rigging foreign exchange markets and Libor benchmark	Federal Reserve
Royal Bank of Scotland	395	Million	5/20/2015	Market Manipulation	Guilty plea and fine for price manipulation in foreign exchange markets	Department of Justice
Royal Bank of Scotland	274	Million	5/20/2015	Market Manipulation	Settled allegations of rigging foreign exchange markets and Libor benchmark	Federal Reserve

UBS	342	Million	5/20/2015	Market Manipulation	Settled allegations of rigging foreign exchange markets and Libor benchmark	Federal Reserve
UBS	203	Million	5/20/2015	Market Manipulation	Guilty plea and extra fine for Libor	Department of Justice
Deutsche Bank	55	Million	5/26/2015	Market Manipulation	Settled allegations of hiding losses of more than $1.5bn during the financial crisis	Securities and Exchange Commission
Citigroup	735	Million	7/21/2015	Lending/Consumer Practices	Penalty for unfair billing practices and deceptive consumer marketing. $700m to be paid as restitution to consumers, $35m as penalty to the agency	Consumer Financial Protection Bureau
Citigroup	35	Million	7/21/2015	Lending/Consumer Practices	Penalty for unfair billing practices and deceptive consumer marketing	Office of the Comptroller of the Currency

Source: Martin Stabe 2015 "Bank Fines: get the data" Financial Times/FT.com 22/May. Used under licence from the Financial Times. All Rights Reserved.

Appendix Ten:
Community Conversations for a Golden Civilization

Imagine a thousand generations into the future. A Golden Civilization has arrived. What does it look like? Feel like? How do people engage with each other, communicate, exchange goods, and govern themselves? Bring your wildest ideas and most personal values to a conversation about the future. Then together, map out a path to get there starting now.

Individuals around the globe have chosen to be leaders in their communities by hosting conversations about a Golden Civilization, its vision, and how to create it. Consider becoming one of them and host conversations in your own communities.

Here is the basic structure of a community conversation that you might follow:

Length: 2 hours

Roles: Two hosts, a facilitator and a recorder, who can switch roles.

Mood: Positive, empowered, compassionate, empathetic, and inspired. A feeling of community and togetherness.

Goal: Create participative democracy based on your communal vision of a Golden Civilization that supersedes negativity and polarization. And then find the paths to action.

Objective: Develop two action areas that the community can focus on at a personal, local, national, or global level.

Resources: Flip chart/white board with markers, or a simple tablet.

Location: Any place of gathering, including community centers, libraries, places of worship, fitness studios, picnic shelters, places of learning, living rooms, and kitchen tables.

Audience: Any group that you are part of currently, or in partnership with an entity that has access to a community. Even friends and family would be great.

Follow through: Continue to meet and revision a Golden Civilization as action steps are taken. Consider joining groups in other areas working on similar actions steps. You may find them on Golden Civilization websites.

Want to be a leader in your community? Become trained in the group facilitation and listening skills that lead to a shared vision of what is possible. Visit www.AGoldenCivilization.com for more details.

Appendix Eleven:
Books by George Kinder

Life Planning for You – How to Design & Deliver the Life of Your Dreams (Serenity Point Press, 2014). You can use this book and its accompanying website LifePlanningforYou.com to develop your own life plan using the EVOKE methodology, or to find an adviser trained and credentialed to do so.

The Seven Stages of Money Maturity – Understanding the Spirit and Value of Money in Your Life (New York, NY: Random House, 1999). A philosophy and psychology of money interlaced with practical information. This is the book that launched the Life Planning movement.

Transforming Suffering into Wisdom – Mindfulness and The Art of Inner Listening (Serenity Point Press, 2015). A book that is filled with practical exercises that make meditation and emotional intelligence accessible to all, from the novice to the sophisticated practitioner, leading to more joyous and meaningful lives.

Lighting the Torch – The Kinder Method of Life Planning (Denver, CO: FPA Press, 2006). A "how-to" for advisers who want to create Life Planning practices, this is the textbook on the EVOKE® method of Life Planning.

A Song for Hana & the Spirit of Leho`ula (Serenity Point Press, 2007). A love story dedicated to a sacred stretch of the Maui coastline, threatened by development. Filled with lyric prose, poetry, and photographs that illuminate the beauty of that spiritual and historic region of Hawaii.

www.georgekinder.com for more of George's work.

Endnotes

1. Yanis Varoufakis "Marx predicted our present crisis – and points the way out." The Guardian, (April 20, 2018) and from his introduction to The Communist Manifesto, Karl Marx & Friedrich Engels (London: Penguin Random House, Vintage Classics, 2018).

2. Matthew A. Killingsworth and Daniel T. Gilbert, "A Wandering Mind is an Unhappy Mind," Science, Vol 330, (November 12, 2010).

3. Edward O. Wilson, The Meaning of Human Existence (New York: Liveright Publishing Corporation, 2014), 176.

4. His Holiness the 14th Dalai Lama of Tibet, "Message for the New Millenium," January 1, 2000, https://www.dalailama.com/messages/world-peace/millennium-message.

5. His Holiness the 14th Dalai Lama of Tibet, "Human Rights, Democracy and Freedom," 2008, https://www.dalailama.com/messages/world-peace/human-rights-democracy-and-freedom.

6. David Gelles, "Want to Make Money Like a C.E.O.? Work for 275 Years," New York Times, May 25, 2018. From the Equilar 200 Highest-Paid C.E.O. Rankings. "Equilar calculated that the median pay ratio [between CEOs and their employees for publicly traded corporations in the United States] was 275 to 1."

7. Huanchu Daoren, Back to Beginnings, trans. Thomas Cleary (Boston: Shambhala Publications, 1994).

8. "Uruguay's Pepe Mujica: 'Inequality Is the Enemy of Democracy'," teleSUR, September 24 2016, https://www.telesurtv.net/.

9. "Reward Work, Not Wealth" Oxfam International, January 2018, https://d1tn3vj7xz9fdh.cloudfront.net/s3fs-public/file_attachments/bp-reward-work-not-wealth-220118-en.pdf.

10. Based on the Dollar Cut-Off from 1980-2014 of the Minimum Adjusted Gross Income for Tax Returns to Fall into Various percentiles–Thresholds Not Adjusted for Inflation and also Summary of the Latest Federal Income Tax Data.
Scott Greenberg, "Summary of the Latest Federal Income Tax Data," 2016 Update, February 1, 2017, https://taxfoundation.org/summary-latest-federal-income-tax-data-2016-update/.

11. Greenberg, "Summary of the Latest Federal Income Tax Data."

12. Oxfam International, "Reward Work, Not Wealth."

13. If you are interested in basic income, here are four articles and a book referencing studies and arguments regarding its many benefits:

Tyler Prochazka , "Will basic income lower crime?" Basic Income Earth Network published December 12, 2016, https://basicincome.org/news/2016/12/will-basic-income-lower-crime/;

Scott Santens , "Why we should all have a basic income," World Economic Forum, January 15, 2017, https://www.weforum.org/agenda/2017/01/why-we-should-all-have-a-basic-income/;

Sam Dumitriu, "Basic Income Around The World: The Unexpected Benefits of Unconditional Cash Transfers", Adam Smith Institute, January 19, 2018, https://www.adamsmith.org/research/basic-income-experiments;

Andrew Yang , "What are the benefits of Universal Basic Income?" Yang 2020 accessed June 28, 2018, https://www.yang2020.com/blog/ubi_faqs/benefits-universal-basic-income/.

Annie Lowrey, Give People Money: How a Universal Basic Income Would End Poverty, Revolutionize Work, and Remake the World (Crown, July 10, 2018).

14. Thom Hartmann, "President Jimmy Carter: The United States is an Oligarchy...",video, July 28, 2015, 1:27 minutes, https://www.thomhartmann.com/bigpicture/president-jimmy-carter-united-states-oligarchy.

15. Thomas Ferguson, Jie Chen, Paul Jorgensen, "Fifty Shades of Green: High Finance, Political Money and the U.S. Congress," The Roosevelt Institute, May 2, 2017, http://rooseveltinstitute.org/fifty-shades-green/.

16. Huanchu Daoren, Back to Beginnings, 43.

17. Ferguson, Chen, Jorgensen, "Fifty Shades of Green."

18. Huanchu Daoren, Back to Beginnings.

19. Shantideva, The Bodhisattva's vow as translated by Tenzin Gyatso, 14th Dalai Lama.

20. WWF, "Living Planet Report 2016, Risk and resilience in a new era." WWF International, 2016, Gland, Switzerland.

21. His Holiness the 14th Dalai Lama of Tibet, "The Reality of War," https://www.dalailama.com/messages/world-peace/the-reality-of-war.

22. His Holiness the 14th Dalai Lama of Tibet, "The 14th Dalai Lama's Nobel Lecture," December 11, 1989, https://www.dalailama.com/messages/acceptance-speeches/nobel-peace-prize/nobel-peace-prize-nobel-lecture.

23. His Holiness the 14th Dalai Lama of Tibet, "The Message of the Dalai Lama Sent to the Millennium World Peace Summit," August 23, 2000, http://www.commongood.info/DalaiLama.html.

24. Huanchu Daoren, Back to Beginnings, 111.

25. His Holiness the 14th Dalai Lama of Tibet, "Message on the 50th Anniversary of the Universal Declaration of Human Rights," December 7, 1998, https://www.dalailama.com/messages/world-peace/universal-declaration.

26. "Why 'Bushmen banter' was crucial to hunter-gatherers' evolutionary success." The Guardian, October 29, 2017, https://www.theguardian.com/inequality/2017/oct/29/why-bushman-banter-was-crucial-to-hunter-gatherers-evolutionary-success.

27. Marcus Aurelius, Meditations, Trans. A.S.L. Farquharson, (CRW Publishing Ltd, London, 2011.) Thoughts from the emperor of Rome, the most powerful figure in the world of his day.

28. Huanchu Daoren, Back to Beginnings.

29. Here's an article on the six companies that own 90% of media in America:
Ashley Lutz, "These 6 Corporations Control 90% Of The Media In America," Business Insider, June 14, 2012, http://www.businessinsider.com/these-6-corporations-control-90-of-the-media-in-america-2012-6?r=UK&IR=T.

When you add in a handful of the billionaires on the following list, including Zuckerberg and Bezos, you have well over 90% of the media covered (see Kate Vinton, "These 15 Billionaires Own America's News Media Companies," Forbes, June 1, 2016, https://www.forbes.com/sites/katevinton/2016/06/01/these-15-billionaires-own-americas-news-media-companies/#883baeb660ad).

One additional company to watch is Sinclair, who has gathered a huge network of local media companies all over the country as reported by Alvin Chang, "Sinclair's takeover of local news, in one striking map," Vox, April 6, 2018, https://www.vox.com/2018/4/6/17202824/sinclair-tribune-map.

30. Rumi, Birdsong, trans. Coleman Barks (Maypop, 1993) published in Mala of the Heart 108 Sacred Poems, edited by Ravi Nathwani and Kate Vogt (New World Library, 2010).

31. Milton Friedman, "The Social Responsibility of Business is to Increase its Profits," New York Times Magazine, September 13, 1970. Copyright @ 1970 by The New York Times Company.

32. Dominic Rushe, "Wall Street Wolves Still on the Prowl as Survey Reveals Taste for Unethical Tactics," The Guardian, May 19, 2015.

33. Huanchu Daoren, Back to Beginnings.

34. The Book of Leadership & Strategy, Lessons of the Chinese Masters, trans. Thomas Cleary (Boston & London: Shambhala Publications, 1996).

35. Rushe, "Wall Street Wolves Still on the Prowl as Survey Reveals Taste for Unethical Tactics."

36. Researchers at The University of Notre Dame and Labaton Sucharow LLP, "The Street, The Bull and The Crisis." May 2015. 1223 participants surveyed; employed in the financial services/banking industry in the US (925) and UK (298) as account executives, financial/investment/wealth advisers, financial analysts, investment bankers, branch/operations management, and portfolio managers; conducted Dec 22, 2014 – Jan 23, 2015.

37. Huanchu Daoren, Back to Beginnings.

38. Labaton Sucharow, U.S. Financial Services Industry Survey, July 2013.

39. The chief executives of publicly held companies with at least $1 billion in annual revenue that filed proxies by April 30, 2018 are featured in the Equilar 200 Highest-Paid CEO Rankings. "The Highest-Paid C.E.O.s in 2017" New York Times, May 25, 2018. https://www.nytimes.com/interactive/2018/05/25/business/ceo-pay-2017.html.

40. Rebecca Riffkin, "Americans Rate Nurses Highest on Honesty, Ethical Standards" Gallup, December 18, 2014, http://www.gallup.com/poll/180260/americansratenurseshighesthonestyethicalstandards.aspx, accessed June 21, 2016.

41. US Department of Labor, "Occupational Outlook Handbook", 2017, www.bls.gov/ooh/healthcare/registered-nurses.htm, accessed June 6, 2018.

42. Valerie Strauss, "How much (or little) teachers earn — state by state" The Washington Post, March 5, 2018, https://www.washingtonpost.com/news/answer-sheet/wp/2018/03/05/how-much-or-little-teachers-earn-state-by-state/?noredirect=on&utm_term=.1cc70e70f4e4, accessed June 7, 2018.

43. Oxfam, Oxfam International, January 18, 2016, p. 36, www.oxfam.org/en/pressroom/pressreleases/2015-01-19/richest-1-will-own-more-all-rest-2016, accessed on February 22, 2016.

44. Deborah Hardoon and Finn Heinrich, "Global Corruption Barometer 2013," Transparency International, 2013, https://www.transparency.org/gcb2013/report.

45. "Corruption Perceptions Index 2014," Transparency.org, 2014, https://www.transparency.org/cpi2014/results.

46. BBC, "Corruption 'impoverishes and kills millions'," BBC World News, September 3, 2014, www.bbc.com/news/world-29040793.

47. For more information on methodology visit, https://rsf.org/en/detailed-methodology.

48. V-Dem Institute, "Democracy for All? V-Dem Annual Democracy Report 2018," University of Gothenburg, 2018, Gothenburg, Sweden.

49. "Honesty/Ethics in Professions", Gallup, December 8-11, 2014, www.gallup.com. 805 adults were surveyed in the US.

50. Ipsos Reid and Reader's Digest Release Annual Trusted Brand Survey, www.ipsos-na.com, January 19, 2015. Over 4,000 Canadians were asked to rate their trust on a list of professions and industries. Conducted August/September 2014.

51. Roy Morgan Image of Professions Survey for Australia 2014, roymorgan.com, April 11, 2014.

52. Ipsos MORI Trust Poll for Great Britain, Ipsos MORI, February 9-11, 2013. 1,018 adults were surveyed.

53. "Financial services industry faces bigger problem than lack of trust - apathy," PwC Research, October 2 2014, UK, http://pwc.blogs.com. The report from Price Waterhouse Cooper's is based on an analysis of a survey of over 2000 people across the UK.

54. Martin Stabe, "Bank fines: get the data," The Financial Times Ltd., May 22 2015.

55. "Martin Stabe, "Bank fines: get the data," The Financial Times Ltd., May 22 2015.

George Kinder, international thought leader, has authored three books on money: *The Seven Stages of Money Maturity*, *Lighting the Torch*, and *Life Planning for You*. He is known as the father of the Life Planning movement. Winner of numerous awards, as founder and CEO of the Kinder Institute of Life Planning he has revolutionized client-centered financial advice with in-depth trainings of thousands of advisers from thirty countries across six continents. A mindfulness teacher, Kinder also leads weekly meditation classes and retreats around the world and wrote *Transforming Suffering into Wisdom: Mindfulness and The Art of Inner Listening*. Kinder is also a published poet and photographer. He lives in Massachusetts with his wife and daughters, and spends several months each year in London and Maui.

CPSIA information can be obtained
at www.ICGtesting.com
Printed in the USA
FSHW011854260219
55953FS